DATE DUE			
Dec 18 '74			
Oct 22 '75			
Oct 22 '75			
Jun 16 '76			
Aug 10 '76			
Sep 28 '80			
Nov 25			
Nov 6 '81			
10 AM Nov 11			
10 AM Nov 12			
10 AM Nov 12			

Rethinking
Sociology

PRENTICE-HALL INTERNATIONAL, INC., *London*
PRENTICE-HALL OF AUSTRALIA, PTY. LTD., *Sydney*
PRENTICE-HALL OF CANADA, LTD., *Toronto*
PRENTICE-HALL OF INDIA PRIVATE LIMITED, *New Delhi*
PRENTICE-HALL OF JAPAN, INC., *Tokyo*

IRVING M. ZEITLIN

Rethinking Sociology

A Critique
of Contemporary Theory

Prentice-Hall, Inc., Englewood Cliffs, New Jersey

Again for Esther, Ruthie,
Michael, Bethie, and Jeremy

3 0 /·0 /

Z e 3 r

9 / / 2 7

Dec. 1974

ISBN: 0-13-778654-9

Library of Congress Catalog Card Number: 73-1835

10 9 8 7 6 5 4 3 2 1

ACKNOWLEDGMENTS

Excerpts appearing throughout this book are reprinted from the following sources (page numbers in the sources are cited on the page where quotes appear):

Talcott Parsons, THE SOCIAL SYSTEM (New York and London: The Free Press and Routledge & Kegan Paul Ltd., 1951). Reprinted with permission of Macmillan Publishing Co., Inc. Copyright 1951 by Talcott Parsons.

Talcott Parsons, ESSAYS IN SOCIOLOGICAL THEORY (New York: The Free Press, 1949 and 1954). Reprinted with permission of Macmillan Publishing Co., Inc. Copyright The Free Press, a corporation, 1949, 1954.

Talcott Parsons, SOCIOLOGICAL THEORY AND MODERN SOCIETY (New York: The Free Press, 1967). Reprinted with permission of Macmillan Publishing Co., Inc. Copyright ©The Free Press, a Division of The Macmillan Company, 1967.

George C. Homans, SOCIAL BEHAVIOR: ITS ELEMENTARY FORMS (New York: Harcourt Brace & World, 1961; London: Routledge & Kegan Paul Ltd.). © 1961 by Harcourt Brace Jovanovich, Inc. and reprinted with their permission.

George C. Homans, "Fundamental Social Processes," in SOCIOLOGY: AN INTRODUCTION, edited by Neil J. Smelser (New York: John Wiley & Sons, Inc., 1967). Copyright © 1967 by John Wiley & Sons, Inc. Reprinted by permission.

Peter M. Blau, EXCHANGE AND POWER IN SOCIAL LIFE (New York: John Wiley & Sons, Inc., 1964). Copyright © 1964 by John Wiley & Sons, Inc. Reprinted by permission.

Ralf Dahrendorf, CLASS AND CLASS CONFLICT IN INDUSTRIAL SOCIETY (Stanford: Stanford University Press, 1959; London: Routledge & Kegan Paul, 1959). Reprinted with permission of the publishers.

Hans Gerth and C. Wright Mills, editors and translators, FROM MAX WEBER: ESSAYS IN SOCIOLOGY (New York: Oxford University Press, 1946).

Harold Garfinkel, STUDIES IN ETHNOMETHODOLOGY (Englewood Cliffs, N. J.: Prentice-Hall, 1967), ©1967. Reprinted by permission of Prentice-Hall, Inc., Englewood Cliffs, New Jersey.

Erving Goffman, ASYLUMS (New York: Doubleday Anchor Books, 1961), copyright ©1961 by Erving Goffman. Reprinted by permission of Doubleday & Co., Inc. Erving Goffman, ASYLUMS (London: Penguin Books Ltd. [Pelican], 1967). Copyright ©1961 Erving Goffman.

George Herbert Mead, THE PHILOSOPHY OF THE ACT (Chicago and London: University of Chicago Press, 1938). Copyright ©1938 by The University of Chicago. All rights reserved.

George Herbert Mead, MIND, SELF, AND SOCIETY (Chicago and London: University of Chicago Press, 1934). Copyright 1934 by The University of Chicago. Copyright 1962 by Charles W. Morris. All rights reserved.

Contents

Preface *vii*

I   STRUCTURAL FUNCTIONALISM

1   The Concepts of Traditional Functionalism   *3*
2   Talcott Parsons: Action Theory and the Social System   *17*
3   Is There a Second Talcott Parsons?   *35*
4   The Rediscovery of Evolution   *51*

II   SOCIAL EXCHANGE THEORY

5   The Exchange Theory of George C. Homans   *63*
6   Exchange and Power in the Work of Peter Blau   *81*

III   CONFLICT THEORY

7   A Note on Coser's Functionalized Conflict   *103*
8   Dahrendorf's Postcapitalist Society   *109*
9   Toward a Marx-Weber Model of Social and Historical Analysis   *123*

IV   PHENOMENOLOGY

10   Husserl and the Crisis of Science and Philosophy   *139*
11   Max Scheler   *151*
12   The Phenomenological Dimension in Max Weber   *167*
13   The Intersubjective World of Everyday Life:
       The Ideas of Alfred Schütz   *171*
14   Garfinkel's Ethnomethodology   *183*

V   SYMBOLIC INTERACTION

15   The Social Psychology of Erving Goffman   *191*
16   Herbert Blumer's Symbolic Interaction   *215*
17   The Dialectical Philosophy of George Herbert Mead   *219*
18   The Rudiments of Marx's Epistemology and Social Psychology   *243*
19   Toward a Synthesis of Marx, Mead, and Freud   *251*
       Epilogue   *257*

Index   *259*

Preface

The present effort seeks to develop a new synthesis of sociological theory. I begin the task critically by taking a close and careful look at the five main theoretical currents in contemporary sociology:

1. functionalism, or structural functionalism,
2. social exchange theory,
3. conflict theory,
4. phenomenology and ethnomethodology, and
5. symbolic interaction.

Each part of the book is devoted to one of these currents as represented by several key thinkers. Each chapter provides an exposition of the theory in question while pointing to problems, ambiguities, and defects.

Although these chapters may be read independently of one another, together they unfold the central thesis of the book. I argue that functionalism is so one-sided and its shortcomings so basic as to cast serious doubt on its scientific fruitfulness. Exchange theory is also encumbered with problems, particularly in the hands of one of its major representatives. Conflict-coercion theory is a vague omnibus term embracing heterogeneous elements that are occasionally contradictory.

The unsatisfactory state of these theoretical currents challenges us to provide an alternative framework that is potentially more fruitful. With this aim I present the rudiments of what I term a Marx-Weber model. This is a programmatic statement that accentuates the complementarity of Marx's and Weber's theories and methods, and calls for their integration into one paradigm.

Because the Marx-Weber model is predominantly structural, however, it does not answer our need for a social psychology. We must search for and develop an adequate social psychology, a task that is facilitated by closely scrutinizing phenomenology and symbolic interaction.

I conclude that George Herbert Mead's dialectical approach most adequately grasps the nature of human interaction and its emergent qualities. Yet there are weaknesses in Mead's conception when it stands alone.

In the final chapters of the book, therefore, I indicate these weaknesses and suggest what elements must be built into Mead's conception. Borrowing these elements from Herbert Marcuse's critical reinterpretation of Freud, I try to show that a reconstructed Mead is epistemologically compatible with Marx's view of man; and that a proper integration of Marx, Mead, and Freud yields the most efficacious social psychology available. When this social psychology is combined with the Marx-Weber model it results in a synthesis that most adequately considers both the structural and situational dimensions of the social process.

I

STRUCTURAL FUNCTIONALISM

1

The Concepts of
Traditional Functionalism

There is a tradition in sociological thinking that has variously been dubbed "functionalism," "structural functionalism," "the functional approach," "functional orientation," "functional analysis," and "functional theory." The relative merits of this tradition have long been not merely debated but also subjected again and again to fundamentally damaging criticisms. Nevertheless, the tradition still has strongly committed adherents.

Some of the best-known contemporary theorists, notably Talcott Parsons and Robert K. Merton, are widely regarded as leading representatives of the tradition. A host of less-known sociologists also employ the language and concepts of functionalism—often without examining these concepts critically or appreciating the implications of their use. It may therefore be worthwhile to have another critical look at this tradition.

What are the main concepts and ideas associated with the functionalist approach? Its fundamental postulates are that all social structures, or at least the major ones, contribute to the integration and adaptation of the system in which they operate. The existence or persistence of a given structure or pattern is explained by means of its consequences or effects, which are presumably both necessary and beneficial to the society in question. Functionalists generally have tried to show that a given pattern fulfills some vital "system need" and that this fulfillment "explains" the existence of the pattern.

Since the bulk of Part I is devoted to a careful scrutiny of the work of Talcott Parsons, the present discussion is confined to other representatives of this tradition. What are the most important questions and issues that one may raise conerning the functionalist conception as outlined above?

There is, first, the question of concepts and how they are defined. Although it is characteristic of traditional functionalism that it taxes the reader's

3

patience with a seemingly endless proliferation of definitions and distinctions, the terms are rarely clear, consistent, adequate, or applicable.

Let us take a concept as rudimentary as "society," which Marion J. Levy, following Parsons, has defined as "a system of action in operation that (a) involves a plurality of interacting individuals of a given species . . . who are recruited at least in part by the sexual reproduction of members of the plurality involved, (b) is . . . *self-sufficient* for the action of this plurality, and (c) is capable of existing longer than the life span of an individual"[1] (italics added).

"Self-sufficiency" is the key criterion that for Levy distinguishes a society from any other social system. One must ask: Is there such a thing as a self-sufficient social system or group, and is there some definite empirical entity that one can unambiguously label a society according to Levy's criterion? Evidently Levy wishes to define that social entity which is larger than the family, village-community, city, province (or state), or region—what we call the nation-state.

Is there any nation-state so self-sufficient that it can dispense with economic, political, cultural, linguistic, and other relations with other states? If the answer to this question is no, we are forced to conclude that societies as defined by Levy (and also by Parsons, as we shall see in due course) do not exist.

Equally vulnerable is another master concept, the "social system," which Levy defines as "any system of social action involving a plurality of interacting individuals," or "any patterned collection of elements." As numerous critics have observed, this is so vague and general as to be meaningless. It does not enable us to distinguish among the various kinds of social groups we all know about—families, friendship groups, residential communities, formal and complex organizations, etc.—all of which are "social systems."

The fact that concepts as fundamental as "society" and "social system" are inadequate suggests that all the associated concepts, together with their accompanying assumptions, are also defective. If one has no clear and precise idea of what "society" or "social system" refers to, how can one speak of "system needs," which purportedly are met or fulfilled by various "structures" (leaving aside, for the moment, the question of what is meant by "structure")? Similarly, in the absence of a precise empirical referent for the term "society," how can one speak of the so-called "functional requisites" of *any* society? Take, for example, the now famous functionalist assertion, made by D. F. Aberle, A. K. Cohen, A. K. Davis, Marion J. Levy, and F. X. Sutton in their essay "The Functional Prerequisites of a Society," that a society cannot prevail unless it avoids all of the following four conditions:

1. The biological extinction or dispersion of the members.
2. Apathy of the members.
3. The war of all against all.

[1] Marion J. Levy, Jr., *The Structure of Society* (Princeton: Princeton University Press, 1952), p. 113.

4. The absorption of the society into another society.[2]

That this assertion is a tautology becomes evident upon critical examination. When is a society terminated? Under what conditions must it cease to exist? When its members either suffer destruction or are stricken with universal apathy (!) or degenerate into a situation described by the Hobbesian metaphor or lose their identity and self-sufficiency. And what constitutes proof that these are *the four* conditions that terminate the existence of a society? Ultimately the proponents of this theory must have recourse to a tautology: the very persistence of any given society demonstrates that the conditions are inoperative.

Nor are the authors' "functional prerequisites of a society" any more satisfactory from either a logical or an empirical standpoint. The list of such prerequisites includes:

1. Provision for adequate relationships to the environment and for sexual recruitment.
2. Role differentiation and role assignment.
3. Communication.
4. Shared cognitive orientations.
5. A shared set of articulated goals.
6. The normative regulation of means.
7. The regulation of affective expression.
8. Socialization.
9. The effective control of disruptive forms of behavior.[3]

The authors have decided that there are nine such prerequisites, but acknowledge that there may be more or—who knows?—even fewer.

To the extent that these presumed prerequisites are true, they are also banal. Who could derive any real intellectual satisfaction from the assertion that for a society to exist, its members must achieve a minimal control of the environment, divide and assign tasks, and communicate? Besides, like the four conditions discussed earlier, these prerequisites resolve themselves into tautologies. One posits certain conditions for a society's survival or operation and then points to its survival as proof that the functional prerequisites have been fulfilled.

In a similar vein, functionalists maintain that patterns or structures persist only if they are adaptive; that is, fulfill functional needs. The persistence of a pattern is thus used to prove its adaptive character while its adaptive character is "proved" by its persistence. One remains neatly enclosed in the circle.

The trouble with these functionalist types of explanation, even the most sophisticated, is that key concepts are defined so loosely and ambiguously that any and all social patterns may be regarded as adaptive or maladaptive as the

---

[2] D. F. Aberle, *et al.*, "The Functional Prerequisites of a Society," *Ethics*, 60 (January 1950): 100–111.
[3] Ibid.

case may be. Not only are the concepts vague, but their accompanying or underlying assumptions are empirically unverifiable.

How can one verify what the so-called "system needs" of a society are? But a scientific explanation must define clearly what is meant by "needs," "adaptive," "functional," "integrative," and so on; and ultimately it must also establish the validity of its underlying axioms. Traditional functionalists have met none of these requirements. They define "system needs" so broadly that, as Francesca M. Cancian has observed,

> almost any social process can be seen as contributing to at least one of them, and, being a list, there are few constraints on adding more needs. But a limited set of prerequisites is essential to functional explanation; without it, an imaginative investigator can "explain" any social pattern merely by describing some consequence or effect of a pattern and arguing that the consequence is a functional prerequisite.[4]

Piling abstraction upon abstraction, as representatives of this school are accustomed to do, does not really help us to comprehend empirical social systems or to analyze social realities. Furthermore, some of their assertions appear to be false.

Aberle and his co-authors tell us, for instance, that among the functional prerequisites of any society one must include "shared cognitive orientations" and "a shared set of articulated goals." Commenting on the inclusion of these two assertions in particular, Pitrim Sorokin observed:

> Since . . . social systems of slaves and masters and of the conquered and their conquerors have existed in many areas of the world for many centuries at a time, and since we are certain that the overwhelming majority of prisoners, slaves, and the conquered have not shared the goals and cognitive orientations of their rulers, this "requisite" is *not* a requisite for the existence and functioning of any and all societies. . . . As a matter of fact, all coercive societies of the past and of the present have lived without it.[5]

Similarly, the neologisms that Levy presents us with in *The Structure of Society*—"eufunction," "dysfunction," "eustructure," and "dystructure,"—he defines in terms of their usefulness or harmfulness for society's "integration," "adaptation," and so forth. Nowhere, however, does he inform us how we would

---

[4] Francesca M. Cancian, "Functional Analysis," *International Encyclopedia of the Social Sciences*, ed D. L. Sills (New York: The Macmillan Company and The Free Press, 1968), 6:29–43.

[5] Pitrim A. Sorokin, *Sociological Theories Today* (New York: Harper & Row, 1966), p. 442.

go about determining whether his reified but elusive "society" is integrated or adapted. Again Sorokin's remarks are instructive:

> Whether the activities of Socrates, Jesus, Washington, and Marx are "eufunctional" or "dysfunctional," whether the movements of the early Christians, the Communists, or the civil-rights workers are the movements of "adaptation" or "maladaptation" of a "society" or "social system" or "social unit," depends upon with which side or with which party we identify ourselves in respective societies. Once we make such an identification, we merely demonstrate our subjective sympathy or bias with the chosen party—which fact hardly increases our knowledge of the sociocultural reality involved. If, on the other hand, we do not make such an identification with one of the parties involved and, generally, do not specify *from whose standpoint and for which party* a given state of affairs appears to be the "eufunction or dysfunction," an "adaptation" or a "maladjustment," these terms become meaningless. Whether we identify or do not identify with one of the parties involved, these inherently subjective and evaluative terms do not increase our knowledge of the "given state of affairs."[6]

MERTON'S REVISIONS

Some students of sociological theory, while agreeing that these criticisms are justified when leveled against traditional functionalism in its cruder form, would defend Robert K. Merton's well-known and sophisticated revisions of the functionalist postulates. Certainly Merton's criticisms of the traditional functionalist postulates and concepts are interesting and lucid. Yet his revisions fail to avoid the usual functionalist pitfalls.

The reader may recall the three traditional postulates that Merton criticized and revised. They were:

1. that standardized social activities or cultural items are functional for the *entire* social or cultural system;
2. that *all* such social and cultural items fulfill sociological functions; and
3. that these items are consequently indispensable.[7]

Merton's revisions may be summed up as follows: A society's unity ought not be posited in advance but ought rather to be an empirical question. One must specify the unit for which a given item is functional; and one must beware of

---

[6] Ibid., p. 443.

[7] Robert K. Merton, *Social Theory and Social Structure*, enlarged edition (New York: The Free Press, 1968), p. 79.

accepting as an unqualified postulate the view that all items fulfill vital functions. Functional analysis must allow for diverse consequences, including dysfunctions as well as functions. Finally, one must not assume that one and only one item or structure can fulfill a given function. Rather, social scientists should allow for the fact "that alternative social structures (and cultural forms) have served . . . the functions necessary for the persistence of groups. Proceeding further, we must set forth a major theorem of functional analysis; *just as the same item may have multiple functions, so may the same function be diversely fulfilled by alternative items.*"[8]

Let us examine the last of Merton's revisions first—his doctrine of functional and structural equivalents, alternatives, or substitutes. If we accept for a moment the assumption that several patterns, x plus others, can fulfill the same function—say, "controlling disruptive behavior"—this is meaningful (i.e., testable in some empirical sense) only if one can distinguish such patterns from nonequivalent ones or, in short, only if one can specify a finite list of such patterns. Moreover, this must be done in such a manner that one could conceivably prove the assumption false—i.e., by finding a society that controls disruptive behavior in the absence of x or any of its presumed equivalents.

If one does not adhere to these rules, discovering equivalents will always be fairly easy. Even these rules, however, should leave us dissatisfied if we are unable to explain why, among structural alternatives, y was present instead of z. Ideally, one should be able to specify which pattern will occur under what conditions—which, in effect, would involve the study of causation: patterns and the cause of their persistence.

Causation, however, is precisely what traditional functionalism has not concerned itself with. Typically, according to this tradition, one "explained" the persistence of a given structure by reference to the presumed functions it fulfilled. If we translate functions into what is commonly meant by that term, namely, consequences or effects, we see that the functionalist is indeed attempting to explain the persistence of a structure by means of its effect rather than its cause. This circumstance has prompted some philosophical critics to question "whether an event can be caused by another later than itself."[9]

Of course, what is usually implied in this type of functional explanation is an interactionist model, a definite reciprocity according to which x causes itself—that is, has "certain effects on y that in turn cause x." This is the only instance in which traditional functionalist explanations refer to causes at all. As Cancian describes it: "In the paradigm of functional explanation, social pattern x is explained by its effects and not by its causes, 'cause' here meaning the necessary or sufficient antecedent conditions for pattern x."[10]

   [8] Ibid., pp. 87–88, italics in original.
   [9] See Ernest A. Gellner's interesting article, "Time and Theory in Social Anthropology," in *Mind*, 67 (1958): 182–202.
   [10] Cancian, "Functional Analysis."

Apart from these considerations, Merton finds himself unable to avoid the very pitfalls he cautions us against. "*Functions*," he writes, "are those observed consequences which make for the adaptation or adjustment of a given system; and *dysfunctions*, those observed consequences which lessen the adaptation or adjustment of the system."[11]

As we see, he retains in his "paradigm for functional analysis" the very concepts he himself describes as "the cloudiest and empirically most debatable," namely, "prerequisites," "system-needs," "adaptation," and the like. The very next item of the paradigm is intended, apparently, to aid us in overcoming the traditional obstacles. "We have observed the difficulties entailed in *confining* analysis to functions fulfilled for 'the society,' since items may be functional for some individuals and subgroups and dysfunctional for others. It is necessary, therefore, to consider a *range* of units for which the item has designated consequences: individuals in diverse statuses, subgroups, the larger social system and culture systems."[12]

But does this actually enable us to overcome the basic problems of functional analysis? So long as we continue to speak of something as being "functional" or "dysfunctional" for a group or social system, so long as we continue to speak of "adaptation," "adjustment," and "system-needs," we remain encumbered by the problems of traditional functionalism. And all this quite apart from the superhuman powers that the paradigm would require if we actually tried to employ it in research.

The first step in the logic of the functional approach, according to Merton, is to establish "certain functional requirements of the organisms or [social systems], . . . requirements which must be satisfied if the organism [or social system] is to survive, or to operate with some degree of effectiveness."[13] But how in the world can one know what an organism or social system requires for its survival or effective operation in advance of having studied it? Sorokin's remarks in this connection are as incisive as they are humorous. Commenting on the first step of Merton's prescription, he writes:

> So, according to this recipe, if we want to make a functional analysis of a bird, our first problem is to find out what the functional requirements are that enable a bird to survive and fly effectively. I am certain that biologists do not follow this recipe in their study of birds, for no biologist can list in advance all the fantastically numerous requirements for survival or effective performance of a single bird under all the different conditions of its life-course. Still less can he compile such a list of requirements applicable to *all* organisms of all species under all the infinitely diverse conditions of their lives. Instead, the biologist studies the anatomical,

---

[11] Merton, *Social Theory and Social Structure*, p. 105.
[12] Ibid., p. 106.
[13] Ibid., p. 103.

histo-chemical, physiological, and behavioral properties of birds and concludes that "Birds fly because they have wings."[14]

Sorokin rightly insists that Merton's revisions have not answered the major objections to traditional functionalism. One need only think of any significant social development to recognize the cogency of his criticism. Are civil rights demonstrations, he asks, functions or dysfunctions? For whom?

> For what sort of adaptation? For the realization of what sort of values and objectives? In which way can each of these processes be scientifically diagnosed as function or dysfunction? If these questions cannot be answered, then the terms are meaningless. If they can be answered, the terms inevitably become subjectively evaluative and arbitrary (which fact is clearly shown by the opposite evaluations of, say, the civil-rights movement by the Negro leaders of the movement and by Southern politicians).[15]

OTHER FORMS OF FUNCTIONAL ANALYSIS

Some social scientists readily acknowledge all or most of these criticisms of traditional functionalism. They believe, however, that there are other types of functional analysis that are not subject to the same objections and which, therefore, may prove to be fruitful. Cancian, for example, has distinguished among the great variety of functional approaches three basic orientations or modes of analysis. All three have one element in common: "an interest in relating one part of a society or social system to another part or to some aspect of the whole." The three orientations are:[16]

1. The *traditional* approach (the one we have so far been examining), based on the postulate that all major social structures "operate to maintain the integration or adaptation of the larger social system."

2. The *sociological* approach, resting on the common concepts and assumptions of sociology. This is the orientation that Kingsley Davis, in his address to the American Sociological Association, argued is equivalent to sociological analysis, pure and simple, therefore requiring no special name. Guided by the rudimentary canons of scientific procedure, this orientation has led to careful description, a search for the determinate relationships among significant sociological variables, and general patterns and regularities. This is the methodological approach associated with the classical tradition of sociological thinking and shared, despite other important differences, by such thinkers as Marx, Weber, Durkheim, and Pareto, to name just a few.

[14] Sorokin, *Sociological Theories Today*, p. 450.
[15] Ibid., p. 449.
[16] These remarks are based on Cancian, "Functional Analysis," pp. 29–43.

3. The *cybernetic* approach, based "on a model of self-regulating or equilibrating systems." Here one abandons all the postulates of traditional functionalism and makes no assumptions about so-called "system-needs," or the "adaptive" or "integrative" effects of patterns. Nor, finally, does one attempt to explain a pattern by its effects or consequences. Cancian calls this formal functionalism, for

> [it] is concerned with homeostatic, or equilibrating, systems, and so with feedback and self-regulation. It abandons the two distinctive attributes of the traditional approach. The effects of a trait for some part of the system are used to explain that part and not to explain the trait; and there is no restriction on the kinds of consequences to be considered. They may or may not be beneficial or necessary to society. This approach is called "formal" because it does not include a theoretical orientation or a substantive hypothesis about empirical events. It is a model of kinds of relationship between elements, like a mathematical model.[17]

Of course, in this third approach too there are minimal requirements of scientific explanation that must be adhered to: assumptions must not be empirically false, propositions must be clearly stated so that a negative case might conceivably be discovered, and so forth.

As Cancian notes, because this is a formal model—that is, lacking in substantive propositions—one cannot, strictly speaking, explain anything by means of it until one has demonstrated a correspondence between the model and a specific social system. Correspondence would constitute a "precise description of the system" and perhaps even a "little theory"—"a 'theory' because it would explain and predict how variance in one part of the system would affect other parts of the system, and a '*little* theory' because the propositions would be limited to one specific system. In order to construct a general theory or explanation, it would be necessary to add an assumption stating that the model fits a certain class of systems, of which the specific system was a member." Again, however, the fruitfulness of this model depends on the degree to which social phenomena do in fact appear to be governed by equilibrating, feedback, and self-maintaining processes.

Are there any examples of the application of this model to observable social phenomena? I have selected one study that, for illustrative purposes, seems to fit the model. Since the bulk of Part I will focus on advanced industrial societies, I have chosen my example from the anthropological literature on "underdeveloped" societies.

In an interesting article entitled "The Myth of the Sacred Cow," the anthropologist Marvin Harris challenges the commonly held notion that Indian ideology, particularly the doctrine of the sacred cow, compels the population to

---

[17]Ibid., p. 30.

deprive itself of foods that are both abundant and highly nutritive and to subsist instead on other foods that are both scarcer and less valuable.[18]

Harris' main thesis is that "the taboo against the slaughter and eating of Indian cattle is consistent with an ecological balance in which human material welfare takes precedence over the welfare of animals." The idea that cattle in India are "useless" animals, wandering about, disrupting work, and damaging crops, is false. Two important questions are relevant to the thesis: (1) Are the cattle competing with the Indian population for scarce resources to the point of lowering the rate of reproduction and chances of survival of that population? (2) Would Indian food production increase substantially with the removal of the Hindu taboo on the slaughter of cattle?

The relationship between cattle and humans in India, Harris argues, is not competitive but symbiotic. "Indian farming is based on plough agriculture, to which cattle labor contributes as much as 46 per cent of the labor cost exclusive of transport and other supporting activities. . . ."

Far from a surplus, therefore, there is rather a shortage of cattle. A pair of bullocks appears to be a minimum for cultivation, and as many as two-thirds of India's farmers may be short of this technical minimum. This shows the usefulness and shortage of bullocks. But what about the cows? To this Harris replies that one must note the obvious: "No cows, no bullocks." Cows produce not only milk (admittedly with highly uneconomical results) but approximately 69 million male traction animals. Cows also produce dung, which turns out to be quite essential to the Indian economy. In addition to a minor use in plastering houses, dung serves as India's main cooking fuel in the absence of alternative combustibles, such as coal, that are prohibitively expensive for most peasants. The amount of dung consumed in cookery (some 300 out of the 800 million tons annually laid down in the countryside) is the "BTU equivalent of 35 million tons of coal or 68 million tons of wood." And the largest proportion of the remaining 500 million tons is used as organic fertilizer for the essential task of manuring.

Furthermore, Harris argues, "the most important point to note about the fuel and manure functions of India's cattle is that old, dry, barren animals do not cease to provide dung. On this score alone, one might expect more caution before the conclusion is reached that the sacred cow is a useless luxury." In addition, dead cattle are not entirely wasted as their hides are employed for a variety of leather products vital to the traditional agricultural technology.

Also of importance is the fact that a substantial amount of beef is in fact eaten despite the proscription. One must remember that there are millions of people in India with no caste to lose. "Not only are there some 55 million members of 'scheduled' castes, many of whom are under no obligation to spurn

[18] See Marvin Harris, "The Myth of the Sacred Cow," in *Man, Culture, and Animals: The Role of Animals in Human Ecological Adjustment*, ed. Anthony Leeds and Andrew P. Vayda (Washington: American Association for the Advancement of Science, 1965), pp. 217–28. The present discussion summarizes Harris's article.

beef, but there are also several more million who are pagan, Christian, or Moslem. It seems likely that a high proportion of the 20 million bovines which die each year get eaten." Thus cattle in India are far from being useless creatures; they provide the human population with milk, meat, bullocks, manure, fuel, and hides. From the peasant's standpoint, these contributions far outweigh the resources the cattle consume.

From this analysis Harris concludes that "the power of the sacra, surrounding the Indian cattle complex, is thoroughly circumscribed by the material conditions under which both man and beast must earn their livings." Given the prevailing property relations in India, the peasants and other poor are benefiting from the cattle and, hence, from the taboo.

Although Harris himself employs neither the concepts nor the assumptions of functional analysis in his essay, Paul W. Collins, a philosopher invited to comment on the contributions to the volume in which the essay appears, sees Harris's analysis as resting on functional premises.[19]

First, the variables Harris employed may be viewed as parts of a system. Second, there appear to be mechanisms at work that maintain "environmental variables at values conducive to the survival or expansion of human populations."

In Collins' view, this most closely approximates what we have called the "formal functional" model, characterized by feedback, self-equilibrating processes. The process Harris observes is not unlike the one governing a thermostat, or the numerous biological processes that serve to maintain the blood sugar level, or the blood cell level.

The formal functional system Collins discerns in Harris' analysis is the following:

1. An R variable (apparently crucial to the system, which in Harris' analysis would be the cattle);
2. disturbing factors (all factors operating to reduce the R variable); and
3. Compensating mechanisms (the taboo).

Harris, Collins agrees, has supported his hypothesis that the cattle population must be maintained *above* certain levels and that the taboo contributes to this.

But an important question remains: Does the interpretation in terms of the "formal functional" model add anything to our understanding that was not already included in the original analysis? Would the employment of this model at the very outset have been a research strategy superior to the one Harris in fact employed? Harris sought a connection between the "irrational" taboo and the prevailing social practice and found that under the existing socio-economic and political system the taboo is not what it has been presumed to be. He neither employed the formal functional model nor concluded from his analysis that a self-equilibrating, cybernetic process was at work. The cybernetic model has,

---

[19]Paul W. Collins, "Functional Analysis in the Symposium "Man, Culture, and Animals," in Leeds and Vayda, *Man, Culture and Animals.*

however, been so little tried in the study of human systems that its potential fruitfulness for research has yet to be determined.

THE ROLE OF HISTORY

Before any attempt is made to apply the cybernetic model, however, one ought to appreciate its definite limitations. One can employ formal functional analysis to explain relations among the *extant* variables of a given system as well as changes in their *quantitative* values; but one cannot explain by this means the emergence or appearance of new variables and processes. The "problem of explaining the origins of new variables and mechanisms requires recourse to explanatory procedures independent of functional analysis."[20]

In other words, formal functionalism is totally nonhistorical—but traditional functionalism has also been largely so. It is therefore no idle accusation to assert, as many critics have, that functional analysis may help to explain how a system works but not how qualitative social change comes about. The study of the changes a social system undergoes requires, among other things, a study of its history. Unfortunately, this is a truth that the adherents of functionalism have either not recognized or that they have ignored. Is it not the height of naiveté to suppose that one can explain the present exclusively by means of the present—to suppose that the chain of events leading from the past has no effect on the present? Some social scientists with a functionalist orientation liken themselves to their opposite numbers in the physical and biological sciences—an analogy with fatal flaws. In physiology, for example, "history" is relatively unimportant because physiologists can rely on "cycles." In the study of human society, however, to rely on cycles alone and to ignore history is to deprive oneself of the study of causality. The social scientist who studies a social structure without studying its history will never truly understand any given state of that structure or the forces operating to change it.

A denial of history and its causal role is peculiar to contemporary sociology. It would have been unthinkable for, say, Marx, Weber, or Durkheim to ignore history. Durkheim, who was the most explicitly functional of the three thinkers and who relied more than the others on organismic analogies, nonetheless emphasized the methodological importance of history. Although Durkheim, in his *Rules of the Sociological Method*, called for "an analysis of the functions of . . . social facts in terms of the social ends they serve," he also insisted that an adequate explanation of social facts requires an historical account of how the facts came to be what they are, i.e., a causal explanation in terms of antecedent social facts.

Let us summarize the major criticisms of traditional functionalism, many

---

[20]Collins, "Functional Analysis," p. 280.

of which, as we shall see, are also applicable to Talcott Parsons' conception of social life. Traditional functionalism

1. exaggerates the unity, stability, and harmony of social systems;
2. imputes a predominantly positive character to all social institutions;
3. is a nonhistorical approach to social systems;
4. tends to regard existing institutions as necessary and indispensable and therefore entails a conservative bias;
5. fails to account for social change.

With these critical points in mind, I turn to the works of Talcott Parsons, commonly regarded as the major structural-functionalist theorist in the United States, in order to explore further the main ambiguities and problems that beset the functionalist orientation.

2

Talcott Parsons: Action Theory and the Social System

When one reads Parsons' early writings on what he was later to call "action theory," with their emphasis on the subjective elements of human conduct, one finds it difficult indeed to understand his subsequent development. In an article published in 1935, entitled "The Place of Ultimate Values in Sociological Theory," he laid out the main elements that he later elaborated in his first major work, *The Structure of Social Action*.

The latter was intended as a study in the history of ideas as well as a contribution to social theory and systematic social science. Taken alone, Parsons argues, the works of Hobbes, Locke, and the Utilitarians were deficient in accounting for the phenomenon of social order. Hobbes placed overwhelming emphasis on the role of the State in assuring order; Locke attributed order to contractual relations, which he treated as given and unproblematic; and the Utilitarians never fully appreciated that if everyone relentlessly pursued his own interests, there was nothing, in the absence of either force or moral restraints, to prevent society from degenerating into the Hobbesian "war of all against all." Therefore one has to seek elsewhere for an adequate conception of order.

Looking over the development of social theory, Parsons discerned a dichotomy corresponding roughly to what the Germans called *Naturwissenschaft* and *Geisteswissenschaft*. The former advocated the application of the natural science model to the study of human behavior, and in its extreme positivist and behaviorist form banished all elements of consciousness from the human pale—or at best treated them as impotent epiphenomena. The latter, in contrast, committed the opposite error. As philosophical idealists they elevated ideas and moral and subjective elements to so high a status that they accorded no significant role to "material" factors in human conduct. What was essential about the human being was his "spirit." Society and culture were essentially spiritual phenomena and indeed each culture was a unique configuration or *Gestalt*—a position that appeared to deny the possibility of a social science in the comparative and generalizing sense.

There were thinkers among both the positivists and idealists, however, who departed from the extremes of their respective traditions and converged toward a more balanced position. Emile Durkheim and Vilfredo Pareto started from a positivist position but soon came to recognize the crucial role of values, ends, purposes, ideals, etc., both in motivating human conduct and accounting for social order. Max Weber, Georg Simmel, and Ferdinand Toennies, presumably starting from an idealist position, also underscored these elements—but without excluding the role of "causes" and "conditions." In other words, thinkers from both traditions converged towards what Parsons evidently regarded as his original contribution, a theory of social action and social order rooted in a society's "common value system."

There are several serious problems with this interpretation of the work of the earlier theorists. To begin, the thesis has something of the contrived about it. It is very doubtful that there is, as Parsons claims, a direct parallel "between my terms 'end' and 'value-attitude' and Pareto's 'residue' and 'sentiment.' "[1] A careful reading of Pareto's *Traité* shows that the "sentiments" and "residues" are more often than not biopsychic forces or what an earlier school of psychology called "instincts." Parsons himself, immediately after claiming the parallel, seems to acknowledge the fundamental ambiguity of Pareto's concepts, for he adds: "I do not, however, adopt Pareto's terminology because he did not clearly draw the line between positivistic and value elements in action which is absolutely essential to me. His terms include both categories."[2] Whatever Pareto's "sentiments" are, they certainly are not the value elements of action theory.[3] On the other hand, what Parsons definitely borrowed from Pareto, and has retained to this day, are concepts of a definitely positivist cast: system, equilibrium, functions, etc.

Similarly, it is also rather doubtful that Durkheim, in the course of his intellectual development, moved toward and discovered only late the important place of values in social conduct. Values and norms are just as evident in his early studies, for instance the *Division of Labor* and *Professional Ethics and Civic Morals*, as in his last major work, *The Elementary Forms of Religious Life*. More important, however, is what Parsons ignores in Durkheim.

Durkheim certainly appreciated the role of moral values in motivating social conduct and maintaining social order. But he also recognized the place of

---

[1] Talcott Parsons, "The Place of Ultimate Values in Sociological Theory," *International Journal of Ethics* 45 (1935): 306.

[2] *Ibid.*, pp. 306–7.

[3] For a detailed critical analysis of Pareto's concepts, see the essay on Pareto in my *Ideology and the Development of Sociological Theory* (Englewood Cliffs, N. J.: Prentice-Hall, 1968).

interest conflicts and force. The "organic solidarity" he posited as resulting from the increasingly complex division of labor depended ultimately on abolishing two pathological forms of this division, the "anomic" and the "forced." Without reducing social inequalities by abolishing inheritance and otherwise restricting the institution of private property, no amount of normative adjustment would suffice to engender the higher form of social order he so strongly desired. Yet this dimension of Durkheim's work never really finds its way into Parsons' conception, where values and other moral elements remain paramount while conflicts of interest and coercion are relegated to an insignificant position.

Another criticism relates to what is perhaps the heart of Parsons' convergence thesis. We are asked to believe that none of the classical theorists whose work he reviews in *The Structure of Social Action* grasped the need to mediate between the extreme positivist and idealist positions; and that it was he, Parsons, whose original contribution it was to have explicitly formulated such a mediation. But this is a curious view, for it denies the methodological contribution of Max Weber. What was Weber's contribution if not the careful exploration of the "middle ground" between the extremes of the *Geisteswissenschaften* and the *Naturwissenschaften*, the insistence that the study of human conduct requires a concern with values and ends as well as causes and conditions? Was it not Weber's ideal to provide explanations that were adequate both *causally* and on the level of *meaning* and *intentionality?*

The impression we get from Parsons' work is that while he acknowledges Weber's effort in this direction, he wants nevertheless to fault him for failing to integrate his disparate insights into a general theory of action, including a theory of social systems. Presumably it is the provision of the latter that Parsons regards as his own significant contribution.

We must, however, seriously question whether Parsons has in this way bested Weber. To anticipate one of the arguments of the following pages, I would hold that when Parsons remains on the level of the postulates of action theory, his position is not significantly different from Weber's. Indeed, it even bears some resemblance to the standpoint of those phenomenologists, existentialists (Sartre, for instance), and philosophical historians who deny the possibility of a social *science* and who therefore regard the study of man and society as a philosophical and historical discipline.[4] On the other hand, Parsons' attempt to build into action theory his functionalist conception of social systems tends to vitiate the major postulates of his action theory—"voluntarism" and the active, creative, and evaluative sides of man. These and other problems may best be explored by examining some of his major writings. Let us first examine *The Social System*.[5]

---

[4] See T. B. Bottomore's review of Parsons' recent essays, "Out of This World," *New York Review of Books*, 13, no. 8 (November 6, 1969): 34–39.

[5] Talcott Parsons, *The Social System* (New York: The Free Press, 1951). Page references to this work will be cited in parentheses immediately following the quoted passage.

THE SOCIAL SYSTEM

We might begin by asking whether or not Parsons' effort constitutes a theory. In *The Social System,* he himself alternately describes it as a "conceptual scheme for the analysis of the structure and processes of social systems"; a "statement of general sociological theory" (vii); and "a theory of systems," which, in turn, is "an integral part of the larger conceptual scheme which we have called the theory of action" (537).

While he acknowledges that ultimately the usefulness of his scheme must be demonstrated in empirical research, he asserts in the same breath that the direct concern of the work "will be neither with empirical generalization as such nor with methodology. . . ." His conception of scientific theory is that it develops in relative isolation from empirical research and that it does so rapidly: "The development of theoretical ideas has been proceeding so rapidly that a difference of a few months or even weeks in time may lead to important changes . . ." (x). The "field is in a process of such rapid development," he adds, that he anticipates "substantial changes" in about five years.

Commentators often have noted how elusive Parsons' abstract scheme is and how rapidly he modifies it. But his modifications are not of the kind usually meant by the term in science—that is, adjusting theory to the findings of empirical research. It seems instead to be a matter of substituting new terms and distinctions for old, independent of any research.

Parsons' modifications are part of a highly eclectic process in which he incorporates diverse elements without regard for their theoretical compatibility or the damage they may be doing to his framework. Voluntaristic, rational, functionalist, Freudian, and still other elements are brought together and uncritically fused into one analytical scheme—a scheme, moreover, with no apparent applicability. For, as we shall see, he himself never employs his grand framework and abandons it altogether when he wishes to explain or interpret a relatively concrete social phenomenon such as Nazism or McCarthyism. But it is best to leave these considerations for later when we have gained a firmer grip on Parsons' major ideas.

His point of departure is the interaction of individual actors under conditions that enable us to treat their "interaction as a system in the scientific sense and subject it to the same order of theoretical analysis which has been successfully applied to other types of systems in other sciences" (3). The simplest system of interaction is a "dyadic" one, as between Ego and Alter, who are, in the final analysis, organisms but whose actions cannot be adequately understood by reference to their biological or physiochemical systems. Social interaction must be grasped on its own level and not reduced to nonsocial factors, although, of course, these may be relevant. This is why Parsons prefers to speak of the "action of the actor" and the "situation of action" instead of the "behavior of the organism" and its "environment." His position is thus quite clearly distinguished from that of the behaviorists.

Ego and Alter are social actors playing specific and reciprocal roles so that a certain "complementarity of expectations" is formed between them. This "complementarity," as we shall see, is the basis of the system's equilibrium. Ego rewards all of Alter's actions that conform with Ego's expectations and, conversely, punishes all actions that do not thus conform; similarly, Alter reciprocally rewards and punishes Ego's actions.

Analytically speaking, the interaction process is *social*; but as it involves values, norms, goals, and motives, one cannot conceptualize social interaction without considering two other systems—culture and personality—that are analytically distinguishable from the social system. Society, culture, and personality are empirically inseparable but analytically distinguishable "spheres."

One cannot adequately understand a *social* system if one fails to take into account that it is simultaneously a cultural system that manifests itself in the personality systems and motives of the individual actors. In Parsons' words, "We cannot speak of the structure of the social system in theoretical terms at all without speaking of the institutionalization of cultural patterns, notably of course patterns of value-orientation. . . . Similarly . . . the motivational processes of the social system are *always* processes within the personalities of the component individual actors" (538).

Thus personality is an aspect of the sociocultural system. Individuals internalize aspects of the institutionalized value patterns and typically act out their roles accordingly—and when they don't, i.e., when they deviate, they are brought back into line by means of negative sanctions. In these terms, there is a "common sector" of both the personality and the social system.

> [It] consists in the value-patterns which define role expectations. The motivational structures thus organized are units *both* of personality as a system and of the social system in which the actor participates; they are need-dispositions of the personality and they are role-expectations of the social system. This is the key to the "transformation formula" between the two systems of personality and social system. . . . This fundamental relationship between need-dispositions of the personality, role-expectations of the social system and internalized-institutionalized value-patterns of the culture, is the fundamental nodal point of the organization of systems of action. (540)

It is the action systems, in this sense, that are abstracted and "studied." They are, Parsons insists, boundary-maintaining systems in that they constitute a frame of reference analytically independent of, say, biological theory.

For Parsons, then, a social system consists of a plurality of actors interacting in a sociocultural situation (as distinguished from the physical environment, or *means* and *conditions* of action) to which their interaction is motivationally relevant and oriented. Each actor derives the energy required for action from his organism and strives to optimize gratification and avoid deprivation, processes always retaining an organic significance. The entire interaction process is mediated by a "system of culturally structured and shared symbols" (6).

The three major aspects of action that Parsons discerns he calls the cognitive, cathectic, and evaluative: the "three basic modes of motivational orientation." These more or less correspond to the old and well-known psychological distinctions of the cognitive, affective, and conative dimensions. The cognitive, for Parsons, refers to the actor's definition of the situation in terms of his interests; the cathectic, to the actor's quest for gratification; and the evaluative, to the actor's choice and ordering of alternatives. An actor may wait passively for events to take place, a state called "anticipation"; or he may seek actively to bring them about or avoid them, a state called "goal-directedness"— the latter being "a fundamental property of all action-systems" (8).

Action theory rests on the fundamental postulate that human social interaction is based on complex and abstract systems of symbolic communication, notably language but also the other shared symbolic meanings of the cultural tradition. It is always in the context of some such tradition that social interaction takes place and assumes certain forms (structures itself). A most important element of this shared tradition may be called a "value," "which serves as a criterion or standard for selection among the alternatives of orientation which are intrinsically open in a situation . . ." (12). When such standards or partial elements thereof are internalized by an actor, they provide the content of his motivational orientation.

Three logically independent systems, the social, the cultural, and the personal, are therefore involved in action. To take the cultural first, its elements are learned, shared, and transmitted.[6] The last of these characteristics, transmissibility, the fact that elements are not only passed on to the next generation but may also be diffused from one system to another, "serves as a most important criterion for distinguishing culture from the social system. . . . Relative to the particular social system, it is a 'pattern element' which is both analytically and empirically abstractable from that particular social system" (15).

Although a social system cannot but operate in the context of a cultural tradition, there is always a disparity between the actual patterns of interaction and those ideally prescribed by the cultural tradition. This is inevitable since individuals internalize cultural ideals only partially and imperfectly. Individual motives never fully embody the institutionalized value patterns of the culture. Each of the three systems, the social, cultural, and personal, thus retain some capacity for independent variation.

Parsons' view of action systems, as I have summarized it thus far, is not

---

[6] All these processes are much more problematic than Parsons apparently assumes. We shall take up this issue later.

without its problems, but it may have some usefulness as a logical clarification of concepts. At this point, however, the trouble begins. For as he proceeds to elaborate the system side of his action "theory," Parsons employs all the functionalist assumptions and terms that we have found to be so problematic from several standpoints. Parsons recognizes that a scientific theory of social systems requires criteria for their empirical separation; his success in providing them, however, is no greater than that of the other functionalists.

What is a "society" for Parsons? It is an "empirically self-subsistent social system." He continues:

> If we add the consideration of duration sufficiently long to transcend the life span of the normal human individual, recruitment by biological reproduction and socialization of the oncoming generation become essential aspects of such a social system. A social system of this type, which meets all the essential functional prerequisites of long term persistence from within its own resources, will be called a *society*. It is not essential to the concept of society that it should not be in any way empirically interdependent with other societies, but only that it should contain all the structural and functional fundamentals of an independently subsisting system (19).

So we see that Parsons' definition is almost identical with the one encountered earlier. Indeed, since Parsons explicitly relies on Aberle et al., our earlier criticisms apply equally here. Despite his insistence that it is of the "greatest importance to specify what the system is which is being used as the object for a sociological analysis, whether or not it is a society, and if not, just how this particular social system is located in the society of which it is a part," Parsons never succeeds in informing us precisely what empirical social reality he is talking about. His definition remains a futile neoscholastic exercise that attempts to overcome one ambiguity by means of another. His "clarification" of "self-sufficiency" certainly sheds little light, for, as we have seen in our earlier examination of functionalism, to say that a society must "contain all the structural and functional fundamentals of an independently subsisting system" is meaningless.

The trouble with Parsons' approach, apart from its functionalist defects, is that it is the wrong way to approach the task of constructing scientific theory. If one is genuinely interested in empirical social systems, one ought to have questions about their workings that one would like to answer. To do this, one does not begin with "society" in the abstract but with a specific society (or several of them) and with an interesting problem. Take these arbitrary examples: How did the slave system of the antebellum South compare and contrast with the slave systems of Greece and Rome? What were the causes of the Russian Revolution and why did that social convulsion occur there and not elsewhere? Why have some societies achieved considerable economic development while others have remained relatively "backward"? Or, finally, why was "modernization" achieved in the context of liberal-democratic institutions in some cases (England, the United States, France) and in the context of authoritarian, fascist, or totalitarian regimes in others (Germany, Japan, Russia)?[7]

In each of these examples, the "society" about which one is talking is quite evident, as is the reason for studying it. This is a problem-oriented approach to social science, including theory building, and is quite the opposite of Parsons' practice, which is to talk about a reified, abstract "society" with prerequisites and needs. Apparently Parsons does not realize that most of the statements that can be made about *any* society are bound to be banal. One of the main reasons, then, for Parsons's ambiguities is that he defines his terms without any research purpose or problem in mind.

THE FUNCTIONAL PREREQUISITES

Parsons' "functional prerequisites" are similar to those we earlier encountered in Aberle et al. A social system must not be incompatible with the functioning needs of its individual, participating actors or with the stable integration of the cultural system. In turn, the cultural and personality systems must support the social system. Actors must be motivated to fulfill the roles required of them, and the cultural patterns must conduce to a minimum of order.

Yet we are never told precisely what the various "system-needs" are, whether of the personality, culture, or society; nor how certain structures concretely fulfill the so-called functional needs. There is not a single illustration suggesting how these fundamental postulates of functionalism might be verified, or a single example of a system or society whose termination might justifiably be attributed to the absence of one or more of the so-called prerequisites. The only conclusion possible is that Parsons' analytical scheme, together with the doctrine of functional prerequisites and system equilibrium (to be considered later), resolves itself into a futile quest for some indeterminate requirements of a vaguely conceived "equilibrium" of an ill-defined social system.

PATTERN ALTERNATIVES OF VALUE ORIENTATION

A scientific theory requires variables, and so Parsons provides some—the now famous pattern variables. He deduces them from Toennies' dichotomy, *Gemeinschaft–Gesellschaft,* and forms them into a series of alternative value

---

[7] For a superb example of this type of study see Barrington Moore, Jr., *Social Origins of Dictatorship and Democracy* (Boston: Beacon Press, 1966)—a study in which the author finds it unnecessary to define "society" even once.

orientations which every actor faces. The alternatives, or dilemmas, and their resolution, are presumably associated with definite role expectations and types of social system, and one sort of resolution would be expected in a predominantly *gemeinschaftlich* system or situation and the polar opposite in a *gesellschaftlich* situation.

Here are the five main dilemmas:

1. Affectivity versus affective neutrality: either the actor orients himself to the gratification of affective needs or he is affectively neutral. The first would be appropriate in a husband-wife relationship, for example, the second not.

2. Self-orientation versus collectivity orientation: The actor pursues either his own private interests or those of the collectivity.

3. Universalism versus particularism: the actor relates to another individual either according to criteria equally applicable to all or according to select standards. To illustrate, an application of universalistic standards would be the recruitment to a job, office, school, or whatever by means of an examination system designed to assess the competence of candidates. Examples of particularistic standards, in contrast, are nepotism or the exclusion of certain ethnic, racial, or other social groups.

4. Quality versus performance: This is similar to Ralph Linton's ascription-achievement dichotomy. Does the actor orient himself to another in accordance with what he *is*, or what he *does*? That is, the actor takes into account either the qualities of the other or his performance.

5. Specificity versus diffuseness: either the actor relates to another individual as the incumbent of a specific status, or he relates to him as a whole person. The former situation would be expected in a place of business, as in the way a customer relates to a salesclerk, for example; the latter situation is characteristic of a family.

The ambiguities are numerous. Why are these dilemmas more useful for thinking about social relationships and systems than, say, the classical dichotomy from which they are derived? Are they binary or opposite ends of continua? What does it mean to say, as Parsons does, that "they may be held to constitute a system" (66)? How does one use these variables? If they are significant variables, why doesn't he who conceived them employ them?—for Parsons does not, as we shall see, either in the further elaboration of his scheme or in his analyses of specific social phenomena.

EMPIRICAL STRUCTURES

It is not true, as some have supposed, that Parsons ignores altogether such important aspects of social reality as stratification, power, force, and conflict. He has given a great deal of attention to these and related matters in his numerous articles and essays. Even here, in his theoretical work, *The Social System*, these matters find their place.

Criticism of Parsons' theorizing is deficient if it stresses only how he has slighted problems of institutionalized inequality, power, and social conflict; it should also be directed against his conception of "empirical clusterings of the structural components of social systems," and the uses to which he puts this conception.

Parsons draws attention to what he regards as the four fundamental empirical clusterings of every society: kinship, social classes, territorially based organizations of force, and religious institutions and associations. His thesis here is that these structures are indispensable to any society and that their variation both historically and crossculturally is severely limited. As a consequence there are definite limits to social change. The argument is essentially polemical, apparently directed against Marxists who have emphasized the variability of societies and their potential for change. It may therefore be instructive to examine Parsons' argument.

1. *Kinship Systems.* Kinship "looms large" in every human society: kinship units universally ascribe one's initial status, and it is within such units that highly significant socialization takes place "with kinship personalities serving as strategically important socializing agents" (154). In addition, regulation of sexual conduct is universal, as are several incest taboos, for example the taboo on intercourse within families, except, of course, for spouses. Finally, kinship units are, in Parsons' terms, everywhere functionally diffuse and collectivity oriented, and it could never be otherwise. What Parsons wants to bring into relief is that there exist universal constraints, and that these account for the fact that kinship units "fall within a narrow sector of the total range of structural variability of types of collectivities" (154). Or again, "the important point is the near universality of the limitation of variability to such narrow limits both with respect to function and to structured types" (155). To explain the "narrow sector," Parsons reviews some of the well-known arguments regarding the extreme dependency of the human infant, the "need" for a sexual division of labor, and the like.

Past and present kinship forms suggest that there are definite structural and functional imperatives that no society can circumvent. As "proof" Parsons cites the experience of the Soviet Union, where there was a brief experiment with so-called free love and the abolition of the family.

The most recent large-scale demonstration of its power [the power of kinship] is the case of Soviet Russia. There is nothing in Marxist ideology in favor of preservation of the family; indeed the balance is strongly the other way. In the early days of the revolution it was taken for granted that the family was mainly a "bourgeois prejudice" and was in process of immediately "withering away." Then came a very powerful reaction so that in legislative terms a far stricter level of enforcement of family obligation than in most Western countries emerged. (156–57)

But what does Parsons prove by his example? The argument is tautological, resting on the assumptions and concepts of functionalism. He reflects on
societies of the past and present, including one that professes to be fundamentally different, and all of which have kinship forms falling within what he defines
as a "narrow sector." From this he infers the existence of certain functional
imperatives—which, in turn, he employs to argue the necessity of the "narrow
sector." Even worse, in one breath he argues the functional necessity of a narrow
range of variation and in the next he says: "It is, of course, by no means
excluded that fundamental changes in any or all of these respects may
sometimes come about" (155). Apparently the functional imperatives may
change.

This is speculation, not science, and may even be ideology. After all,
Parsons could just as easily have selected and underscored quite the opposite
characteristics of kinship forms—their immense variety and changeability. The
point is that if one has a scientific interest in studying kinship phenomena, one
does not go about the task as Parsons does. Instead, one studies the variety of
kinship forms, the historical changes they have undergone, and their relation to
other aspects of their respective social systems. If one believes that Soviet
experience is relevant to the issue, one ought at least take serious account of
both objective conditions and policy decisions. Barrington Moore, a close
student of the Soviet society, has, for example, written in this connection:

> In the first place, the Soviets, I think, adopted their conservative policy
> toward the family *faute de mieux*. That is to say, with their very limited
> resources, and with other more pressing objectives, they had no genuine
> alternatives. Steel mills had to be built before crèches, or at least before
> crèches on a large enough scale to make any real difference in regard to
> child care. In the meantime the services of the family, and especially of
> grandma (*babushka*), had to be called upon. In the second place, with
> consolidation of the regime in the middle thirties, Soviet totalitarianism
> may have succeeded in capturing the family and subverting this institution
> to its own uses. At any rate the confidence and vigor with which the
> regime supported this institution from the early thirties onward suggests
> such an explanation. Thus the Soviet experience does not constitute by
> itself very strong evidence in favor of the "functional necessity" of the
> family.[8]

If Parsons proceeds less cautiously than this, it may be due to ideological
elements in his thinking—elements of which he may be unaware but which
become evident in his handling of the other empirical clusterings.

  2. *Social Stratification.* Here, too, Parsons wishes to establish the severe

---

[8] Barrington Moore, Jr., *Political Power and Social Theory* (Cambridge: Harvard
University Press, 1958), pp. 162–63.

limitations on the variation of structures. "The essential fact," he writes, "seems to be that there are rather sharp limits to the independent variability of the instrumental structure and the distribution of facilities, on the one hand, [and] the distribution of rewards, on the other" (157). Stratification and inequality are inherent in the "instrumental complex itself." "With the elaboration of the division of labor," he continues, "there is an inherent tendency to differentiate along two axes both of which have inferiority-superiority implications." One reason for this is that achievement is always evaluated: people perform their tasks either well or badly and their comparative skill and competence have to be assessed and presumably even ranked.

But there is, according to Parsons, another important reason: role differentiation (division of labor) requires organization, and organization, in turn, requires the allocation of responsibility for the "affairs of the collectivity." Parsons states:

> [The] imperatives of effectiveness demand that with differentials of competence and of responsibility there should go differentials in facilities. It would clearly not be efficient to place the best tools in the hands of the least efficient workers in order to compensate them for their lower efficiency status, still less perhaps to entrust the most important facilities to those carrying least responsibility. . . . There is, therefore, an inherent tendency to allocate greater facilities to those on the higher levels of competence and responsibility.
>
> This tendency is *both* a functional imperative of effectiveness and efficiency of instrumental structures, *and* an inherent implication of the valuation of instrumental achievement. But the valuation of instrumental achievement *itself* means that achieving higher levels of competence and/or responsibility, and having larger facilities at one's command *are in themselves rewards*, and rewards which are inherently differential. It is literally impossible to have an instrumental system sanctioned by the valuation of achievement without the internal differentiation of the role and facility structure coming *also* to be a differentiation of rewards, an internal stratification. (159)

The first observation one might make about this formulation is that it fails to distinguish between two social processes, differentiation and stratification. Although they are often found as corollary processes in social systems, it is dogmatic to insist that stratification (inequality of rewards and life-chances) must accompany differentiation. There is also, a logical defect in the formulation. Parsons says that when one has facilities at one's command they are in themselves rewards; but if facilities are rewards by definition, then differentiation is also stratification by definition and Parsons has formulated no proposition. What he probably means to allege is that stratification inevitably accompanies differentiation.

But is it true that differential access to facilities, or responsibilities for them must be accompanied by unequal rewards? Most probably not. We do know of contemporary social systems, based on modern technology and industry, where this is not the case. The *kibbutz* is an outstanding example of a system in which some members have greater responsibility than others over large, complex, expensive facilities but do not receive greater rewards in the form of wealth, power, or privilege. The factory manager, for instance, receives a very specific mandate from the collectivity; and it is in the context of the factory alone that he exercises authority over the productive facilities. Even here, however, his authority is severely limited, since the members of the collectivity as a whole make the large policy decisions affecting both the factory and its relation to other economic and social aspects of *kibbutz* society. But what one certainly will not find in the *kibbutz* are institutionalized inequalities: there are no differential rewards that accrue to the manager and his family as a result of his responsibility over important facilities. Parsons' main error lies in his elevating of material incentives to the status of a universal imperative. As we shall see presently, his own treatment of the "profit motive" would seem to impose crippling qualifications on his so-called imperatives.

Parsons is also altogether uncritical of the proposition that expertise and efficiency require hierarchy and stratification. He ignores altogether the question to which Max Weber and other serious students of social organization have drawn attention: To what degree is the hierarchical structure of an organization a "requirement" of efficiency and expertise and to what degree a requirement (under historically specific property and power relations) of social control, domination, and discipline? This is a difficult question, to be sure, but an important one. What is certain is that this and other questions raised by Parsons' theoretical position cannot be answered—any more than his "imperatives" can be proved—by pointing again and again, as he does, to Soviet experience.

Kinship structures, Parsons continues, contribute to and reinforce the imperative inequality in industrial society. The integration of the kinship and occupational structures is such that facilities and rewards available to one member of a family will unavoidably be shared by the others. "The consequence of this is that the combination of an occupationally differentiated industrial system and a significantly solidary kinship system *must* be a system of stratification in which the children of the more highly placed come to have differential advantages, by virtue of their ascribed kinship status, not shared by those lower down" (161). Again, what does Parsons adduce as "proof"? This "generalization is amply confirmed," he writes, "by the history of Soviet Russia" (161). He goes even farther: "unless the need for kinship solidarities can be radically reduced below, for instance, the present American level, there is an inherent limit to development, not only of absolutely egalitarian societies, but even of complete equality of opportunity" (161). He speaks of "absolutely egalitarian societies" and "complete equality of opportunity" as if we had so closely approximated these conditions that his "iron law" might console us for not attaining them absolutely. The point is that Parsons is not really exploring the question in a scientific and critical manner but simply affirming—on the basis of a discussion that has nothing to say about property and power relations—the inevitable continuation into the future of present-day social forms.

3. *Territoriality and Force.* Parsons' entire discussion of empirical clusterings is a curious one. Here, in one very small section of his book, he speaks of force, power, and conflict, but neither before nor after does he actually apply these concepts in his abstract analytical scheme—where his "common value system" occupies the stage almost alone. When he does turn briefly to force, power and conflict, he gives them a curious twist.

For Max Weber, it will be recalled, a state successfully "claims the monopoly of the legitimate use of physical force within a given territory." The "state is a relation of men dominating men."[9] This, for Weber, is a definition. What does Parsons do with it? He transforms the definition into a functional necessity: "[No] paramount integrative structure of a society could perform that function [the prevention of undesired action] effectively unless it were intimately tied in with the control of power relations in general and force in particular" (162).

After emphasizing the central role of the internalization of values in maintaining social order to the virtual exclusion of other elements, he now adopts a quasi-Hobbesian position. But he fails to deal with the problem of the role of force in the maintenance of order in a logical or an empirical fashion. Why is it that in some societies internalized values predominantly account for social order and the use of force is truly a last resort? Why is it that in other societies fear constitutes a much larger ingredient in the obedience of its members, and the coercive apparatus plays a major role in exacting this obedience? Nowhere are we offered enlightenment on these or related questions.

4. *Religion and Value-Integration.* There are functional imperatives, Parsons maintains, that make religion a necessary institution in any society. Fear of death, the disparity between ideals and their actualization, undeserved suffering and unpunished evil, are a few of the conditions that make religion indispensable. Once again Parsons cannot resist pointing to the Soviet experience as "proof" that social institutions must remain within a narrow band of possibilities, and that when societies attempt experiments on the edge of the band or beyond it, they are bound to fail. The religion of Communism, he says, has repudiated coercion and force in its ideal state; yet, in reality, "far from repudiating the use of force, the Communist movement has magnified and glorified it" (166).

It is true that Parsons does remind the reader that "some things certainly become possible at certain stages of ... [a society's] development which were previously not so ..." (167). In the main, however, he ignores such qualifica-

---

[9] H. H. Gerth and C. Wright Mills, trans. and eds., *From Max Weber: Essays in Sociology* (New York: Oxford University Press, 1958), p. 78.

tions, for what interests him most is to persuade us that there exist functional exigencies assuring that the future will be merely, or little more than, a repetition of the past.

THE CONCEPT OF EQUILIBRIUM

Parsons' explicit assumption is that the social equilibrium, the continuity and maintenance of social patterns, is *not* problematic and requires no explanation; only change requires explanation.

It is certainly contrary to much of the common sense of the social sciences, but it will nevertheless be assumed that the maintenance of the complementarity of role-expectations, once established, is *not problematical*, in other words that the "tendency" to maintain the interaction process is the *first law of social process*. . . . Another way of stating this is to say that no *special mechanisms* are required for the explanation of the maintenance of complementary interaction-orientation. (205, italics in original)

This fundamental assumption is clearly untenable. If we begin by taking Parsons' simple dyadic model of Ego and Alter, we can readily see that an equilibrium is very problematical indeed and that special mechanisms are in fact required to maintain it. Alvin Gouldner has shown that if Ego continues to act precisely in accordance with Alter's expectations, the end result might very well be to weaken and undermine the relationship.[10] If, for example, a husband consistently and predictably brings his wife flowers and candy on certain ceremonial occasions, such as anniversaries and birthdays, and only on those occasions, one logical possibility is that she will experience a diminishing gratification and respond accordingly by rewarding him less and less for the same conduct. On the other hand, if he resorts to special mechanisms such as surprising her with a gift on a nonformal occasion, when she least expects it, this might serve immeasurably to reinforce and revitalize the relationship. Even this homely example shows that something more than Parsons' law of inertia—a mechanical conception of equilibrium—is required for an understanding of human relationships.

There is nothing unproblematic or automatic about the maintenance of normative expectations or value systems. Parsons' view, according to which social order is based on a "common value system," takes no note of what Max Weber emphasized—a society is characterized by a "polytheism" of values in combat with one another. Values neither fall from the skies nor prevail

---

[10]See his "Organizational Analysis" in Robert K. Merton, Leonard Broom, and Leonard S. Cottrell, Jr., eds., *Sociology Today* (New York: Basic Books, 1959), p. 425.

independently of specific social groups and strata. When attempts are made to institutionalize a more unified value system, they typically serve the interests of the powerful and privileged. Often, therefore, these attempts meet with resistance and opposition. Finally, it cannot be assumed that each generation will be as receptive to certain values as the last.

In sum, by isolating values from interests, social classes, and the state, and by positing inertia, Parsons ignores the fact that implanting and maintaining values often involves "great pain and suffering," as Barrington Moore puts it. Commenting on Parsons' assumption of inertia, Moore writes:

> To maintain and transmit a value system, human beings are punched, bullied, sent to jail, thrown into concentration camps, cajoled, bribed, made into heroes, encouraged to read newspapers, stood up against a wall and shot, and sometimes even taught sociology. To speak of cultural inertia is to overlook the concrete interests and privileges that are served by indoctrination, education, and the entire complicated process of transmitting culture from one generation to the next.[11]

SOCIAL CHANGE

Since Parsons assumes that the maintenance of a social system, its equilibrium state, is unproblematic, we are left with a "theory of systems" that does not explain order. At the same time we are told that *"a general theory of the processes of change of social systems is not possible in the present state of knowledge"* (486, italics in original). By his own admission, then, his so-called "theory of systems" accounts for neither order nor change—to which one can only respond: "Then what does it account for?"

Although a general theory of change in the strict sense is presently impossible, Parsons writes, "we can still say a number of empirically relevant things about the general *nature* of such processes, which derive from the fact that they are processes occurring within the social system" (491).

At this point, he introduces the term "vested interests" and notes that "change is never just 'alteration of pattern' but alteration *by the overcoming of resistance"* (491, italics in original).

> The term vested interests seems appropriate to designate this general resistance to change which is inherent in the institutionalization of roles in the social system. . . . It is not confined to "economic" or "material" interests though it may include them. . . . The phenomenon of vested interests, then, may be treated as always lying in the background of the problem of social change. With the exception of processes of institutional-

[11] Moore, *Social Origins of Dictatorship and Democracy*, p. 486.

ized change, change in the social system is possible only by the operation of mechanisms which overcome the resistance of vested interests. It is, therefore, always essential explicitly to analyze the structure of the relevant vested interest complex before coming to any judgment of the probable outcome of the incidence of forces making for change. These considerations will often yield the answer to the questions of why processes of change either fail to occur altogether or fail to have the outcomes which would be predicted on a common sense basis. (492–93)

There are several observations to be made regarding the introduction of this concept at this late date. It is introduced quite arbitrarily and has no relation whatsoever either to his general analytical scheme or to functionalism. If, however, this valuable concept is to be introduced, why not employ it in relation to the phenomenon Parsons calls equilibrium? Had he done so, Parsons would have been compelled to acknowledge that this equilibrium is quite problematic and that there are social groups organized to resist change in a variety of ways. Such an analysis would have required a study of power, domination, and the conflict of interests—concerns wholly foreign to the main thrust of his work. Thus his belated introduction of the concept is unsatisfactory, for he puts it to no good use.

Opposed on general grounds to theories emphasizing key factors or sources of change, Parsons tells us that his "central methodological principle . . . is that of the interdependence of a plurality of variables" (493). But we never learn which variables these are, what the principle is by which he selects them, or why a dogmatic eclecticism is necessarily superior to a dogmatic one-factor theory.

Parsons' discussion of social change is not very illuminating. Towards the end (530), he takes a final opportunity to let us know once again that the Soviet experience "proves" that radical equality is strictly a wish fantasy and that real social movements, such as Christianity and Communism, fall short of their founders' ideals.

As one reads the final passages of *The Social System*, and reflects on the obscure language, the endless classifications and distinctions and the numerous problems to which attention has been called, one cannot but agree with numerous harsh judgments[12] of this work.

[12] It has been described, for example, as "vicious circles and empty and pretentious verbal formulae" (George Gurvitch); arid vagueness "often taken for wisdom" (Leopold Von Wiese); and "about 50 per cent verbiage, 40 per cent well-known textbook sociology, and only 10 per cent of possible—although rather vague—ideological use" (C. Wright Mills).

3

Is There a Second Talcott Parsons?

Numerous commentators have observed that when Parsons turns his attention to empirical phenomena he also turns his back on his general analytical scheme. Some critics, notably Alvin Gouldner, have gone even farther, noting that when called upon to explain concrete social developments, Parsons not only abandons his general orientation but often implicitly adopts another, antithetical to his own. Gouldner describes it as a double bookkeeping operation, in which Parsons employs a consensual or functionalist model in his theoretical writings and a quasi-Marxian or "conflict" model in his empirical essays. It is this other side of Parsons that I shall explore here, to determine whether his alter-ego is what it appears to be.

Let us begin with his 1942 article, "Democracy and Social Structure in Pre-Nazi Germany."[1] What strikes one immediately is that Parsons places at the center of investigation classes and class interests and their connection with economic developments. In his comparative analysis of Germany and the United States he is interested in the structural similarities and differences of the two societies, his aim being to explain why Nazism developed in Germany while the United States retained its liberal-democratic framework.

First, what were the similarities between the two societies? Parsons stresses "the high development of industrialism, under the aegis of 'big business' " In the economy, this involved "a high development of large scale organization, with a large, propertyless industrial class, a high concentration of executive authority and control of industrial property, and an important element of highly trained technical personnel, especially in engineering, but also in relation to legal and

---

[1] In Talcott Parsons' *Essays in Sociological Theory* (Glencoe, Ill.: The Free Press, 1954). Page references to this essay will be cited in parentheses immediately following the quoted passage.

administrative functions" (104). The vast majority of each population was involved in the market economy and, more specifically, it was "mainly dependent on money income from salaries, wages or the profits of enterprise or disposal of services" (105). Finally, Parsons mentions the segregation of ownership from political authority and other statuses, and a certain degree of individual freedom and mobility of resources that appear to be characteristic of the " 'liberal' type of industrial economy."

These similarities, however, are less significant than the differences between the two societies, Parsons argues. The most obvious structural difference is that Germany, in common with other European societies, had an old regime, with its corresponding class structure and institutions; while the United States never had a landed nobility, a peasantry, or as numerically large a *petite bourgeoisie* of artisans and shopkeepers as did Germany. The transition to industrial capitalism must be studied keeping in mind that "feudal, militaristic, bureaucratic, and authoritarian features" of the old regime remained in effect in capitalist-industrial Germany. The Junkers dominated and controlled the countryside, kept the lower classes in a state of dependency, and enjoyed "a position of high social prestige enforced by rigid conventions."

As for the position of the Junkers in the state, their main role was not so much in civil administration as in the armed forces; which, in turn, were responsible not to the civil administration but directly to the Kaiser, thus assuring "solidarity of social status between the nobility and royalty, the two elements of the traditional 'ruling class' " (107). Finally, the power of the nobility was reflected in the Junkers' distinctive "style of life which was in sharp contrast with everything 'bourgeois,' involving a strong contempt of industry and trade, of the bourgeois virtues, even of liberal and humane culture" (107). Insofar as feudal and bourgeois elements fused in Germany as they did elsewhere in Europe, the fusion resulted in a more pronounced feudalization of the bourgeoisie, so that industrialists, for example, assumed the style of life of the Junkers rather than vice versa.

Parsons goes on to argue that the feudal elements continued to play an active and central role in shaping German society and politics even after industrial capitalism had firmly established itself. The reduction of the army after 1918 and the abolition of the monarchy significantly weakened the feudal regime, but this "process was not sufficiently thorough to break up its social identity nor to destroy its traditional prestige, especially in view of its close integration with other 'conservative' elements in the social structure" (107). The most important of these elements was perhaps the state bureaucracy (civil service), a highly professional and formalized organization that, though comprising some individuals of bourgeois origin, viewed itself as owing its allegiance to the dominant class of the old order. We should note that Parsons' main thesis here is that the failure to smash the bureacracy and other elements of the feudal state apparatus had fateful consequences for the development of German democracy: "the higher civil service was not, in the Weimar Republic, displaced from formal participation in the operation of Government. If anything their power was probably on the whole increased because short of really radical revolution their knowledge and competence in administrative affairs was indispensable for keeping the essential governmental services in operation in a time of crisis" (109). The Junkers and the bureaucracy shared an ideology "which is perhaps best called 'Prussian conservatism.' " Although hardly absolutist and holding to a Kantian conception of devotion to duty, "this [ideology] was combined with a strong sense of prerogative and authority which would not brook the 'democratic' type of control by persons without authority, or any presumption, of elements not authorized by their formal status to interfere in the functions of duly constituted authority" (109).

In addition, the Lutheran Church and doctrine were bound up with these conservative elements and in fact bolstered their often harsh authoritarian and "cynical pursuit of power in defiance of the welfare of the masses of the people" (110). All this severely limited the influence and effectiveness of parliament, which, to a greater degree than in England or the United States, became "structured as a system of representation of rather specific interest groups such as agrarian interests, big business, labor unions, the Catholic Church, a tendency which came to full flower under the Weimar Republic and had a good deal to do with its instability." The dominant role of the state in industrial development, notably its ownership and operation of the railways, also severely limited the independence of the business interests.

Contributing to the inhibition of liberal democracy in Germany were her severe economic difficulties as well as

> the development of the relations of capital and labor, in the sense in which that tension is structurally inherent in all capitalistic industrial econo-mies. . . . The Weimar regime put the trade unions and the parties of the left in a position of greatly enhanced power; wages were continually pushed up; and undoubtedly many business people became frightened and were ready to accept almost anything which would protect them from the danger of expropriation. (116)

Parsons thus emphasizes that the tensions and conflicts attendant upon the existence of classes and groups with sharply opposed interests requires close attention if one is to explain why Germany succumbed to Nazism. In a remarkable theoretical reflection that would seem to repudiate much of his subsequent theorizing, particularly his general analytical scheme, Parsons writes:

> In our common-sense thinking about social matters we probably tend greatly to exaggerate the integration of social systems, to think of them as neatly "exemplifying" a pattern type. For purposes of sheer [?] comparative structural study this need not lead to serious difficulty, but when dynamic problems of directions and processes of change are at issue,

> it is essential to give specific attention to the elements of malintegration, tension and strain in the social structure. (117)

So Parsons calls attention to the disorganizing effects in all Western countries of rapid social change—urbanization, migration, war, inflation, depression, and class and other social conflicts—aggravated in Germany by an additional factor, a "mobilization of the extremely deep-seated romantic tendencies of German society in the service of a violently aggressive political movement incorporating a 'fundamentalist' revolt against the whole tendency of rationalization in the Western world . . ." (123).

We see, then, that in order to explain concrete social developments Parsons is compelled to deal with factors to which Marxists and other conflict theorists give close attention.[2] This is characteristic of several other of his articles dealing with significant social issues. In "Some Sociological Aspects of the Fascist Movements," for example, he tells us that the Marxists may be right in relating Fascism "to fundamental and generalized aspects of Western society."[3] Fascism, he emphasizes, is a "radicalism of the right." Based not on the old conservative elements but on newer privileged elite groups with "vested interests" in their position, it nevertheless appeals to the masses, who are insecure and in a state of severe anomie as a result of the various changes and dislocations accompanying the industrial revolution. Equally important is the great antipathy to what Weber called the rationalization of the West—an antipathy emanating from specific social classes and groups, mainly those of the old order. This conservative ideology repudiates rationalization and modernization. Fascist ideology "characteristically accepts in essentials the socialist indictment of the existing order described as capitalism, but extends it to include leftist radicalism and the whole penumbra of scientific and philosophical rationalism" (135). Yet while fascism, with its demagogic use of "socialist" slogans, appears to threaten capital and other vested interests, it actually furthers the interests of big business by smashing the power of labor and mobilizing the economy for war.

In still another essay relating to Germany and problems of fascism, the quasi-Marxian approach becomes even more evident. Published in 1945, "The Problem of Controlled Institutional Change" addresses itself to postwar Germany and the problem of putting an end once and for all to German aggressive expansionism. The main thesis of the article rests on a fundamental and rudimentary sociological postulate: in order to change character structure, the underlying institutional structure must be changed.

What is revealing here is the aspect of the institutional structure that

---

[2] I use the term "conflict theory" with several misgivings, for reasons I hope to make clear in Part III of this book.

[3] Parsons, *Essays in Sociological Theory,* p. 125. This volume also contains the next two essays discussed, "The Problem of Controlled Institutional Change" and "Population and the Social Structure of Japan." Page references will be cited in parentheses immediately following the quoted passage.

Parsons chooses to discuss: the "vested interests." These are the factors in a social structure resisting change, for "they are oriented to the maintenance of objects of interest which have already become established" (241). What the Allies must do in Germany after its defeat is to break up or suppress the various vested interest groups—without, however, generating renewed resentment among the Germans. Essentially, Parsons' recommendation is to find an apolitical outlet for the German romantic complex, with its accompanying submissiveness of the lower strata and authoritarianism of the higher. It is more important, however, "to eliminate or seriously reduce the structural role of the hierarchical, authoritarian, and formalistic elements in the 'conservative' German institutional structure—in particular its focus on the army and military class should be broken." Finally, it is essential "to displace the conservative pattern and to reduce the tension by systematically fostering those elements of the pattern of modern Germany, especially of industrialism, which are closest to their counterparts in the Democratic countries" (251).

The "Nazi party and all its subsidiary organizations and the Junker class" must be compulsorily and immediately suppressed. The Junkers should be attacked "at their most vulnerable point—the economic basis" (253). Two other institutional elements of the conservative complex, the higher civil service and the big industrialists, must be transformed. As the former was so integral a part of the traditional structure, its direct liquidation would probably "be attended by very formidable guilt feelings." Besides, as it would constitute an important element in any orderly transition to a postwar society, Parsons concludes that an indirect attack would be best. Since "probably the most important single defense of the old conservative patterns here is the *class* basis of recruitment of the higher personnel," it is essential "to facilitate *effective*, not merely formal, equality of opportunity in the civil service" (255, italics in original).

As for the big industrial interests, Parsons continues, it is clear that historically they developed "within a conservative pre-industrial social structure" and indeed fused with and remained dependent on the traditional, conservative, upper strata of Germany, and of course on the Nazi party. The danger of German industrialism to the United Nations should therefore be seen not in its industrial power per se but rather in its "integration with a militaristic state and conservative class structure"; which in turn suggests that so drastic a policy as deindustrialization, the "Morgenthau plan," is unnecessary. Instead, "a reorientation of German business in the direction of a liberal industrialism . . . seems most desirable" (256).

Still other policy recommendations rest on class analysis. It "is essential that the occupying authority should not 'identify' with the old, upper classes, but should remain aloof from them" (258). In order to distintegrate the authoritarian-submissive complex among German women one must make "domestic service more expensive and servants less submissive," thus "throwing more responsibility on middle-class women" (260). In sharp contrast to Parsons' later theoretical scheme, in which value orientations appear to be unanchored in classes and unrelated to interest, he here emphasizes that changing a people's character is not simply a matter of "indoctrination with the proper attitudes and values" (260). Power is of paramount importance: "The *first* question to ask about a person, an organization, or a group is, what is its position in the *German* social system? Is it in a sufficiently strategic position to exert an important influence in the right direction?" (262).

In the balance of the article Parsons argues that the economic and occupational structure may well be the most strategic lever of change; for insofar as achievement in the economy is institutionalized, "roles in which an established status was the main emphasis, as in large sections of the peasantry, the old *Mittelstand* and the older elite groups, would be correspondingly weakened" (263). At the same time, instituting the achievement principle would contribute to the progressive weakening of hierarchy and formalism. Finally, of course, stability in the postwar period is unthinkable in the absence of a "highly productive, full-employment, expanding economy . . ." (265).

We can read these essays and others as implicit critiques of Parsons' theoretical work. Indeed, in addressing himself to the problem of changing the German ideology, Parsons makes a theoretical statement so clearly pointing up his quasi-Marxian alter ego that it deserves special attention: "Every society has important elements of conflict. Hence, an ideology which has unifying functions will tend to 'play down' the element of internal conflict and thus be 'skewed' in another way. In the United States, for example, from the 'official' ideology one could get little insight into the actual divergences and conflicts between religious, ethnic and class groups" (267–68).

JAPANESE SOCIAL STRUCTURE

In an essay published in 1946 entitled "Population and the Social Structure of Japan" Parsons addresses himself to Japan's remarkable industrial achievements, the transition from a predominantly "feudal" to an industrial system, and classes and class relationships are at the center of his inquiry. He begins by noting a significant difference between Japanese "feudalism" and its European counterpart. Although tokugawa Japan knew both a nobility (daimyo) and a gentry of sorts (samurai), and although rural tenancy prevailed, there were unique aspects of the traditional social structure that account for the comparative lack of resistance to modernization during the Meiji period.

In the first place the samurai owned no land of their own. They depended for their income on the daimyo, who owned the land and paid their retainers rice stipends. In addition, the tokugawa regime had managed to drive wedges between the various levels of nobility, which therefore remained relatively isolated from each other and powerless vis à vis the central power. The nobility was a divided and weak class with only an attenuated hold over the samurai. The latter, with no vested interest in their local communities, were rather easily pried away from the smaller nobles and attached to the courts of the big lords and the central regime, where they acquired power and influence. Soon the samurai became a higher civil service group with more power than the daimyo; while the latter, in their already weakened position, were easily deprived of their special feudal status. Together with the court nobility and the great nobles of outstanding wealth the samurai amalgamated into one stratum, forming a "new centralized national nobility" (280).

Like Europe, Japan had something of a "bourgeois class." Its role was different, however, from that of its counterpart in the European "bourgeois revolutions." Feudal-military values continued to dominate Japanese culture while the merchant and tradesman were held in contempt—traditionally having even less social honor than the peasant. Expanding wealth and low prestige and power combined to make the Japanese bourgeoisie highly discontented with the tokugawan regime and staunch allies of the leaders of the Meiji reforms. They financed and generally supported the restoration, whose leaders in turn rewarded them with positions in the new national aristocracy. Merchants and tradesmen now fused and intermarried with daimyo and samurai. The result was not so much the *embourgeoisement* of the nobility as the feudalization of the bourgeoisie. In Parsons' words, this

> was very different from the "bourgeois revolutions" which took place in Europe. In various respects the older aristocratic groups remained dominant; it was their values and patterns of life which set the principal tone for the new Japan. Important as the mercantile elements were as the direct vehicle of Japan's economic modernization, it was only for brief periods, as in the 1920's, that they acquired anything like the upper hand. (281)

Thus, although there were some alterations of the preindustrial social structure, it remained largely unchanged in the course of industrialization: the traditional classes retained hegemony, the peasant base stayed intact, and the samurai acquired a new field of expression for their military code, namely, "the armed forces of a modern nation, supported by a nationalistically tinged system of universal education."

Underscoring the differences between European and Japanese modernization, Parsons points to the greater role of the state in the latter case in both subsidizing and supervising business and industry. Other important differences were the retention of traditional patterns and values by the lower classes; the fusion of religious and nationalistic elements legitimizing territorial expansion and militarism; and, finally, the relative weakness and dependence of the Japanese middle classes.

So we see still another case in which Parsons' analysis of a significant problem is hardly distinguishable from what I have, for want of a better term, called a quasi-Marxian approach. Faced with a significant question, Parsons talks not at all about "system-needs," "functional imperatives," "equilibrium states," "system integration," "adaptation," "goal attainment," or "common value system." Instead he turns to classes, strata, and other concrete structural conditions to deal adequately with the question at hand. Equally striking is that Parsons' analyses have both a comparative and historical dimension.

In sharp contrast to his theoretical writings, the essays we have been considering treat values in their immediate and direct connection with specific and concrete social groups, strata, and classes. Thus if, as we have seen, aristocratic values remained dominant in industrializing Japan, this is explained by the continuing hegemony of the older classes. Their wealth and power, and not any alleged functional contribution to "system-needs," explain the dominance of their values.

THE TWO APPROACHES COMPARED

The approach that Parsons takes in the essays we have been discussing is hardly compatible with the one we encountered in *The Social System* or the one found in his essay "A Revised Analytical Approach to the Theory of Social Stratification," written in 1953.[4] In this essay he posits a "common value system" as the basis and sine qua non of the stability of social systems and he stresses throughout the *valuational* aspect of stratification. Are we to believe that in pre-Nazi Germany Junkers, peasants, industrial workers, Catholics, Protestants, Communists, Social Democrats, and Nazis all shared a common value system? Or that in Japan the various strata of daimyo, samurai, peasants, merchants, and industrialists shared a common value system? By his own testimony they did not. Where, then, does one see evidence of a "common value system" and how does one go about verifying it?

Yet this assumption is characteristic of his recent theoretical works. In these terms the "other" Parsons is chimerical, a brief aberration. For our purposes, however, the aberration is important, for it demonstrates that Parsons himself was unable to analyze significant social issues and developments by means of a general scheme and was forced to resort to a quasi-Marxian analysis.

It is, however, of interest to note that whether it was Nazism, fascism, Japanese militarism, or McCarthyism, Parsons gave his attention to these developments only after they became "history." T. B. Bottomore has observed, "Parsons did not analyze the rise of Fascism, and the consolidation of its power, at the time when these events were taking place. He published his essays . . . when the ideas which he formulated had already become common currency. For this sociology, as for Hegel's philosophy, the owl of Minerva spreads its wings only with the falling of the dusk."[5]

---

[4] Reprinted in, *Essays in Sociological Theory*. Page references to this essay will be cited in parentheses immediately following the quoted passage.

[5] T. B. Bottomore, "Out of This World," *New York Review of Books*, 13, no. 8 (November 6, 1969): 37, n. 9.

POWER

The extreme one-sidedness of Parsons' conception of power may not become immediately evident in a casual reading of his theoretical writings. In "A Revised Analytical Approach to the Theory of Social Stratification," for example, he begins his discussion of stratification and power by emphasizing the valuational aspect (e.g., "stratification in its valuational aspect . . . is the ranking of units in a social system in accordance with the standards of the common value system"), but goes on to say: "The valuational aspect must be analytically distinguished from the others entering into the total 'power' system of a society" (388). And in distinguishing the other aspects, it does appear for a moment that interests, force, coercion, the dominance of one individual over another, the struggle for power, and the like, will be given adequate attention. In this essay, as in *The Social System*, he draws attention to the central importance of "possessions" and "facilities."

"Possessions" are transferable valued objects, valued either actually by their possessor or potentially by others. Individuals and/or collectivities acquire "control" of these objects and hence "in the institutionalized case rights to their use, control or disposal differentiated from those held by other units in the system," (390). One may discern in possessions two orders of significance: they may serve as "facilities" or as "rewards," which are analytically but not necessarily empirically distinct. Facilities are means to an end or "means-objects relative to instrumental goal-attainment processes" (390).

Since facilities are scarce resources, every social system must provide mechanisms for their allocation. Facility allocation therefore relates directly to the problems of order and power. In *The Social System*, Parsons says that, with a single qualification, he will accept Hobbes' definition of power, namely, "a man's present means to any future good." The qualification is this:

> that such means constitute his power, so far as these means are dependent on his relations to other actors; the correlative is the obligation of alter to respect ego's rights. Hence *in one aspect* all possession of facilities is possession of power because it is at least in an implied and contingent sense a control over the actions of others, at least in the sense of ability to count on their non-interference.[6]

In "The Theory of Social Stratification" Parsons similarly defines power "as the realistic capacity of a system-unit to actualize its 'interests' (attain goals, prevent undesired interference, command respect, control possessions, etc.) within the context of system-interaction and in this sense to exert influence on processes in the system" (391). So we see that power is a matter of controlling facilities, and thus gaining control over the actions of others and actualizing one's interests.

---

[6] Talcott Parsons, *The Social System* (New York: The Free Press, 1951), p. 121.

The extent and reach of one's power depends, for Parsons, on three conditions, which he lists in *The Social System* as the "extensity of the system of actual or potential exchange relationships through which it ramifies"; "the incidence of universalistic orientation within the system," enabling power to transcend specific sets of relationships; and the "gradient of effectiveness or 'drasticness' of means."[7] In plain English, this means that institutionalized limits to force and fraud exist in every social system. In the absence of such limits the "war of all against all" would result. Resorting to ever more drastic means by ego and alter leads to a vicious, upward-spiraling struggle for power that can only be stopped by imposing controls on both.

Parsons explicitly states in "The Theory of Social Stratification" that "the concrete 'position' of a system-unit in a social system cannot be only a function of its place in the scale of valuation relative to an integrated common value-system, because no social system is ever perfectly integrated in this sense" (390). And he further notes that one might conceptualize the discrepancy between the " 'ideal' ranking order and the actual state of affairs" in terms of power—which, in turn, results from three sets of factors: (1) how one is evaluated in terms of the common value standards, (2) the degree to which one is allowed to deviate from these standards, and (3) "the control of possessions [including facilities] which is a source of differential advantage in bringing about a desired result (including preventing one not desired)" (391). Moreover, access to possessions and facilities are "always to some degree a function of factors which are 'adventitious' from the point of view of the value-standards of the system . . ." (392).

I have quoted Parsons at length in order to highlight how confusing and even contradictory his procedure is. First he posits a common value system without a word about the ambiguities that this concept entails. How does one verify this assumption? Why is the assumption required at all in the study of stratification and power? Granting for a moment some semblance of a common value system, how does it come about? This is the omission I have already called attention to in criticizing him for treating the so-called equilibrium state of a system as given and unproblematic, thereby ignoring altogether the various coercive measures that accompany the "common values," whether in the family, community, or society at large.

Yet, as soon as he posits common values and assigns them central importance, he hedges them in with crippling qualifications: factors affecting power are "adventitious" with regard to the value standards of the social system in question; and in the study of any concrete system, the nonvaluational components are "extremely important." Following this, he says, "However, the point of view from which we approach the analysis of stratification prescribes that analysis should focus on the common value-pattern aspect" (393). As to *why* this focus is prescribed, he offers this "explanation": "Only through this

[7] Parsons, *The Social System*, pp. 122–23.

[focus] can we gain stable points of reference for a technical theoretical analysis of the empirical influence of the other components of the system-process. This is essentially because on general theoretical grounds we can state that the 'focus' of the *structure* of a system of action lies in the common value-pattern aspect of its culture" (393). Clearly, this is no more than an arbitrary assertion; but Parsons remains true to his word and all further discussions of social order, stratification, and power retain this focus.

What this means in effect is that power, as the control of strategic facilities that, in turn, enables some men to control the actions of others, receives no serious attention and is relegated to so subordinate a "causal" status as to figure not at all in the analysis. Throughout his work he adopts a conception of power diametrically opposed to this. Power, he writes, is "a facility for the performance of function in, and on behalf of, the society as a system . . ."[8] Or power refers to the *"capacity of a social system to get things done in its collective interest."*[9] So we are back to the functionalist framework: power works for the "society" and gets things done in its collective interest.

The least one can say of this approach to the problem of power is that Parsons is guilty of the same errors of which he accuses others. In a well-known review article of *Power Elite*, for instance, he takes C. Wright Mills to task for adopting a particular conception of power "without attempting to justify it. This is what may be called the 'zero-sum' concept; power, that is to say, is power *over* others.[10] Parsons does not like this and likes even less Mills's view that "politics is a struggle for power." For Mills, Parsons continues, "power is not a facility for the performance of function in, and on behalf of, the society as a system, but is interpreted exclusively as a facility for getting what one group, the holders of power, wants by preventing another group, the 'outs,' from getting what it wants. What this conception does is to elevate a secondary and derived aspect of a total phenomenon into the central place."[11]

Parsons goes on to argue that power, like wealth, has not only a distributive aspect (it has to be allocated and divided) but a collective one: it serves the interests and goals of "society," which Mills ignores. "He is interested only in *who* has power and what *sectoral* interests he is serving with his power, not in how power comes to be generated or in what communal rather than sectoral interests are served."[12]

If in fact Mills focuses exclusively on sectoral interests and Parsons on

---

[8] Talcott Parsons, "The Distribution of Power in American Society," in *Structure and Process in Modern Societies* (Glencoe, Ill.: The Free Press, 1960), p. 220.

[9] Talcott Parsons, " 'Voting' and the Equilibrium of the American Political System," in *Sociological Theory and Modern Society* (New York: The Free Press, 1967), p. 255, italics in original.

[10] Parsons, "The Distribution of Power," p. 219. But of course one can have power over others without this necessarily implying the zero-sum concept. Yet Parsons tends to equate the two.

[11] Ibid., p. 220.

[12] Ibid., p. 221.

communal interests, both are one-sided. Nonetheless, without defending Mills' specific thesis in *Power Elite*, I would suggest that Mills at least makes an effort to provide some empirical-historical evidence for his particular conception of power. Parsons, in contrast, provides none.

More, Parsons has alleged that Marxism is one-sided. But Marx readily acknowledged the role of values, i.e., the ruling beliefs and ideas, in contributing to the submission and compliance of the subject classes; whereas Parsons denies or ignores the relationship of ruler-subject as well as the coercive, nonvaluational components of consent and compliance.

"NEW IDEAS" ABOUT POWER AND FORCE

In recent years Parsons has thought it useful to draw out the main characteristics of power by likening it to money. In his essay "On the Concept of Political Power," written in 1963, he argues that power and money are analogous phenomena.[13] To see the parallel, it is necessary to remember that money is a symbolic, circulating, medium of exchange. It is symbolic in that it stands for value or utility; and it manifests this quality by having only exchange value but never use value. It is therefore a mode of communicating one's ability to buy and sell.

The more "primitive" a monetary system, the more likely it is that money will appear in the form of a commodity, e.g., precious metals, and that the commodity will be regarded as the "real" determinant of the money's value. In more advanced economies the volume of trade and exchange actually utilizing the metal is only a very small fraction of the total volume, which employs "valueless" symbolic money and complex instruments of credit. In these terms, the metal is primarily a "reserve," used mainly in certain contingencies. Symbolic, "valueless," money is mutually acceptable only within the confines of a definite network of relationships, which can conceivably become worldwide; it therefore rests "on a certain institutionalized confidence in the monetary system" (307). Money thus communicates reciprocal commitment and obligations within a definite system of relations so that the fulfillment of obligation or failure to do so carry with them appropriate positive and negative sanctions.

By analogy, then, Parsons defines power as the "generalized capacity to secure the performance of binding obligations by units in a system of collective organization when the obligations are legitimized with reference to their bearing on collective goals and where in case of recalcitrance there is a presumption of enforcement by negative situational sanctions—whatever the actual agency of that enforcement" (308). What Parsons insists upon in his definition is that the "threat of superior force, is not an exercise of power"; further, "the capacity to

[13]Talcott Parsons, "On the Concept of Political Power," in *Sociological Theory and Modern Society*, pp. 297–354. Page references to this essay will be cited in parentheses immediately following the quoted passage.

secure compliance must, if it is to be called power in any sense, be generalized and not solely a function of one particular sanctioning act which the user is in a position to impose, and the medium used must be symbolic" (308). He maintains that power is a strictly "symbolic" phenomenon necessarily involving legitimation. Parties to a relationship have nothing but symbolic expectations vis à vis one another. "Legitimation is therefore in power systems, the factor which is parallel to confidence in mutual acceptability and stability of the monetary unit in monetary systems" (309).

The general and legitimate aspects of power are connected in that the calling into question of legitimacy leads to increasingly "secure means of gaining compliance" which, because they are "more effective 'intrinsically,' [are] more tailored to the particular situations of the objects and less general." Thus the decline of both the generality and legitimacy of power culminate, in the last resort, in "the use of force as the most intrinsically effective of all means of coercion" (309); at this point, having arrived at force and coercion—specific and nonlegitimate means of gaining compliance—we have exited, according to Parsons, from the house of power.

Continuing the analogy, if the value of money is grounded in precious metals held in reserve, so the "value" or effectiveness of power is correspondingly related to force and coercion, also held in reserve. Just as the exclusive use of gold as money could never serve a modern, complex system of exchange, so the exclusive use of force as a negative sanction could never "function to mediate a complex system of organizational coordination . . ." (313). If money is to be a general medium of inducement, it must have legitimacy, for it is this quality that inspires confidence and engenders compliance to act for money. Similarly, power must not merely deter actions but offer positive inducements to fulfill commitments.

THE HIERARCHICAL ASPECTS OF POWER

Just as some have more money than others, so do some have more power than others. Yet the analogy is not perfect, Parsons acknowledges. For money measures value "in terms of a continuous linear variable," or quantitative dimension, while power "involves a quite different dimension which may be formulated in terms of the conception that A may have power over B" (317). But this is not what it appears to be, as we shall soon see. Power requires "the focusing of responsibility for decisions, and hence of authority for their implementation. This implies a special form of inequality of power which in turn implies a priority system of commitments" (317).

The hierarchical ordering of the collectivity reflects the respective contributions of each echelon to the fulfillment of the system of commitments. It is these functional contributions of each that make the hierarchy of power, e.g., A over B over C, etc., legitimate, for it is in "the interest of the effectiveness of the collective operation as a whole" (318). Since the hierarchy exists in a normative context, one may speak of compliance not merely when subordinates obey but also when superordinate echelons observe the prevailing norms. The institutionalized normative order is what Parsons defines as *authority*, which bears the same relationship to power as does the institution of property to money.

In pursuit of his analogy, Parsons wishes to tie all this together in order to deliver another blow to the "zero-sum" conception of power. If one may speak of "utility" as the criterion of the economic function, then, he suggests, "effectiveness" may be regarded as the standard governing the political function. This standard, he characteristically maintains, is the "success of collective goal-attainment" of the system in question. In the economy a business firm is the best example of a collectivity in which standards of both "utility" and "effectiveness" coincide. Inputs of power and money increase productivity which, in turn, brings with it increments in both money income and power. Surpluses of power and money are invested in the expansion and enhancement of the collectivity's "power position" in a plurality of competing units (338).

In the "polity" one may also see a process of power enhancement parallel to economic investment. In democratic electoral systems, for example, one may observe a kind of "banking phenomenon" according to which voters or constituents "deposit" power with their elected officials. "The 'deposits' of power made by constituents are revocable, if not at will, at the next election—a condition analogous to regularity of banking hours" (339). Such deposits are invested by the officers so that the power of the collectivity as a whole is enhanced. "In any case," Parsons continues, "I should like to conceive the process of power enhancement as strictly parallel to economic investment, in the further sense that the pay-off should be an increment to the level of collective success in the sense outlined above, that is enhanced effectiveness of collective action in valued areas which could not have been expected without risk-taking on the part of leadership in a sense parallel to entrepreneurial investment" (341).

For Parsons, then, wherever one turns one sees that the expansion of income and the enhancement of power serve the collective interests. Everyone benefits—so one ought not speak as if the gains of some imply the losses of others. Once again Parsons has given us a "scheme"—this time in the form of an analogy replete with terms like power inflation and deflation. He "resolves" what he calls the old dilemma of whether power is a matter of coercion or consensus by concluding that "it is both."

He himself acknowledges the "inherent arbitrariness" of his concepts but makes no real effort to justify them. What insights, we must ask, do we gain from his analogy that we did not have before? He suggests, for example, that when "power-credit" has been extended too far, obligations and performance will be inhibited by resistance. In a disintegrating collectivity a certain formal office may be "worthless" because it loses its "basis of effectiveness." This decline in effectiveness is the analogue of inflation in the monetary field. But in discussing the phenomenon of McCarthyism in the 1950s, he says that it may be understood as "a *deflationary* spiral in the political field" (342). How does he define "deflation"? A power system is deflated, he writes, "by undermining the essential basis of trust on which the influence of many elements bearing formal and informal leadership responsibilities, and which in turn sustained 'power-credit,' necessarily rested" (343).

This definition, as T. B. Bottomore has pointed out,[14] indicates that Parsons' analogy is a poor one: his power deflation has the characteristics associated with monetary inflation. Besides, his definitions of inflation and deflation both stress the decline of effectiveness, so that he actually may be using two distinct terms to describe one process. Even if his distinctions were unambiguous, we would have to ask: What, besides a label, does he add to our understanding by telling us that McCarthyism is a deflationary spiral?

Apart from this, as we examine Parsons' analogy we see that he has remained faithful to his functionalist-consensualist position. He has done so, moreover, not by means of either a theoretical or empirical analysis of the elements of order and power but rather by "a trick of definition."[15] For as we have seen, all the real problems and issues are indeed defined away. To take some examples:

1. Power is consistently conceived, by Parsons, as serving "collective goals" and interests; he thus conveniently absolves himself from dealing with the numerous conflicts of values and interests among those with unequal amounts of wealth, power, and privilege in any social system.

2. Power is defined as an essentially *symbolic* medium, so that the control of concrete means or resources and the resulting domination of others is ignored.

3. Power is defined as a *generalized* and *legitimized* medium, thereby ignoring

   a. the classical distinction between power and authority (legitimized power, as defined by Weber, for example);

   b. the fact that some hold power illegitimately; and, most importantly,

   c. the various processes, including force, fraud, and deceit, by means of which power gains legitimacy.

4. Power is defined so as to exclude force *except* as a symbolic reserve, so that again, by definition, force or coercion never play any direct role in the "stabilization" of systems—despite so much historical evidence to the contrary.[16]

5. Power may be arranged in a hierarchy, but this invariably serves the common interests of the collectivity. Hierarchical power systems are functionally and organically integrated. They are characterized by the absence of either conflict or coercion among the various echelons or strata. Hence, any dichotomy

[14] Bottomore, "Out of This World," p. 38.

[15] The apt phrase is Anthony Giddens's. See his " 'Power' in the Recent Writings of Talcott Parsons," in *Sociology*, 2 (September 1968): 265.

[16] Cf. ibid., p. 267.

between those who command and the others who obey is altogether unthinkable.

6. Power, when enhanced and aggrandized, results rather simply in larger units in a "competitive system"—a conception clearly designed to push out of sight the patterns of domination that emerge among the units.

7. Power works so unswervingly for the common interest and in a normative context hallowed by a common value system, that "compliance should . . . not be limited to 'obedience' by subordinates" (318), but include, as well, the obedience to norms of superordinate echelons.

8. Power, finally, is likened to money. Parsons treats the two as analytically parallel but never examines the relation between them. How, for example, money becomes power and vice versa is never accorded attention. Similarly, Anthony Giddens has observed that

> The parallels which Parsons is determined to pursue between the polity and the economy serve, in fact, to separate political and economic processes from one another. That economic and other "material" factors themselves play a key part in power deflation is ignored because Parsons is above all concerned to show how the polity and economy are "analytically" similar, not how they intertwine. Parsons' many discussions of the relationships between sociology and economics, including his and Smelser's *Economy and Society*, are all stated in terms of highly formal . . . categories, and rarely suggest any substantive generalizations linking the two.[17]

In sum, Parsons stands firmly in the functionalist-consensualist camp.

[17] Ibid., p. 266.

4

The Rediscovery of Evolution

In 1964, in "Evolutionary Universals in Society," published in the *American Sociological Review*[1] Parsons made it known that he had become interested in the concept of evolution as applied to human society, launching his exposition with not even the briefest discussion of nineteenth-century evolutionary theory. But we must ask: What were the main merits and defects of nineteenth-century evolutionary theory? Why was it eventually rejected, and was the rejection justifiable on scientific grounds? In what respects is Parsons' perspective similar to the nineteenth-century view and therefore intellectually indebted to Spencer, Morgan, Tyler and others? What changes, corrections, or additions is he introducing that might justify his posture of "discovering" or "rediscovering" evolutionary theory? We search in vain for any attention to these and related questions here or in later elaborations of this essay. Instead, Parsons rests content with the assertion, made in *Societies: Evolutionary and Comparative Perspectives*, that he is not "merely reviving old ideas" and that he has considered "the idea of social evolution in the context of the major theoretical and empirical advances that have accumulated since the earlier evolutionists wrote."[2] He does not, however, specify what these advances have been, though he believes that his own formulation has successfully avoided what he calls the deadly scientific sin of the nineteenth-century thinkers, namely, monism, or theories based on a single factor.

It is more likely, however, as we shall see, that (1) his own "theory" is

[1] Talcott Parsons, "Evolutionary Universals in Society," *American Sociological Review*, 29 (June, 1964); reprinted in *Sociological Theory and Modern Society* (New York: The Free Press, 1967), pp. 490–520. Page references to this edition of the essay will be cited in parentheses immediately following the quoted passage.

[2] Talcott Parsons, *Societies: Evolutionary and Comparative Perspectives* (Englewood Cliffs, N. J.: Prentice-Hall, 1966), p. 109.

51

perhaps more monistic than various nineteenth-century perspectives; (2) his conception may hardly be regarded as an advance beyond ideas more than a century old; and, finally, (3) his formulation is a forced marriage of evolutionist and functionalist ideas and hence subject to the criticisms made of his other theoretical work. Once again we encounter the emphasis on normative elements, "system-needs," and societal goals, but this time it is accompanied by a conception of social evolution devoid of force, conflict, or power.

In "Evolutionary Universals in Society" Parsons begins by seeking after certain social evolutionary universals. An "evolutionary universal," he writes "is a complex of structures and associated processes the development of which so increases the long-run adaptive capacity of living systems in a given class that only systems that develop the complex can attain certain higher levels of general adaptive capacity" (493).

We meet again the familiar but still ambiguous functional term "adaptive capacity" combined with the evaluative assumption of a "higher" developmental stage, defined as an allegedly greater capacity to adapt. So we continue to face the numerous conceptual problems of functionalism. "Adaptive capacity" to what conditions? How do we know whether or not certain social structures heighten the adaptive capacity of a social system?

In contrast with the theory of "natural selection," Parsons tells us, the criterion in the sociocultural realm is not necessarily the extinction of the unadaptive societies. The relatively disadvantaged do survive. But he does not proceed to inform us how, therefore, one distinguishes the advantaged from the disadvantaged systems from an evolutionary standpoint.

Another important difference between natural selection and social evolution is that cultural patterns, unlike genes, "are subject to 'diffusion' " (494). In these terms, the evolutionary "prerequisites" of society and culture are those in which the "symbol" increasingly replaces the gene. "System-needs" are therefore determined by both the genetic constitution and the cultural tradition. Characteristically, Parsons first mentions "normative expectations" that pertain to "man's relation to his environment" and that delineate "the ways in which adaptation should be developed and extended. Within the relevant range, cultural innovations, especially definitions of what man's life *ought* to be, thus replace Darwinian variations in genetic constitution" (494–95).

The cultural value patterns, the orientational aspect of the simplest and most rudimentary social systems, Parsons terms "religious" in Durkheim's sense. Together with mechanisms of symbolic communication (language), the value patterns rest on social organization, exclusively kinship at the earliest stage; which organization, in turn, employs technology, i.e., "empirical knowledge and practical techniques," in however rudimentary a sense. In Parsons' words:

> These four features of even the simplest action system— "religion," communication with language, social organization through kinship, and technology—may be regarded as an integrated set of evolutionary universals

at even the earliest human level. No known human society has existed without *all* four in relatively definite relations to each other. In fact their presence constitutes the very minimum that may be said to mark a society as truly human. (495)

But this is merely a definition, since Parsons nowhere tells us whether we know of "fossil" societies that have perished as a result of lacking one or more of the so-called prerequisites. After all, the important consideration in an evolutionary theory postulating prerequisites is to show that certain empirical conditions contribute to a society's adaptive capacity and that their absence leads to its dissolution, conspicuous disadvantage, or the like. But as Parsons insists that "extinction" is not the criterion, and nowhere clearly provides criteria for distinguishing the "advantaged" from the "disadvantaged," we are left with a definition of the alleged prerequisites of an undefined state called "adaptive capacity." We are therefore back to the old ambiguities of functionalism.

When Parsons attempts to deal with the transition from the "primitive stage" to the next, his "explanation" runs somewhat parallel to the nineteenth-century view. Associated with the process of "breaking out," he says, are two evolutionary universals: "a well-marked system of social stratification, and that of a system of explicit cultural legitimation of differentiated societal functions, preeminently the political function, independent of kinship." The evolutionary significance of stratification "lies in the role in primitive societies of *ascription* of social status to criteria of biological relatedness" (496).

Stratification manifests itself in prestige differences between "senior" and "cadet" lineage groups, with the former acquiring certain economic advantages over the latter, as well as greater political power. The "kinship units with lesser claims to preferment, are 'forced' into peripheral positions. They move to less advantageous residential locations and accept less productive economic resources, and they are not in a position to counteract these advantages by the use of political power." But this idea is dropped in favor of the familiar functional formula: "on the other hand," Parsons continues, "the society as a system gains functional advantages by concentrating responsibility for certain functions" (497). And he provides a justification for stratification in these terms: "The main point is that the differentiation of groups relative to an advantage-disadvantage axis tends to converge with the functional 'need' for centralization of responsibility" (498).

Parsons, then, does not totally overlook the phenomena of the pursuit of economic advantage and power. But he assigns them no real causal role in social development. Throughout he stresses the positive functions of stratification for the "society." The motor, or motors, of development and change are not the struggles resulting from the inequalities, but rather the functional need of the system as a whole. Parsons is capable of speaking of the emergence of "an 'upper,' a 'leading' or, possibly, a 'ruling' class set over against the 'mass' of the population" (498), but he gives this no serious or sustained attention.

There is no discussion whatsoever of the connection between economic surplus and classes. No attention is given to the proposition, now generally accepted among social scientists, that with the emergence of a significant surplus over and above the subsistence requirements of the producers themselves, a group other than the producers manages in various ways to gain control of the surplus as well as the productive resources; and that a system of domination thus emerges that ensures the maintenance of the producers' subsistence at a minimum level and continued economic and other advantages for the rulers. This economic basis of stratification, the resulting conflicts of material interests, the struggles over access and control of the surpluses and key resources, the use of force and the threat of force to gain or retain control of resources, war within and among societies, the institutionalization of political power to maintain the privileges of the dominant class—all this receives no treatment in Parsons' conception of social change and "evolution."

Indeed, among the three major variables of stratification it is *prestige*, for Parsons, that is the most strategic; for wealth and power soon drop out of sight. "Stratification in the present sense, then, is the differentiation of the population on a prestige scale of kinship units such that the distinctions among such units, or classes of them, become hereditary to an important degree" (498). And again: "First, what I have called a 'prestige' position is a generalized prerequisite of responsible concentration of leadership (499).

Why is stratification a primary condition of evolution? Because it disposes of the "obstacles posed by ascription," and "gives the advantaged elements a secure enough position that they can accept certain risks in undertaking collective leadership (500–501). Similarly, Parsons' conception of legitimation is divested of its problematic aspects and thoroughly accommodated to his functionalist framework. What he consistently highlights are "solidarity," the "integrity of the system as a whole," "common loyalties and common normative definitions of the situation"—in short, that the collectivity always remains a "societal community" (503).

At certain stages two additional evolutionary universals emerge: bureaucratic organization, and money and markets. Power, at the earlier stage, though "backed up by coercive sanctions . . . including the use of physical force, *at the same time* . . . rests on the consensual solidarity of a system that includes both the users of power and the 'objects' of its use." Power, then, as we have come to expect, "is the capacity of a unit in the social system, collective or individual, to establish or activate commitments to performance that contributes to, or is in the interest of, attainment of the goals of a collectivity" (504). Money and markets are viewed in much the same way: they make possible a greater mobility of resources "for use in the interests of the collective goals in question" (507).

With respect to generalized universalistic norms, Parsons makes a grand sweep through the three main stages of law in continental Europe: Roman law, Catholic canonic law, and the revival of Roman secular law in Renaissance Italy that culminated in the modern European *Rechtsstaat*. As for England, the crucial development occurred when "Justice Coke asserted the independence of the Common Law from control by royal prerogative" (513). According to this view, law developed in a conflict-free social vacuum: it is Justice Coke and not the English revolutions of the seventeenth century that is crucial for an understanding of English history.

Not surprisingly, the ultimate stage in Parsons' evolutionary scheme is the democratic association—in which leadership is an elective office and the members participate "in collective decision-making through the election of officers and often through voting on specific policy issues" (515–16). Thus Parsons gives us a scheme of evolution through the main stages of *"primitive, intermediate,* and *modern,"*[3] and we are hard put to see in what sense this scheme may be regarded as an advance over the nineteenth-century view.

In his essays on evolution as occasionally elsewhere it is clear that Parsons is waging a polemic against Marxism.[4] He thinks he has bested Marx and, for that matter, all other thinkers who, Parsons alleges, put forward "single-factor theories [that] belong to the kindergarten stage of social science's development."[5] Parsons is confident that he himself has progressed beyond this stage. "Any factor," he instructs us, "is always interdependent with several others"—as if the outstanding nineteenth-century theorists did not understand this.

What is striking is Parsons' apparent unawareness that he is presenting a "factor" theory of his own. It is surely fatuous to suggest that Marx's conception of history presented "material" or economic interests as the sole determining factor of social change. Rather, he assigned to economic interests, relationships, and developments a causal priority within a causal hierarchy in which noneconomic elements definitely contributed their share; he did so, moreover, on empirical-historical grounds.

On the other hand, when Parsons presents his own "hierarchical ordering of the factors," it becomes an actual single-factor theory, perhaps even a dogma. For in his case it appears to be based on an article of faith: " . . . I believe," he writes, "that, within the social system, the normative elements are more important for social change than the 'material interests' of constitutive units."[6]

What is equally striking about Parsons' evolutionary perspective is that, despite his having formulated it in the latter part of the twentieth century, he presents an even more naive law of progress than did the nineteenth-century thinkers. As every careful student of the history of ideas knows, progress was a Comtean dogma; while Marx held out the possibility of mankind's reverting to barbarism. Marx never let his reader forget that for the gain in material comfort and cultural elevation that some men enjoyed, countless others paid dearly—with their lives and, short of that, with pain, suffering, and blood. Parsons, in

[3] Parsons, *Societies*, p. 22.
[4] See Ibid., p. 115.
[5] Ibid., p. 113.
[6] Ibid., p. 113.

contrast, concludes his "Evolutionary Universals in Society" by asserting that the combination of evolutionary universals and the accompanying structural complexes confer "on its possessors an adaptive advantage far superior to the structural potential of societies lacking it" (520). Presumably Parsons has in mind the "modernized" as opposed to the "underdeveloped" societies.

Not only does this way of talking obscure the price that the masses of people have paid for the so-called "adaptive advantage" of their society; it also ignores the fact that the "adaptive advantage" of the modernized societies includes means of dominating, subjugating, and even destroying the inhabitants of the "underdeveloped" society.

But Parsons also begs several other questions. Does "modernization," in the form we know it, in fact confer greater adaptive capacity? To take the most obvious point first, how can one speak of greater adaptive capacity in the present period of history, when all men live in the shadow of a possible nuclear holocaust? Even if we set this aside, it is evident that Parsons' proposition remains problematic. It may very well be a supreme irony that the "modernized" societies ultimately have *less*, not more adaptive capacity than the underdeveloped. We may, for example, be forced to witness passively the starvation of millions, even tens of millions, of Indians during the coming decade. Yet India may continue to sustain hundreds of millions of people long after the United States, for example, may be incapable of doing so, unless present trends are reversed. For while famine may destroy great masses of people in the underdeveloped areas, the United States may become

> a desolate tangle of concrete and ticky-tack, of strip-mined moonscape and silt-chocked reservoirs. The land and the water will be so contaminated with pesticides, herbicides, mercury fungicides, lead, boron, nickel, arsenic and hundreds of other toxic substances, which have been approaching critical levels of concentration in our environment as a result of our numbers and affluence, that it may be unable to sustain human life.[7]

The point, of course, is not that this will or must occur but simply that these tendencies find no place in Parsons' uncritical, naively optimistic, functionalist-evolutionary perspective. While Parsons regards "modernization" as an unmixed blessing (an unqualifiedly superior adaptive capacity), and continues to view existing instutitional arrangements as basically functional and adaptive, ecologists and biologists warn us, as one writer puts it, that "We must halt land destruction. We must abandon the view of land and minerals as private property to be exploited in any way economically feasible for private financial gain. Land and minerals are resources upon which the very survival of the nation depends, and their use must be planned in the best interests of the people."[8]

---

[7] Wayne H. David, "Overpopulated America," *The New Republic*, January 10, 1970, p. 15.
[8] Ibid.

VALUES AND SOCIAL SCIENCE

In these concluding remarks I shall not review the criticisms made so far either of functionalism in general or of the Parsonian variant in particular, but rather address myself to an additional problem: the relation of social values to social science and the nature of this relation in Parsons' work.

Parsons accepts the methodological assumption that the values of particular groups or strata of society definitely affect our knowledge. Following Weber, Parsons believes that this is true of all scientific knowledge but probably more true of the social sciences than it is of the natural sciences.

According to this view, summed up under Weber's concept *Wertbeziehung* (value relevance or relatedness), there is no escaping the fact that the *selection* of a scientific problem or aspect of society for study is related to the scientist's values and interests; moreover, values and interests affect not merely the selection of the problem but the investigation and the conclusions themselves. Explaining Weber's view, Parsons writes: "Essentially what Weber said was that no matter how fully any given empirical propositions are validated, their inclusion in a body of knowledge about society is never completely independent of the value perspective from which those particular questions were asked to which these propositions constitute answers."[9]

In these terms all social scientific propositions are value relevant or value relative. Therefore, although one may adhere to the well-established universal standards for determining empirical validity, there always remain value and interest elements in one's propositions, so that "reality" is presented in a selective and perhaps even biased and distorted fashion.

A proposition may be "true," and nevertheless present a one-sided and partial view of the social reality in question. This is because all knowledge is *perspectival*, that is, acquired from a particular standpoint. This is especially true of social knowledge because the social observer, his values, and his interests are themselves constituent elements of the subject matter. The observer is a part of the society he is studying. Consciously or not he selects problems and phenomena for study from a definite value or interest standpoint, which in turn, is associated with one or another social group, stratum, or class of the society.

If one conceives of society as a plurality of social groups and strata (as in fact Weber did), each with values and interests peculiar to it, then the social scientist is bound to carry the values of one or more of these groups and likely to study the world from the *partial* standpoint of one of these groups. Does this mean that social science is impossible and that what passes for science is merely ideology? Weber's answer is that it is not impossible but exceedingly difficult.

For Weber, the first step in overcoming these difficulties was for a social scientist to recognize the one-sidedness of his perspective, or the value and interest relevance of his approach to reality. It was in this connection that he

[9] Talcott Parsons, "An Approach to the Sociology of Knowledge," *Sociological Theory and Modern Society*, p. 149.

introduced the concept *Wertbeziehung*, as well as another, *Wertfreiheit* ("value freedom").

Weber's methodological position has been widely misunderstood and misinterpreted. Students of the social sciences have been taught again and again that for Max Weber objectivity in the social sciences meant achieving *Wertfreiheit*, a condition of being quite literally value free. Objectivity, they have been told, means freeing oneself of all values in the process of scientific investigation. This interpretation of Weber's position has been repeated so often that even those who questioned the possibility of achieving this state never questioned whether Weber himself held such a view.

Of course, this was never Weber's methodological position, and Parsons candidly acknowledges that he discovered this fact late in his career. In 1964 he wrote:

> it has not been nearly so clear to me previously that the former ["value freedom"] did not refer, as so many have claimed, to the absence of all value commitments as a norm for social scientists, but to the *differentiation* between the values of science, in the broad sense of the German *Wissenschaft*, which includes the humanistic disciplines, and the values appropriate to practical social policy.[10]

And, in the same vein, Parsons correctly explains that Weber's doctrine of *Wertfreiheit*

> is not an advocacy that the social scientist abstain from all value commitments. . . . The point is rather that *in his role* as scientist a particular subvalue system must be paramount for the investigator, one in which conceptual clarity, consistency, and generality on the one hand, and empirical accuracy and verifiability on the other, are the valued outputs of the process of investigation.[11]

There are therefore definite values which are most appropriate to the scientist's role, to science as a vocation, and these values are quite different from those, say, of the politician's role, politics as a vocation. In practice, political man may be just as committed to truth, clarity, and consistency as scientific man. Nevertheless, these are predominantly the ideals of *Wissenschaft als Beruf* and one ought self-consciously to strive for these ideals, and to approximate them as closely as possible. This is one precondition of what Weber termed "objectivity."

But there is another. Objectivity, in Weber's sense, is not possible so long as a scientist or scholar remains *unconscious* of the specific social, political, and

[10] Talcott Parsons, "Evaluation and Objectivity in Social Science," *Sociological Theory and Modern Society*, p. 79.

[11] Ibid., p. 86.

moral values that shape his motives and interests. Among the first responsibilities of the scientist, therefore, is self-awareness—the conscious recognition of the values that dominate his thinking and observations. Only such a recognition enables him to overcome systematic distortion of reality, that is, to cease viewing it always from the same partial and biased standpoint. Having achieved a relatively clear awareness of his dominant values and interests, the scientist can deliberately view phenomena from other value standpoints. He can adopt consciously and methodically a variety of perspectives and in this limited sense "free" himself from the possible limitations of one point of view.

Wertbeziehung, therefore—a clear recognition of the relevance of one's values to the selection and investigation of a social problem or phenomenon—is essential for *Wertfreiheit*. Indeed, both are essential ethical injunctions for the scientist and scholar.

It seems in order to ask whether and how well Parsons adhered to these ideals. If he had never made any scientific claims for his work, it would be pointless and unfair to ask this question. However, since Parsons believes himself to be standing squarely in the camp of science, one is in fact meeting him on his own ground by observing that his "theorizing" is anything but scientific.

We have seen how frequently his basic assumptions are unverified and unverifiable; how his concepts are ambiguously defined; how he provides few propositions making clear and unequivocal statements about some aspect of reality; and, finally, how seldom his analytical concepts and distinctions have definite empirical referents. On the one hand, then, one finds precious little of the conceptual clarity and empirical accuracy implied in the concept of *Wertfreiheit*.

On the other hand, Parsons' work is also wanting with respect to *Wertbeziehung*—and to that extent he may be presenting us with a "particular ideology," according to his own definition. Following Mannheim, he writes that a "particular ideology" involves an even greater selectivity than may be necessary, "in that among the problems and phenomena known to be significant for the social science of his time, [scientists] select some for emphasis, and neglect or play down others." Selectivity in this sense, Parsons continues, "shades off into distortion. . . . The criterion of distortion is that statements are made about the society which by social-scientific methods can be shown to be positively in error, whereas selectivity is involved where the statements are, at the proper level, 'true,' but do not constitute a balanced account of the available truth."[1 2]

Parsons understands very well that there are certain "built-in vulnerabilities to ideological 'bias' at the very core of the social-scientific endeavor itself (and indeed, in somewhat lesser degree, in all science)," and that "the scientific community is at best only partially insulated, both culturally and socially, from those other elements in society that in the nature of their structured positions

[1 2] Parsons, "An Approach to the Sociology of Knowledge," p. 153.

cannot give primacy to scientific subvalues and standards of empirical investigation." Scientists are therefore under great pressure, consciously or unconsciously, to yield "concessions" to "outside orientations."[13]

So as we look over Parsons' *oeuvre*, we have a right to wonder whether he has carefully considered the relevance of all this to his own work. Has he confronted himself and asked whether and in what degree his "scientific" statements are characterized by "selectivity" and even "distortion"; whether, and in what measure, he has been yielding concessions to outside orientations and interests? For if he has not asked himself these questions, he has failed to abide by the norms of "science as a vocation."

[13] Ibid., p. 159.

II

SOCIAL EXCHANGE
THEORY

5

The Exchange Theory of George C. Homans

It was out of a dissatisfaction with functionalism, George C. Homans tells us, in his autobiographical introduction to *Sentiments and Activities*,[1] that he turned to psychology and ultimately to his own version of exchange theory. His critical discussion of functionalism in this introduction serves as a brief review of its major problems and defects and suggests what virtues Homans saw in explanations based on psychology and rudimentary economics.

Homans discerned at least three types of statement in which social scientists employed the term "function." In the first type anthropologists, for example, spoke of the functional interrelation of a society's institutions. Each institution was a function of each of the others, and together they formed an integrated social structure. This view, shared by the most famous of functionalists, Malinowski and Radcliffe-Brown, bore a great resemblance to the doctrine of Homans' teacher at Harvard, L. J. Henderson. Henderson, a physiologist and biochemist, had come under the influence of Vilfredo Pareto's *Sociologie Générale* and offered a seminar on Pareto, insisting that mutual interdependence and equilibrium apply no less to social systems than they do to physical or biochemical systems.

The interrelatedness of institutions Homans found to be a useful assumption. What he objected to was the fact that functionalists inevitably tied this assumption to other, untenable ones. Are institutions so interrelated that a change in one will induce changes in all the others? This is hardly to be taken for granted. Quite the contrary, it should be the object of investigation and empirical demonstration. Once this is done, it becomes quite clear that "there is

---

[1] George C. Homans, *Sentiments and Activities* (New York: The Free Press, 1962), pp. 1–49. Page references to this introduction will be cited in parentheses immediately following the quoted passage.

a good deal of play in any institutional structure: institutions do not mesh with others mechanically like the parts of a machine. Instituions *are* the behavior of men; their relations are mediated by the behavior of men." (23).

Within any given social structure, one cannot account for an institution's character solely by its relation to the others. How then could one explain the presence of the same institution in a number of societies differing in other institutional respects? Functional statements of the first type, Homans concludes, "offer in themselves no explanation: given [for instance] that a particular rule of exogamy is associated with a particular form of lineage organization, we must still ask why this should be so." (23).

If this first type of statement, which Homans calls structural, was characteristic of all functionalists, the second type distinguished among them. Malinowski, for example, accounted for an institution not only by relating it to others, but also by relating it to the individual needs of society's members. Canoe magic was associated with deep-sea fishing but not with fishing in the quiet lagoon. The apparent function of magic, then, was to alleviate the anxiety of fishermen under precarious and potentially dangerous circumstances. The underlying assumption here is that anxiety, though generated under specific conditions among the Trobrianders, is an emotional state all men everywhere must cope with and control. This type of explanation differs from the first, therefore, in that it is psychological; it attempts to account for an institution by showing that it exists because it is "functional for men as men."

The third type of functional statement, in contrast, alleges that an institution prevails because it is functional for the society as a whole—that is, it contributes positively to the maintenance, integration, and adaptation of the society itself as a reality *sui generis*. This type, most characteristic of Durkheim and his disciple, Radcliffe-Brown, Homans finds most objectionable. Since it asserts a positive relationship between a particular institution and the structural maintenance of the society of which it is a part, the implication is that if the particular institution changes or disappears, the change will express itself in the disruption or discontinuity of the society. If this is to be more than a vacuous statement (i.e., if a part changes, then the whole of which it was a part must also become different), one needs solid criteria by which to assess the structural maintenance or change of a society.

Homans most emphatically rejects the "solution" of those functionalists for whom a society's very survival constitutes proof of the positive functions of its institutions. When this is more than a tautology, he argues, it proves to be false. In examining monographs dealing with societies that had quite literally failed to survive, Homans found that the records of "such extinct societies showed that they possessed *all* the functions on all the usual lists of prerequisites. If they died it was not for lack of institutions but for lack of resistance to measles, or firewater, or gunfire or something of the sort" (26).

Homans' point is not to deny that institutions have consequences—good (functional), bad (dysfunctional), latent, manifest, etc.—but rather to challenge the view that there is some intellectual advantage in asserting that institutional forms are either functional or dysfunctional for the "society itself," and not merely for certain of its members. Assertions about consequences for a society as a whole have proven to be undemonstrable.

Homans rejects equally, as wholly untenable, the related functionalist form of social Darwinism, which, seeking to demonstrate its assertions, conceives of competition among societies as if it were the competition of organisms in a state of nature. According to this view, those societies survive that possess institutions of the greatest survival value. But this is clearly unsatisfactory, since in the competition among societies, the weak do not perish—they are conquered or absorbed. The history of such cases shows that "The victors were usually content to let the institutions of the weaker people alone so long as they themselves [i.e., the victors] controlled the government and collected the taxes" (27). Societies do not compete as animals do, so the Darwinian argument is false.

Social scientists, says Homans, ought to give up trying to explain the persistence of an institution by means of false analogies and undemonstrable assumptions. Instead, they ought to ask why certain individuals and groups have found a particular institution to their interest, why others have not, "and how the former, in the context of the other institutions of society, have managed to get the institution adopted in the teeth of the opposition" (28).

To sum up, Homans' critical look at functionalism reveals at least three classes of statements: *structural* propositions that are testable but have to be explained by others; *psychological* propositions that are themselves testable but which are also "required for the explanation of Class 1"; and *functional* propositions that are "neither testable nor required for explanation" (30). "I came to the conclusion," he writes, "though I could demonstrate it even to my own satisfaction in only a few cases, that the ultimate explanatory principles in anthropology and sociology, and for that matter in history, were neither structural nor functional but psychological: they were propositions about the behavior of men as men" (29). This conclusion has guided Homans' work and has led him to conceive of social behavior as exchange.

EXCHANGE, JUSTICE, AND POWER

In *Social Behavior: Its Elementary Forms*[2] we find Homans' most complete and detailed exposition of his theory. He begins by noting that elements of the truths he wants to present and test in the form of scientific propositions are already embodied in proverbs and maxims: "Every man has his

[2] George C. Homans, *Social Behavior: Its Elementary Forms* (New York: Harcourt, Brace & World, 1961). Page references to this book will be cited in parentheses immediately following the quoted passage.

price. You scratch my back and I'll scratch yours. Do as you would be done by. You can't eat your cake and have it too. No cross, no crown. Fair exchange is no robbery. To each his own. *Noblesse oblige.* Whosoever hath, to him shall be given. . . . And so forth" (1). These are partial truths that men apply in everyday life in an ad hoc manner, generally grasping neither their interconnections nor the theory they imply. Homans wishes to state these truths in a series of theoretical propositions and to test them; this will enable him not only to describe elementary social behavior, but to explain it.

By social behavior Homans means the actions a person engages in that will call forth some form of reward or punishment from another person. In these terms, actions resulting in reward or punishment by the nonhuman environment would not be regarded as social behavior. If, for example, a farmer's son plants corn in a certain way, his behavior is social only insofar as his actions are oriented to the potential reward or punishment of another person, say, his father. It is *not* social insofar as the son plants corn because it will get him a crop. A further stipulation is that when one person acts in a definite way toward another, the reward or punishment must come from the second and not from some "third party, whether an individual or organization" (2). Finally, Homans' subject matter is actual behavior, the interaction between persons and not the norms or rules that may apply to their situation. He will, he says, treat norms as given—which does not mean he will ignore them but rather take them into account without seeking to explain them. Individuals interacting directly with each other he calls elementary social behavior. Why "elementary"? "Because it is relatively easy to explain, and for no other reason . . ." (3).

To explain elementary social behavior Homans relies on two bodies of theory: behavioral psychology and rudimentary economics. Actually, the two bodies of theory may be merged into one, since both regard "human behavior as a function of its payoff: in amount and kind it depends on the amount and kind of reward and punishment it fetches" (13). Both conceive the exchange of human activities in terms of reward and cost and both seek to explain these activities in terms of what certain actions cost as compared with what they gain for the actor. From this standpoint, social interaction is an exchange of "goods" and services in which each actor strives to reduce costs and maximize profits.

Homans draws his favorite illustration of exchange from Peter Blau's *The Dynamics of Bureaucracy*. The interaction of two office clerks, Person and Other, is paradigmatic of face-to-face, small-group behavior in and out of the laboratory. Person is less skilled at the required paperwork tasks than Other. The office rules stipulate that if a clerk needs help with his work, he should seek it from the office supervisor. But if Person were to follow the rules, he would reveal his incompetence, thereby hurting his chances for promotion and increments. Despite the rules, therefore, Person requests help not from his supervisor but from Other, who, being more skilled, also does his work more quickly and has time to spare. "Other gives Person help and in return Person gives Other thanks and expressions of approval. The two men have exchanged help and approval" (31–32).

Bearing this paradigm in mind, let us look at Homans' propositions:

1. If in the past the occurrence of a particular stimulus-situation has been the occasion on which a man's activity has been rewarded, then the more similar the present stimulus-situation is to the past one, the more likely he is to emit the activity, or some similar activity, now. (53)

This first proposition describes the conditions under which Other is likely to help Person. If any subsequent situation resembles a preceding one, in which Other was rewarded for helping Person, he may help Person not only when he asks for it but even when he merely appears helpless.

2. The more often within a given period of time a man's activity rewards the activity of another, the more often the other will emit the activity. (54)

This proposition asserts a tendency toward proportionality between the frequency of activity exchanged between Person and Other. An increase or decrease in the frequency of one's activities will evoke a corresponding change in the activities of the other.

3. The more valuable to a man a unit of the activity another gives him, the more often he will emit activity rewarded by the activity of the other. (55)

If proposition 2 asserts a direct relationship between the frequency of one activity to the frequency of another, proposition 3 asserts that the value of one's activity is directly related to the frequency of the other's. How does one measure value? By the need one has for a particular activity. The greater Person's need for help, the greater is its value. He will therefore ask for it more often and also reward Other with gratitude more often when he obtains it. A rate of exchange is implicit here: if Person needs (or values) help more than Other values approval, Person is likely to give "relatively more approval than Other gives help."

4. The more often a man has in the recent past received a rewarding activity from another, the less valuable any further unit of that activity becomes to him; and therefore by proposition 3, the less often he will emit the activity that gets him that reward: the more help Person has recently received from Other, the less, for the time being, he needs any further help and the less often he will ask for help or give thanks. Accordingly this

proposition may mask the truth of proposition 2, which says that the more often Other rewards the activity of Person, the more often Person will emit the activity. (55)

To the dyad, Person-Other, Homans adds a third party, whom he calls Third Man. Like Person, Third Man is deficient in skill and in need of Other's help. Person and Third Man are willing to give Other approval for his help; but now Other must divide his limited time between them. Person and Third Man will now receive less assistance than Person did when he was alone with Other. Other's help has become more scarce and valuable so that Person and Third Man are now prepared to "pay" more approval per unit of Other's help. Thus, "Other's bargaining position has improved over what it was when he had only Person to deal with even though no conscious bargaining need take place" (56).

The concepts of cost, profit, and reward are therefore essential for an understanding of behavior as exchange. Cost, for Homans, refers to "value forgone," and not only to the pain incurred in engaging in a specific activity. An activity incurs cost insofar as it causes one to forgo a rewarding and alternative activity. When Other helps Person he inevitably incurs a cost: if he refuses to help and continues instead to do his own work, he forgoes Person's approval; conversely, if he extends assistance, "he forgoes the value of doing his own work" (61). Similarly, if Person does his own work, he loses the value of help; and if in fact he solicits help, he pays in loss of self-respect, since in asking for help, he acknowledges his inferiority to Other.

Hence, the formula that emerges from these exchanges is: Profit = Reward – Cost. "We define psychic *profit*," writes Homans, "as reward less cost, and *we argue that no exchange continues unless both parties are making a profit*" (61, italics added). We shall return to this problematic proposition momentarily.

"The open secret of human exchange," he continues, "is to give the other man behavior that is more valuable to him than it is costly to you and to get from him behavior that is more valuable to you than it is costly to him" (62). This clearly raises issues of distributive justice and brings us to the fifth proposition:

> 5. The more to a man's disadvantage the rule of distributive justice fails of realization, the more likely he is to display the emotional behavior we call anger. (75)

What is a "just" exchange? A "fair" exchange? Generally Homans implies that so long as an exchange continues it is profitable, or regarded as such, by both parties to it. But this conception of things bears a dangerous resemblance to the tautological, functionalist propositions Homans so vehemently repudiates elsewhere. It has definitely conservative implications besides. How does one know that an exchange relationship is just? By observing that it persists!

According to this logic, it follows inevitably that all prevailing dyadic relationships are fair and just. But who could take such an assumption seriously? Nor does it strengthen Homans's case to argue, as he does, that existing relationships are just because if they were unjust the parties to them would have broken them off and sought alternative sources for the service in question. This, too, is an untenable assumption. What right has he to assume that alternative sources are always available?

Homans prefers rather subjective criteria for what is fair and just. Although he calls attention to the possibility of exploitative exchanges, he does so only in passing. Most often justice, for Homans, is a relative and subjective matter. People compare themselves to others and assess their investments, costs, and rewards in relation to the investments, costs, and rewards of others. Person asks whether he is getting all that other men in circumstances similar to his would get; and Other asks himself the same type of question. If and when men find that they are not getting all that they ought, they not only become angry (which they find intrinsically rewarding), but they "avoid activities that get them into unjust exchanges; they learn to emit activities that are rewarded by the attainment of justice . . ." (77). Homans acknowledges that "it is a man like Other who commands a supply of a scarce good that is most in danger of violating Person's notion of distributive justice, or, as we say, of exploiting him" (77). But he glosses over this issue and gives no systematic attention to relationships of domination and exploitation. The subjects of Homan's theory, for some reason he does not explain, "are always free not to enter into exchange at all . . ." (78).

This certainly is not true of the larger social world in which we all live and work. But even if we confine our attention exclusively to the microsocial world to which Homans intends to apply his theory, we find that at the very least, his assertion highly exaggerates the freedom men have to enter or not to enter certain exchange relationships. For Homans glosses over the key question of whether viable and more just alternatives are actually available to an exploited individual. If not, he remains unfree and coerced. Homans's conception of exchange refuses to acknowledge that people remain in relationships in which they are dominated and exploited even when they regard them as unjust.

Deliberately limiting his theory to the interaction of small groups of individuals who are formally equal, Homans fails to consider how the larger context of formal authority and domination shapes their behavior and determines their fate. The microsocial world Homans has abstracted from the larger world he separates and sets aside, and he invests the subjects of this world with unlimited freedom. When they find that they profit less than they would like from a particular relationship, they change their behavior, enter an alternative relationship, and increase their profit. "And," Homans continues, "if whenever a man's behavior brought him a balance of reward and cost, he changed it away from that which got him the less profit, there might well come a time when, other circumstances remaining the same, his behavior did not change further because he has successfully abandoned all the behavior that brought him less profit" (99).

That is the way Homans accounts for stable and persistent behavior. If and when every member of the group attains this happy state, its organization has achieved what he calls a "practical equilibrium."

At the same time his definition of "cost" leads him to a conception of things that is difficult to reconcile with what we know about everyday life. "For an activity to incur cost," he argues, "an alternative and rewarding activity must be there to be forgone" (59). And later he writes: "in ordinary human experience, alternatives are important because they raise the cost of any activity and so render more probable the emission of some other activity. The rule is: no alternative, no cost" (100). Indeed? But one could just as easily argue the opposite: that it is precisely those situations in which no apparent alternatives are available that men find psychically, and otherwise, most costly. It is not necessary to hold the precise opposite of Homans' proposition, however, to see that men find situations costly (repressive and frustrating) where they cannot avail themselves of alternatives.

Although Homans gives some attention to social conflict and takes up some issues of justice in exchange, his treatment of the issues reveals several inadequacies. Part of the reason for this is his exclusive consideration of behavior that is, in his words, "easy to explain." To "explain" elementary behavior he reviews a series of studies and experiments that tend to support the validity of his propositions. It is impossible here to summarize these studies in detail; and in any case it is unnecessary since the problems, ambiguities, and shortcomings of Homans' approach become quite evident in his treatment of distributive justice, which we shall consider next. A critical scrutiny of that treatment, based as it is on "field studies of real-life groups," affords us a more direct view of his approach to justice in everyday life.

JUSTICE

For Homans, justice in social behavior is characterized by this fundamental rule: every man who is a party to an exchange relation expects his rewards to be proportional to his costs; he expects that "the greater the rewards, the greater the costs—and that the net rewards, or profits, of each man be proportional to his investments—the greater the investments, the greater the profits. . . . Finally, when each man is being rewarded by some third party, he will expect the third party, in the distribution of rewards, to maintain this relation between the two of them" (232). The more this "rule of distributive justice fails of realization" for an individual, "the more likely he is to display the emotional behavior we call anger." When justice fails, however, men not only display anger or guilt, "they also learn to do something about it. They learn to avoid activities that get them into unjust exchange . . ." (232–33). Throughout, Homans' definition of justice underscores the proportionality of rewards to investments for the parties concerned. When proportionality ceases to characterize the exchange in question, it becomes unjust, and the party who fails to gain rewards commensurate with his investments turns away from the relationship and seeks and finds another that is just.

What this clearly implies, as we noted earlier, is that all exchange relations, so long as they persist or remain in effect, are characterized by proportionality: each gets out of the relationship rewards proportional to his investment—or at least each perceives such a proportionality. According to Homans, no man remains a party to an exchange relation that fails to realize for him the required proportionality.

Homans goes on to maintain that "the rule of justice says that the more valuable to Other the activity Person gives him, the more valuable to Person should be the activity Other gives him" (233). But a careful look at this proposition reveals that it does not have the same meaning as the one we have just examined. This proposition implies that justice depends on the *symmetry* or *equality* of the exchange; while the earlier proposition stresses *proportionality* of reward to investment. The two propositions do not mean the same thing. It is possible—and indeed, very often the case—that one party to a relation has made greater investments and has obtained profits in proportion to his investments without his service necessarily being equal to the service of the other. Homans insists, however, that the two propositions are in effect identical. He can do so only because his criterion of justice is strictly subjective: the value of the exchanged services is what it is perceived to be by the parties to the exchange; if each feels it is a just exchange, it is one. As for the outside observer, he too has only a subjective criterion of justice: the very fact that the exchange relation continues means that both parties regard it as just; which means, apparently, that the observer must also conclude that it is just. Since there are no independent objective criteria by which the outside observer can decide whether or not the relation is just, Homans in effect solves the problem by definition, in much the same way that traditional functionalism "solved" the problem of whether a society's functional prerequisites had been fulfilled. There are other problems besides.

ALEC AND THE GANG

To test the validity of his theory of justice, Homans draws upon William F. Whyte's *Street Corner Society*, the study of the now famous Norton Street gang. Several nights each week, we are told in that study, the gang members went bowling. Alec, a member of the gang whom the others held in low esteem, regarded himself as a rather good bowler. Indeed, occasionally he did beat the others, including Long John, a highly respected member and friend of Doc, the gang's leader. Yet when Doc set up a tournament among all members, Alec did not bowl well at all. "Good bowling takes confidence," Homans observes, "and Doc and the other members saw to it that Alec's confidence was undermined by friendly heckling. In so doing, *they maintained a state of justice*" (234, italics added). Interpreting the episode further, Homans writes:

> In individual matches and when the leaders of the group did not gang up on him, he could do very well in bowling, but in other activities he did not conform very closely to group standards. He was boastful; he was aggressive in trying to improve his social ranking. He spent more time chasing girls than the other Nortons did, and, what was worse, showed that he was capable of leaving friends in the lurch when on the prowl. If his behavior had improved in these respects, his social rank might then have risen, and his scores in intraclique bowling competition might have been allowed to go up. As it was, his rank remained low. (234)

The rule of justice that Homans discerns here is that "the value of what a member receives by way of reward from the members of the group in one field of activity should be proportional to the value to them of the activities he contributes in another field." Since Alec contributed little of value in one field and violated a number of norms, the group controlled the reward he got in another field—"they kept it down. They kept the value of what he got 'in line' with what he gave" (234).

A few critical comments are in order here. We might begin by asking what all this has to do with "justice." The group's behavior could just as easily be interpreted as a petty, coercive attempt to enforce conformity, a form of group tyranny. How does Homans really know whether the gang's reaction to Alec was a matter of administering justice rather than enforcing conformity? From his strictly behavioristic standpoint, of course, Homans has no real means of distinguishing between the two. Whether a group is enforcing conformity or administering justice is at least in part a question of what *meaning* the members attribute to their actions. In Homans' behavioristic method, however, there is no provision for getting at the meaning of acts or the motives of actors.

Let us assume that Homans would reply that the group was in fact enforcing conformity, but that they regarded this enforcement as just. How can he know this? Perhaps they enforced conformity even while believing that they were behaving unjustly. All Homans has to work with are two pieces of data: that Alec conformed poorly and that he also bowled poorly under certain circumstances. How does Homans know what meaning to attribute to these data? On what grounds does he attribute one meaning rather than another? How would he verify it?

But let us accept for a moment Homans's supposition that the group members were seeking justice and that they judged their punishment of Alec as commensurate with his transgressions. Does it follow from this that the outside observer or social scientist—in this case Homans—must accept the group's judgment uncritically? When Homans says that "they kept the value of what [Alec] got 'in line' with what he gave," how does he know that the two values are "in line"? According to this logic any other reaction of the group, either more severe or less severe, would also be in line. For so long as Alec remains in the group, *anything* the group does to punish him for lack of conformity would, according to Homans, result in an equivalence between what he gives and what he gets. So long as Alec remains in the group (i.e., has neither terminated this exchange relation nor sought a more profitable alternative one), the group, by definition, can do no injustice to him.

Or would Homans argue that a reaction of a certain severity would have been "out of line" and therefore unjust? Again, however, what criterion do we have to determine whether the gang's reaction is in or out of line? The only criterion Homans seems to offer is that men will avoid unjust relationships—from which it follows that since Alex remained a member of the gang, the punishment must have been just.

Justice in everyday life is a complex matter; and surely one does not even begin to cope with this complexity by equating justice with whatever the group does to ensure conformity. One needs, instead, more objective ways of assessing how just relationships are, not merely the subjective criteria of the group itself. Judged from this point of view, Homans's other attempts to validate his theory are no more satisfactory than the first.

THE BANK WIRING ROOM

Homans's rule of justice is that "a man's rewards in exchange with others should be proportional to his investement" (235). To test this he utilizes another well-known body of research that Elton Mayo and his colleagues carried out in the Hawthorne plant of the Western Electric Company. The scene is the Bank Wiring Observation Room, in which there were two main jobs: wiring and soldering. The wiremen received more pay than the soldermen;

> [they] were presumed to be more skilled, and held more seniority. Of the nine wiremen six worked on so-called connector equipment and three on selector equipment. The differences between the two jobs were slight, but the connector wiremen were a little senior and got a little more pay than the selectors. There were three soldermen in all, one for each set of three wiremen, and they soldered in position the wires that the others had connected to terminals on the equipment. (235).

Two cliques emerged, based on the connector wiremen and selectors, the first group holding itself superior to the second in accordance with the higher skill, pay, and seniority of its members.

> To the first, or connector, clique but in a subordinate position as befitted his inferior job-status, belonged Steinhardt, the solderman for the first three connector wiremen. To the second, or selector clique in the same sort of position belonged Cermak, who had replaced another man as solderman for the three selector wiremen. Matchek, the solderman for the middle group of wiremen, suffered from a speech defect and was hardly a member of Observation Room society.
>
> All the men ate lunch in the room, sending out one of their number to pick up their food and drink from the plant restaurant. The question was who should be the "lunch boy"—note the word "boy." It was not a very valuable service; anyone could have performed it for himself, and it was menial: the lunch boy was a servant for the others. At the time the men were first assigned to the room Steinhardt had reluctantly agreed to do the job. But as soon as Cermak came in as a solderman for the selector wiremen and was accepted as a member of their clique, Steinhardt was relieved and Cermak took over as lunch boy. (235–36)

Homans then asks: "was it appropriate that he should do so?" And he replies with an unqualified affirmative. Why was it appropriate? Because Cermak "was a solderman, and soldermen held the lowest job status in the room; of the soldermen he was the least senior and the last to come into the group. Accordingly the group assigned him the least rewarding activity at its disposal: his menial job was in line with the other features of his status" (236). Cermak's rewards were presumably proportional to his investments and hence the treatment accorded him was just.

Now, as earlier, the most obvious defect in this argument is that the situation Homans describes might just as easily and appropriately be labeled unjust. The members of the group delegated a menial and servile task to the man who was already low man on the totem pole. But why is this just? Why is it just and appropriate that one who already receives least should continue to receive least? To this Homans would reply: it is just because he has invested less than everyone else. Who says?

After all, the status and pay distinctions of the various jobs were made not by the workers themselves but by those in formal authority—management. Even if the workers themselves had made these distinctions, should the social scientist accept the validity of this status hierarchy uncritically, thereby automatically regarding as just all actions of the "higher" toward the "lower"?

The trouble with Homans' conceptualization of this situation is that it tends to justify and dignify the status quo; it attributes justice to relationships that might as accurately be characterized by the concepts exploitation, coercion, and domination.

Why exploitation? Let us remember that we are talking about exchange, about some reciprocal exchange of activities or services. Cermak provided a definite service for the others; he brought them their lunch. Homans tries to depreciate its value by saying that "it was not a very valuable service [since] anyone could have performed it for himself . . ." But this is the same as saying that the service the slave performs for the master, the master could perform for himself. Ergo, the slave's service is not valuable.

Obviously this will not do. What is undeniable is that Cermak gave of himself to the group. What did he get in return? Very little and perhaps nothing—though Homans would insist that Cermak received approval for fulfilling his menial, servile function; or, negatively, that he was not punished for refusing either by rebuke or ostracism; or, finally, that he fulfilled his task unwillingly and experienced anger, which was his reward. Yet if we compare in time and effort the daily service Cermak rendered the group with what they gave him in return, it becomes evident—particularly if we abandon Homans' subjective and arbitrary criteria—that Cermak received, both qualitatively and quantitatively, less from the group than he gave, and was to that extent exploited.

Cermak was also, it is clear, coerced and dominated by the group. He could have refused to comply; but this alternative, he probably felt, would be more costly. In any case group pressure won out. The group members effectively coerced him into doing their bidding, successfully keeping him in his place. But this hardly warrants our saying that this is the way things ought to be, that it is a just state of affairs and regarded as such by all concerned.

Homans writes that "we must remember that we are talking about justice as seen by the members of a particular group and not about our own sense of justice, which is of course Olympian." Once again, how does Homans know that the group members regarded their actions toward Cermak as just? Homans has described only their overt behavior and knows nothing about how they assessed their acts. From the available data there is no way of knowing what meaning they attributed to their pressure on Cermak—whether they viewed it as just, whether they questioned its fairness, or, finally, whether they persisted in it even while definitely recognizing its injustice. Poor Cermak! He is not only kept at the "bottom of the heap" but subjected to a mechanical and behavioristic social science that informs him that he has received his just deserts—his reward is proportional to his "investment."

In his chapter on justice and elsewhere Homans centers our attention exclusively on the status distinctions among the workers and employees themselves and ignores the relations between the workers and those in formal authority. Ledger clerks, for example, believed that their job was more responsible than that of cash posters, and they resented the fact that both jobs received equal pay. Ledger clerks also complained when their supervisor temporarily assigned them to cash posting, for they regarded this temporary transfer as a "put down," a loss of status. At the very least, the ledger clerks argued, they ought to get a few more dollars to show that their "job is more important" (240).

"Apparently," Homans offers in interpretation, "distributive justice demands not just that higher investment should receive higher reward in one respect but that it should do so in all" (240). In other words, the ledger clerks were demanding "status congruence."

We must ask again: What this has to do with "justice"? Striving for status congruence and striving for justice are not necessarily the same. The ledger clerks felt themselves superior in some respects and wished to feel superior in all. Why call this the pursuit of justice rather than, simply, the pursuit of self-interest, higher income, and superior status? To take an analogy from the larger social world, would Homans interpret it as the pursuit of justice if whites in the United States, regarding themselves as superior in some respects, sought to achieve superiority in all?

The trouble with Homans' interpretation of the ledger clerk—cash poster situation is that it is so arbitrary. He not only confuses the pursuit of self-interest with the pursuit of justice but regards men's striving for status congruence, profitable investments in their interpersonal relations, etc., as the manifestation of a universal psychological law. "We believe," he writes, "that men are alike in holding the notion of proportionality between investment and profit that lies at the heart of distributive justice" (246). Yet his next statement renders this assertion meaningless. "The trouble is that [men] differ from society to society, from group to group, and from time to time in any one society or group" (246).

There is still another aspect of Homans' procedure that we cannot pass over in silence. Since management was solely responsible for the policy that frustrated the clerks' desire for status congruence, it was quite irrational for the clerks to resent the cash posters, but they did. "Though it was not the cash posters' fault that the ledger clerks' pay was no higher, the latter showed some resentment of the posters as beneficiaries of injustice" (245—46), Homans says, but he has nothing to say about this as an example of "divide and conquer."

Indeed, what Homans never examines is the way in which the distinctions among the workers militate against their common interests. His exclusive focus on the workers themselves, on the distinctions among them, and on their mutual envy obscures the major conflict of interest in the world of work and industry—i.e., between those who control the strategic resources and those who do not.

For Homans, the workers are always questioning the justice of one another's rewards but never questioning either the rewards of those who control the means of production or the system of control itself. In these terms, Homans' sociology, whether he realizes it or not, effectively favors the interests of management.

Homans might seek to defend his procedure by reminding us that he has deliberately confined his attention to informal, or what he calls elementary, exchange relations. But this procedure results in the radical separation of two worlds: here the microworld of informal elementary behavior, and there the macroworld of formal authority. Never the twain shall meet. The result of this radical separation is that we hear much about status differences and mutual jealousy among the workers themselves but nothing about the system of power and domination of which they are a part. We get the impression that Homans' subjects are governed by psychological laws and not by the values and interests of a specific social system in a particular historical epoch.

Furthermore, we learn practically nothing about certain important dimensions of informal behavior itself. In *Social Behavior* Homans gives no attention to power and domination; in a book of some four hundred pages, there is no discussion of the processes leading to power nor even an index reference to the concept. That he himself eventually recognized this omission becomes evident in "Fundamental Social Processes," an essay published a few years later. Let us consider this essay in detail.

HOMANS ON POWER

When two or more individuals enter into an exchange relationship, and one of them is able to change the behavior of others in his own favor, "we say that one man is more powerful than another."[3] Homans assumes that Person and Other originally gained equally from their exchange of approval and advice, and that now, for some reason, the value of Other's advice has gone up—perhaps he has been taking too much time from his own work. Other is now able, whether he intends it or not, to get more approval per unit of advice. "The general condition for differences in power is this: the party to the exchange who gets the lesser net reward from it is less likely to change his behavior than is the other party." This has been called "the principle of least interest." Quoting J. W. Thibaut's and H. M. Kelley's *The Social Psychology of Groups*, Homans continues: "that person is able to dictate the conditions of association whose interest in the continuation of the affair is least" (53).

This becomes evident in a situation in which one man has power over many, and hence a great interest in maintaining his power over the entire group—"more interest, perhaps, than any one of the group has in remaining

[3] George C. Homans, "Fundamental Social Processes," in *Sociology: An Introduction*, ed. Neil J. Smelser (New York: John Wiley & Sons, 1967), p. 53. Page references to this essay are hereafter cited in parentheses immediately following the quoted passage.

under his control; but in exchange with any one of them, he has less to gain. This may make it rewarding for the members of the group to combine and deal with him collectively on more nearly equal terms. But now a new pair relation has been established: the powerful man against the group" (54). (An obvious example of this would be workers organizing themselves to defend and promote their interests vis à vis the employer.)

No sooner, however, does Homans introduce the concept of power and begin to specify its sources, than he proceeds to deny it:

> Note that *after* Person has changed his behavior in order to give Other more approval, the power of the two men is shown in the matrix [not reproduced here] to be once more equal, in that each is now getting equal net reward out of the exchange: Person's 3−2 equals Other's 2−1. We have deliberately set the figures so that the rewards are equal. This was done to indicate that in repeated exchanges between persons, provided that there is no other change in conditions, *power differences tend to disappear*, and neither party unilaterally will change his behavior any further." (54)

Thus, for Homans, when practical equilibrium is achieved, power disappears, and the exchange relation becomes once again a relationship of equality. This is similar to the point of view we encountered in *Social Behavior*, where Homans maintained that so long as a relationship persists, it is just. Now he maintains that it is not only just but equalitarian as well.

What this arbitrary and bizarre conception tends to do is to overlook entirely the perpetuation of power in persisting relationships—with the parties to the relation being not only unequal, but with one of them successfully dominating, subjecting, or coercing the others. If we take Homans' own example, in which the many who are individually weak combine to counter the one who has power over them, we think immediately of industrial workers uniting against an employer. The fact that workers have organized into a union certainly does not mean that their power is now equal to management's. The workers may have improved their bargaining position, they may even have improved it immensely, but this does not alter the fact that they continue to be subject and subordinate to the employer's power and authority, and that they are dependent, for their livelihood, upon the employer. Given the conditions of the prevailing economic and political system, they need the employer more than he needs them. A definite imbalance of power prevails between the two parties, despite the persistence of their relationship.

The main source of this inherent imbalance is the fact that one party controls the means of production while the other does not; one party controls strategic resources and therefore commands, while the other party, if he is to gain his livelihood, must subordinate himself and obey.

But, Homans might object, all this may be true in the macrosocial world of private property and formal-legal authority, but not in the microworld of elementary behavior. Let us return to Homans's original paradigm, in which Person and Other are working together in an office. According to the formal rules, it will be recalled, each employee is required to do his own work; if he should run up against a problem or difficulty, he is to request assistance from the supervisor. But since it is the supervisor's evaluation of the employees that will determine their increments and promotions, they avoid asking him for help. Requesting help from him is tantamount to admitting one's incompetence and is therefore likely to work against an employee's interests. It is in this context of formal authority, a context to which Homans pays scant attention, that Person turns to Other for help.

Other gains power over Person, Homans acknowledges, because Other "has acquired expert knowledge of office procedures, which Person has not had the time to acquire and which he badly needs" (54). The reason Other is more powerful "is that he sets a lower value on approval than Person sets on advice" (55). This power, Homans suggests, results from a *change* in situation, i.e., from one in which Other accepted as equivalent the approval he received for his advice, to one in which Other assigns less value to Person's approval. The change could occur for any number of reasons but comes about in this case as a result of the entry of Third Man. Like Person, Third Man is relatively unskilled; he therefore values advice more than the approval he is prepared to give in return. Other now advises two men and his costs rise accordingly, because he must now take more time from his own work. And though he is now getting more approval, the value of further approval has declined for him "through satiation."

On the other hand, because two men are now seeking advice,

> neither may be getting as much advice as one did earlier. They are in danger of becoming relatively deprived of advice, and thus . . . the value of advice goes up for each of them. Both effects tend to make exchanges in the immediate future less rewarding to Other than to either Person or the Third Man, and it is this that gives Other power over both of them. Power, then, depends on an ability to provide rewards that are valuable because they are scarce. In the office, many men can provide approval, but we have assumed that only Other can give good advice. (55)

This is the way Homans explains the emergence of power—i.e., as resulting from a change in conditions, specifically the entry of Third Man redounding to the benefit of Other.

The question that suggests itself is whether, in the absence of Third Man or any other change, one must assume equality of power in the relationship of Person and Other. In other words, if we go back from Homans's triad to his original dyad of Person and Other, is it true that "in repeated exchanges between [them], provided that there is no other change in the conditions, power differences tend to disappear, and neither party unilaterally will change his behavior any further"? Is it true that "Person, for instance, will not make his approval any more fulsome, since it would cost him too much in the way of confessing his inferiority" (54)? It is hard to see why power differences between Person and Other should disappear. For so long as Other has more expert knowledge than Person and Person must hide his relative incompetence from the supervisor, and so long as Person can neither coerce Other into giving him advice nor find an alternative source for it—so long as these conditions prevail, it would seem that Person needs Other more than Other needs Person. A fundamental imbalance, asymmetry, or inequality is inherent in the relationship.

Other controls a strategic resource and therefore will come to dominate Person, for whom admitting inferiority to Other is less costly or painful than admitting incompetence to his supervisor. Homans' assumption of equalitarian relation of exchange and the disappearance of power rests on the premise that Other's ability to withhold advice gives him no greater power than Person's ability to withhold approval. But this is surely an untenable premise. Given the constraints of the situation, approval is not a strategic resource but advice is.

The point here is not that Homans does not understand all this; he himself remarks in another connection, "Men are powerful when many want what they, the few, are able to supply or many fear what they, the few, are able to withhold" (59). The point is rather that his analysis generally obscures the imbalances of power that characterize all or most exchange relations. For this reason his conception of elementary exchange, though developed with skill, intelligence, and humor, is less adequate than Peter Blau's, to which we now turn.

6

Exchange and Power in the Work of Peter Blau

Unlike Homans, who has limited explicitly the applicability of his theoretical propositions to interpersonal relations, Peter Blau has set himself the problem of deriving "the social processes that govern the complex structures of communities and societies from the simpler processes that pervade the daily intercourse among individuals and their interpersonal relations."[1]

Blau agrees with Homans[2] that one cannot generalize simply from the micro- to the macrosocial world. His task, therefore, is to suggest connecting links between the two. By studying elementary interpersonal processes, he aims to achieve a better understanding of the development of the complex structures of associations among men. "It is this fundamental concern," he writes, "with utilizing the analysis of simpler processes for clarifying complex structures that distinguishes the approach here from that of other recent students of interpersonal processes . . ." (2).

For Blau, an adequate approach to the problem must avoid the extremes of grand theory and psychological reductionism. The former is so highly abstract that it can be related to observable reality only with the greatest difficulty or not at all. The latter reduces complex structures to simple psychological processes and ignores the emergent qualities of human interaction. An adequate

[1] Peter M. Blau, *Exchange and Power in Social Life* (New York: John Wiley & Sons, 1967), p. 2. Page references to this book are hereafter cited in parentheses immediately following the quoted passage.

[2] Homans writes, for instance: "Let us not be in any hurry to generalize from what happens in the small group to what happens in society at large. The status, pay, and other rewards that go to the more public positions in the larger society may not be determined by the supply of, and demand for, valuable services in quite the same way that esteem is determined in elementary social behavior." And similarly, "We should never assume that the informal group is a microcosm of society at large, that what holds good of the one holds good also for the other." See pp. 152 and 357 of his *Social Behavior: Its Elementary Forms* (New York: Harcourt, Brace & World, 1961).

grasp of elementary processes of interaction therefore requires an awareness of the larger structural contexts in which these processes are implicated, just as an adequate understanding of the larger complex structures of social life requires some reference to their more elementary dimensions.

It is therefore most important, Blau says, to grasp the doctrine of *emergence*. According to this doctrine in its most general form, the interaction of elements often results in new qualities that are neither inherent in the elements nor predictable in advance of their interaction from an examination of the separate elements themselves.

As applied to social life, this doctrine not only alerts us to the emergent qualities of large structures, but of interpersonal interactions as well. If one individual extends a service to another, the expectation is that the other will reciprocate when he can. A social bond is thereby created between the two. Further, although the psychological rewards of each tend to reinforce this bond, "the psychological process of reinforcement does not suffice to explain the exchange relation that develops. The social relation is the joint product of the actions of both individuals, with the actions of each being dependent on those of the other" (4).

In contrast to Homans, Blau draws attention at the very outset to the dimension of power in social exchange. Transactions as well as the power relations resulting from them constitute social forces that must be studied in their own right, and not only in terms of the normative or value context that may limit or strengthen them. When one person exercises power over another, whatever satisfaction he derives entails deprivation and cost to the other, who is subject to his power. This does not necessarily imply that social relations are always zero-sum games. Rather it means that while the associating individuals may profit from the association, they do not profit equally. Some profit more than others just as some pay higher costs than others.

Blau posits fundamental processes of attraction among human beings that lead to social exchange. Employing the same dyadic paradigm we found in Homans' work, Blau immediately calls attention to the *imbalances* of power that are so characteristic of exchange and that Homans, as we have seen, overlooks.

Person needs help that Other is able to provide but has nothing with which to reciprocate. "While the other may be sufficiently rewarded," Blau writes, "by expressions of gratitude to help him a few times, he can hardly be expected regularly to devote time and effort to providing help without receiving any return to compensate him for his troubles" (21). Thus, unlike Homans, who equates advice and approval and sees no reason why their exchange should not result in an equalitarian relationship, Blau emphasizes the basic difference between the two commodities and underscores the imbalance of power to which this difference is likely to conduce.

If, for instance, Person needs Other's services and has no really equivalent service to give in return, he has three alternatives: (1) he may coerce Other into giving him assistance; (2) he may obtain assistance from another source; or, (3) "he may find ways to get along without such help." If, however, these three alternatives fail of realization, Person has only one other course of action open to him: "he must subordinate himself to the other and comply with his wishes, thereby rewarding the other with power over himself as an inducement for furnishing the needed help" (22–23). Person's compliance with Other's wishes provides him with a generalized means of attaining various ends.

In these terms "Exchange processes . . . give rise to differentiation of power" (23). Other can command because he commands resources or services that Person needs; and Person obeys because he needs those resources and has found no alternative means of acquiring them. Other's demands or orders are assessed in terms of the service he furnishes to Person. What Other gives and what he demands in return may appear in line, fair, and just to Person; but what Other demands may also very well appear excessive, thus arousing in Person "feelings of exploitation for having to render more compliance than the rewards received justify" (23).

It is on the basis of social norms that subordinates evaluate their superior's demands. If the demands seem fair, they give consent and show approval. If, on the other hand, the demands appear unfair, subordinates regard themselves as exploited and show disapproval. The collective assessment that emerges among subordinates "has far-reaching implications for developments in the social structure." When subordinates collectively approve of the superior's exercise of power, their approval tends to legitimize it. When they collectively disapprove the legitimacy of power is called into question and discontent and opposition are engendered. "It is out of such shared discontent," Blau suggests, "that opposition ideologies and movements develop—that men organize a union against their employer or a revolutionary party against their government" (23–24).

Asymmetrical reciprocity and inequality, Blau shows effectively, are often evident even in a love relation. If a boy is attracted to a girl more than she is to him, he may have to "go out of his way to make associating with him an especially rewarding experience for her," sparing neither time nor money to please her. If he succeeds in impressing her and making himself attractive to her, she will find "associating with him as rewarding as he finds associating with her, as indicated by the fact that both are equally eager to spend time together" (27). But this mutual attraction ought not obscure the fact that "the reciprocity has been established by an imbalance in the exchange." The contribution the two parties make to the relationship are unequal or in imbalance because the boy must make a special additional effort to sustain the relation by pleasing the girl. Since he wants her more than she wants him, she becomes the superior in the relationship and he must provide her with supplementary rewards to induce her to continue to associate with him. Power thus permeates the most intimate of associations, whether love, friendship, or marriage; and reciprocity depends on "one partner's greater willingness to defer to the other's wishes" (27).

Love, then, though an example par excellence of an association based on intrinsic rewards, involves inequalities of mutual commitment and dependence. When lovers quarrel, they test, in effect, their mutual dependence. Since quarrels are liable to culminate in the destruction of the relationship, one party, at least, must swallow his pride, and acknowledge his commitment and dependence, which may entail compliance with the other's wishes and subordination. The "principle of least interest" thus applies to love relations no less than to rational, contractual ones. For the less interested or involved lover "is in an advantageous position, since the other's greater concern with continuing the relationship makes him or her dependent and gives the less involved individual power. . . . This power can be used to exploit the other; the woman who exploits a man's affection for economic gain and the boy who sexually exploits a girl who is in love with him are obvious examples" (78).

Blau follows Homans' conception of social association "as an exchange of activity, tangible or intangible, and more or less rewarding or costly between at least two persons."[3] But Blau gives these exchanges a completely different emphasis. Exchange not only establishes bonds among individuals, but it does so by placing some in superordinate positions and others in subordinate ones. Basing his views on the principles Marcel Mauss derived from his study of gift exchange,[4] Blau notes that he who provides "rewarding services to another obligates him. To discharge this obligation, the second must furnish benefits to the first in turn" (89).

VALUES, NORMS, AND INTERESTS IN SOCIAL EXCHANGE

Blau prefers to limit the term social exchange to voluntary interaction, excluding thereby actions resulting from physical coercion or from the demands of conscience. Thus, the giving of alms to a beggar would be regarded as social exchange only if the giver acts not out of guilt but for the gratitude and deference he will get in return. The term refers to "voluntary actions of individuals that are motivated by the returns they are expected to bring and typically do in fact bring from others" (91).

How does social exchange begin? Addressing himself to this question, Alvin Gouldner argued that the norm of reciprocity "is not only in some sense a defense or stabilizing mechanism but is also what may be called a 'starting mechanism.' That is, it helps to initiate social interaction."[5] Blau disagrees; indeed, he takes the opposite view "that the fundamental starting mechanism of

[3] Homans, *Social Behavior*, p. 13.

[4] See Marcel Mauss, *The Gift* (Glencoe, Ill.: The Free Press, 1954).

[5] Alvin Gouldner, "The Norm of Reciprocity: A Preliminary Statement," *American Sociological Review*, 25 (April 1960): 176.

patterned social intercourse is found in the existential conditions of exchange, not in the norm of reciprocity" (92).

Blau wants to emphasize that it is self-interest rather than a moral norm that is the "necessary condition of exchange." Individuals fulfill their obligations for past services in order to continue to receive them in the future. The advantages one hopes to derive from exchange relations, one's *interest* in them, initiates an exchange. "Not all social constraints are normative constraints, and those imposed by the nature of social exchange are not, at least, not originally" (92–93).

With respect to interpersonal relations, Blau supports his position with this illustration. If an individual repeatedly borrows things from a neighbor without ever reciprocating, the likelihood is great that the neighbor will soon refuse to lend. It is also likely that the neighbor will become less friendly and more distrustful of the individual; hence, for example, he will be "disinclined to trust him to repay for having their common fence painted but ask him for payment in advance" (97). Other neighbors, moreover, would no doubt also learn of the individual's delinquency, so that he would eventually acquire the reputation of being generally untrustworthy. Thus there are numerous disadvantageous consequences that the failure to reciprocate brings in its wake, "several of which do not depend on the existence of a norm of reciprocity" (97). Failure to reciprocate, especially if one is unable to do so, may also result in one's subordination to another—which leads us again to the phenomenon of power.

POWER AND ITS DIFFERENTIATION

Blau follows Weber in defining power as "the probability that one actor within a social relationship will be in a position to carry out his own will despite resistance."[6] The powerful one can realize his will because others depend upon the positive rewards he furnishes and fear their withdrawal. An obvious example is the power of an employer over his employees. Given their dependence upon him and their consequent fear of losing their jobs, they comply with his directives.

Power in these terms is the ability to enforce compliance recurrently by means of negative sanctions. Power is distinguished from direct physical coercion by the element of freedom it entails—i.e., the fact that an individual can always choose not to comply and to suffer the consequences. Power, finally, is "inherently asymmetrical . . . resting on the net ability of a person to withhold rewards from and apply punishments to others—the ability that remains after the restraints they can impose on him have been taken into account. Its source is

[6] Max Weber, *The Theory of Social and Economic Organization* (New York: Oxford University Press, 1947), p. 152.

one-sided dependence. Interdependence and mutual influence of equal strength indicate lack of power" (117–18).

Once again, in sharp contrast to Homans's conception, there is a continuing accentuation of the imbalance, asymmetry, and one-sided dependence that characterize exchange relations. Blau also frames his discussion so that one can apply his concepts to both micro- and macrosocial relations: the power of one lover over another resulting from their unequal commitment, and the power of the employer over his employees by virtue of his legal control of the means of production. In both cases one party controls the availability of services that the other needs.

ALTERNATIVES TO SUBMISSION

Yet there are circumstances that enable men to evade compliance and subjection. Blau follows Richard M. Emerson[7] and presents four logical possibilities by means of which an individual (or individuals) can avoid submission:

1. He can provide an equivalent service in return so that his relation to the other remains one of equalitarian reciprocity.

2. He can "obtain the needed service elsewhere . . ."

3. He can force the other to provide the service, which, however, results in his domination of the other.

4. He can "do without this service" or find some substitute for it.

In the absence of these four alternatives, the individual has no choice but to comply, since he who controls the needed service can make its provision "contingent on . . . compliance" (119). Their presence constitutes the conditions of social independence. For it is the availability of these alternatives that "enables people to evade the fifth one of dependence on services from a given source" (119).

What this suggests is that he who wishes to acquire and sustain power must adopt a certain strategy. To translate his control of resources into control over people, he must close them off somehow from the four alternatives, just as those who wish to avoid subjection must keep these alternatives available and open. There is, then, a clear conflict of interest between those who dominate and seek to dominate and those who are dominated and seek their freedom—a conflict of interest that in the society at large assumes economic, political, legal, and ideological forms.

Power and conflicts of interest are as characteristic of interpersonal relations as they are of large complex organizations and indeed of other groups,

[7] See Richard M. Emerson, "Power-Dependence Relations," *American Sociological Review*, 27 (1962): 31–41.

strata, and classes of the larger society. It is the merit of Blau's analysis that he brings this fact into relief. The very same exchange of approval and advice that Homans treats unproblematically as equalitarian reciprocity, Blau explores as a differentiation of power. If Person recurrently needs Other's advice, he will typically pay for it not merely with approval but with deference to his wishes.

To understand why this is likely to occur it is only necessary to examine the logic of the situation. The fact that Person continually turns to Other for advice means that Person is inferior to Other in at least one important respect. Person lowers his status by continually asking for assistance; so the value of the respect or approval he gives in return depreciates correspondingly. In the short run approval may be adequate reward for advice or some other expert service; in the long run this is highly unlikely. In Blau's words:

> Initially, the high respect of the rest of the group may be sufficient reward for the contribution a group member makes, and short-term discussion groups in laboratories may never advance beyond this stage, but in the long run it is likely to prove insufficient. Since the value of a person's approval and respect is a function of his own social standing, the process of recurrently paying respect to others depreciates its value. (127)

Ultimately, Other will come to regard respect alone as inadequate. Consequently Person will have to obligate himself to furnish an additional form of compensation. Typically, Blau argues, deferring to Other's wishes is the only way Person has of repaying him. Other, then, has not only a higher status than Person (which Homans recognizes) but also power over him (which Homans overlooks).

Furthermore, the power that an individual may have originally established by providing a service, he may sustain and perpetuate even after he has drastically reduced the quality and quantity of that service. This self-perpetuating dimension of power is evident in interpersonal relations but even more so in the structures of the larger society.

THE LEGITIMATION OF POWER

When men join together to carry out some collective effort, they soon find that to achieve their purpose they must divide their labor and coordinate their activities. They must, in short, form an organization. "Power is that resource," writes Blau, "that makes it possible to direct and coordinate the activities of men" (199). But power is no simple resource, for it involves domination, and where there is domination there is also conflict. Domination generates resistance, opposition, and sometimes even revolution.

The effective operation of organizations does not eliminate resistance and opposition. Those who hold power within organizations seek, however, to reduce conflict to a minimum. The superordinates strive to create conditions under which their subordinates will comply most willingly. Among these conditions is the legitimation of power, which is what is meant by the term *authority*.

Max Weber stressed that authority involves "a certain minimum of voluntary submission." However, so-called voluntary submission is the result of complex causes, including fear of the consequences that follow failure to obey as well as a desire to demonstrate approval of those in power and their directives. Frequently sociologists employ the concept of authority in a way that tends to obscure the element of fear and accentuate the element of approval. In Blau's analysis our attention is directed to both elements—although, as we shall see, he too tends to exaggerate the role of a certain type of approval.

Leadership is a form of power that may or may not acquire legitimacy; and it may acquire varying degrees of legitimacy. A leader's power presumably rests on the contribution he makes to the group, which enables him to constrain its members and demand their compliance. In the absence of alternative sources for this contribution, the leader's power becomes inescapable. Obedience and submission entail costs for those who obey. Hence those who obey sit in judgment of those who command, weighing the value of the contribution against the costs of submission.

The demands of the powerful are assessed in terms of "social norms of fairness." If subordinates regard the demands of their superior as being in line with his contribution, they grant their approval; if they regard the demands as excessive, they show disapproval. Given sufficient power, a superior can enforce compliance, "but approval cannot be forced regardless of how great the power." Some degree of approval is precisely what tends to legitimate power, and it appears that "the effectiveness and stability of leadership depend on the social approval of subordinates" (201).

An adequate conception of "leadership" must underscore the fact that men do not merely "follow" a leader out of respect for him. They comply with his directives as an obligation. This obligation empowers the leader "to coordinate the activities of the members of a group, which involves directing individuals to do things that are not to their own immediate advantage" (202). The effective coordination of activities produces rewards, the distribution of which the leader decisively influences. Whether the rewards consist of honor or material benefits, there is the question of how much the leader should take for himself and how much he should leave for the rest of the group.

If the followers regard the benefits derived as adequate or more than adequate compensation "for the costs they have incurred, both by performing services and by complying with directives, their collective approval of his leadership legitimates it" (202). Their reciprocal obligation for the leader's contribution, as well as their agreement that his abilities merit respect, create group pressures to comply with his directives. The legitimation of power therefore means that the leader need not directly enforce obedience himself but can rely on his followers to constrain and control individuals inclined to resist or disobey.

So both "power over others and their legitimating approval of that power" are key elements of stable leadership. Yet Blau perceives the two elements as somewhat incompatible. This "dilemma of leadership," as he calls it, becomes evident in the two different requirements of leadership. On the one hand, his *power* rests on the greater contribution of his services: not only his followers' dependence on his service but his relative independence of any service "they might offer in return" (203). On the other hand, his *authority* requires his followers' approval, "which means that he does not maintain complete independence of them" (203). If he insists on his independence and refuses favors, his followers experience this as rejection and respond with disapproval. His very domination of the group generates antagonism, at least on the part of some, thus lessening the probability of legitimacy. Conversely, if he strives mainly for approval, his ability to base his decisions on strict standards of effectiveness is inhibited, and this diminishes the respect he commands.

LEADERSHIP AND POWER IN FORMAL ORGANIZATIONS

Although there are some parallels between leadership in small informal groups and leadership in large formal organizations, there are also fundamental differences. Especially where the employment contract comes into play, power rests on the "organization's resources that enable it to buy the services of employees and to make them dependent on it for their livelihood, the degree of dependence being contingent on employees' investments in their jobs and the alternative employment opportunities available to them" (205).

Managerial power is formally legitimated by the terms of the employment contract and the formal rules of the organization. A manager may seek to increase his control over subordinates by exercising his formal prerogatives to the limit—rewarding conformity and punishing insubordination and disobedience. He may also seek an alternative means of extending his control: he may providy his subordinates with services that engender obligations of a nonformal sort. Since the manager holds formal power, he may choose to refrain from using it to the hilt, thereby engendering in his subordinates gratitude, approval, and obligations. In this way he "relinquishes some of his offical power in exchange for greater legitimate authority over subordinates" (206).

A manager thus adds to his official power by converting some of it into personal influence. This influence over individuals who owe him a debt of gratitude is not yet legitimate authority. Such authority comes into being, Blau argues, only when the shared values of the collectivity legitimate the superior's power.

In the degree that subordinates come to regard the manager's practices as fair, or conducive to their welfare, they develop an interest in the continuation of those practices and continue to fulfill their obligations to him. "Shared feelings of loyalty and group norms tend to emerge that make compliance with his directives a *social* [i.e., nonformal] obligation that is enforced by the subordinates themselves. The subordinates' common approval of managerial practices that benefit them jointly gives rise to social norms that legitimate managerial authority" (207).

By now, all effective managers no doubt know all this; it is, in fact, the heart of the "science" of management-employee relations. A form of manipulation, it is one of several means the powerful employ to effect greater compliance and to reduce opposition and resistance, thus making their task easier and the operation of the organization smoother—not to mention the reduction of administrative costs and the corresponding increase of profits. But Blau gives only scant attention to the manipulative aspect of what he calls the subordinates' legitimation of managerial practices. When he does give fuller attention to the ideology accompanying manager-employee relations, his analysis yields bizarre conclusions—conclusions that detract, I must say, from his otherwise illuminating discussion throughout.

ON COGNITIVE DISSONANCE

To suggest how subordinates come to rationalize their compliance, Blau avails himself of Leon Festinger's concept of "cognitive dissonance." This refers to a situation in which an individual, faced with more or less equally attractive alternatives, chooses one but remains doubtful as to whether he has chosen the better one. The theory accompanying the concept is that, finding the dissonance disturbing, the individual will strive to reduce it, typically by raising the value of the chosen alternative and lowering the value of the other.

Now, to return to the workers and their manager, Blau argues that they experience dissonance only when they feel an obligation to comply with his directives, but not when they obey out of fear of the sanctions for noncompliance. In Blau's words: "If a superior uses his coercive power to impose his will on subordinates, the serious cost of disobedience makes obedience unequivocally the preferable alternative. Although submission is unpleasant, subordinates have no doubt that the consequences of failure to submit would be more so. There is no cognitive dissonance, and hence no basis for processes of dissonance reduction" (208). If, on the other hand, subordinates feel obligated to repay their superior for his "service," i.e., for having refrained from using all the official power vested in him, "noncompliance is a possible alternative that is not entirely unreasonable."

In this case, the cost of compliance is presumably less than the advantages they gain from the manager's service. Yet they may have some doubts: is the service, they might ask, really worth the hardships submission entails? The cognitive dissonance they experience under these circumstances they tend to reduce or resolve by appreciating the advantages of compliance and depreciating its costs. The manager, they might tell themselves, is after all an expert; he is not exercising the prerogatives of a superior, only doing his duty; and they are not submitting, only fulfilling their responsibilities.

> These beliefs might be considered rationalizations through which individuals adapt to a subordinate position. Social processes, however, transform the individual rationalizations into common values. . . . The social consensus that develops among subordinates in the course of their communication that it is right and proper and not at all degrading to follow managerial orders validates these beliefs and converts what might have been individual rationalizations into a common value orientation. (208)

If this is being advanced as a general proposition and is to be taken literally, it produces some very misleading implications. We are asked to believe that human beings experience no inner cognitive conflicts when they submit to power out of fear; that their recognition of the great costs of disobedience, which "makes obedience unequivocally the preferable alternative," generates no ambivalence within them; that submission out of fear is total resignation, and that there is no residue of doubt as to whether one should resist or even rebel instead.

Blau's version of cognitive dissonance allows for doubt among subordinates *only* when they perceive some "service" that the superior appears to be offering. If the superior exercises self-restraint, and refrains from ruling with the full weight of the heavy hand to which his official power entitles him, the subordinates become grateful and develop obligations that they fulfill by complying fully and easily. Should doubts arise among them as to whether the superior's "service" is really worth full and easy compliance, they typically resolve these doubts in favor of submission, comforting themselves, however, with rationalizations that it is right and proper that things be so and not otherwise.

What this tends to imply is that where men regard the apparent alternatives to submission as more painful than submission, they submit without inner conflicts. More, that they submit without expressing opposition to domination—opposition that might range from subtle, foot-dragging resistance to open strife and rebellion.

Blau's treatment thus emphasizes overwhelmingly the legitimacy of prevailing relationships of domination. Legitimacy is never placed in quotation marks since subordinates never question the relationship of domination itself. Blau allows them to question only one dimension of the relationship and then only under a specific circumstance. This conception of things soon transforms domination into consensus, and consensus into group tyranny. Our attention is drawn away from the structure of power, and the mechanisms for assuring it, and centered on the subordinates' common value orientations, on their internalization of norms of compliance. It is no longer the superior who enforces compliance through the means of power at his disposal; the subordinates now do it for him: "even the potential deviant[8] who for some reason does not feel personally obligated to the superior is under pressure to submit to his authority lest he incur the social disapproval of his peers. A man in authority does not have to enforce compliance with his orders, because the structural constraints that exist among subordinates do so for him" (209).

Blau's aim in all this is to distinguish authority from coercion; but he soon empties his conception of authority of all elements of domination. Authority "entails imperative control," he acknowledges. But it is brought about not by the superior's disposition of the means of domination, but by the norms and sanctions of the subordinate group that "exert compelling pressures on individual subordinates to follow the superior's directives." Hence, Blau continues, "compliance is voluntary from the perspective of the collectivity of subordinates, but it is compulsory from the perspective of its individual members. It is exactly as voluntary as conformity with social norms generally, for example, as our custom of wearing clothes" (209). Blau thus obscures the coercive dimension by speaking of the group's so-called voluntary submission; but the fact that the subordinates may have subjectively willed the relationship should not blind us to the possibility that they may have had little or no choice and that they were therefore objectively forced into it.

Blau's analysis glosses over relationships of domination and plays down the inevitable repression and alienation that accompany them as well as the resistance and opposition they engender. The emphasis on the consensual approval of subordinates, and on the superior's "service" or contribution results in a very one-sided analysis and, hence, in obfuscation.

Even when he draws attention directly to the undeniable power over others that formal leaders such as managers possess, he does so not in order to explore the mechanisms of domination but to contrast their "problem" with that of informal leaders. The latter "must rely on their own qualities and resources to command the willing compliance of followers." The manager's problem, however, "is to win the loyalty and legitimating approval of subordinates, particularly since his power may tempt him to dominate them instead of winning their respect and willing compliance" (210). Taken literally, this means that the men whom the manager commands are not dominated so long as he has won their loyalty. He is only *tempted* to dominate them but insofar as he has effected their willing compliance, he does not. This subjective view of domination is also carried over into the discussion of another important concept, that of exploitation.

---

[8] Note the term *deviant* here, which portrays the individual as one who deviates from group norms rather than as one who resists and opposes those in power.

EXPLOITATION

"Opposition to power arises," writes Blau, "when those subject to it experience shared feelings of exploitation and oppression" (227).[9] If one is powerful, one is capable of enforcing submission and utilizing one's power "to exploit others by forcing them to work in behalf of one's interests" (228). For Blau, the prevailing social norms define whether the demands made by those in power are fair and just or whether they are excessive compared with the services or benefits derived from the powerful. Outright coercion offers no benefits and therefore is "always resisted and, if possible, opposed." Those subject to power resting on the control and provision of services, however, "do not necessarily experience their position as disadvantageous, although they may do so" (228).

The principle that emerges is this: if the benefits received by those subject to power exceed what the social norms of fairness have led them to expect, they will express approval of the leaders and thus fortify their power and legitimate their authority. If benefits barely meet the expectations of subordinates,

> they will neither feel exploited nor express firm legitimating approval of the groups in power. If, however, the demands of the ruling group with a monopoly of vital resources far exceed what social norms define as fair and just, subordinates will feel exploited and seize any opportunity to escape the ruling group's power or to oppose it, inasmuch as their situation is, basically, no different from that of groups subject to coercive force. (228)

Although those in power are guided by considerations other than norms of fairness, they are influenced by such norms. Especially within organizations, where stability requires a minimal approval from subordinates, norms of fairness serve to impose restraints on power. When men come to feel exploited and oppressed, anger, disapproval, and antagonism are aroused within them and directed against those whom they hold responsible for their exploitation and oppression. The exploited have little or nothing to lose from resistance and opposition.

Even if the exploited see no alternative to their condition in the present, "they derive some independence from the fact that the possible alternative of a future change in the power structure is more attractive to them than to those who receive adequate benefits under existing conditions" (231). Furthermore, their outrage at the violation of justice may be so great as to make "retaliation against the oppressors" more gratifying than ensuring the flow of small rewards by submission. Exploitation may lead not only to opposition but also to the formation of a revolutionary ideology, "which effects and completes the

[9] Blau deserves credit for exploring the concept of exploitation. To the best of my knowledge Alvin Gouldner was alone when, a few years before Blau wrote his book, he reminded us of the *general* importance of the concept, justly complaining that it had "almost disappeared from sociological usage." See his "The Norm of Reciprocity," p. 165f.

transformation of social deprivation into a surplus resource, by making exploited and oppressed groups less dependent on material rewards and thus freeing their energies to fight existing powers" (231). Thus, just as values of approval legitimating the ruling group may develop among subordinates who regard its rule as fair, values legitimating opposition may develop among subordinates who regard its rule as exploitative and oppressive.

Retaliation, revenge, feelings of aggression and violence are the initial responses and inclinations of the oppressed. These "base tendencies" the revolutionary ideology transforms "into noble ideals pursued not for selfish reasons but for the sake of relieving the misery of one's fellow men or even for bettering the conditions of humanity at large" (232). That is about all Blau has to say about exploitation per se, for he devotes the remainder of the chapter to the forms opposition assumes in the society at large, primarily to opposition political parties and the classes and strata that tend to support them.

The main problem with Blau's conception of exploitation is that it is so highly subjective. Certainly, in order to know whether and in what degree they are exploited, subordinates must perceive subjectively the presumed service their superiors are rendering as well as the portion of the rewards the superiors take for themselves versus the portion they leave for their subordinates. This "subjectivity" is an essential part of the concept. What is objectionable, however, is the reliance on "norms of fairness" to determine whether in fact an exploitative situation exists.

If the concept of exploitation is to be fruitful a relatively objective criterion of an exploitative relation is needed; what is surprising is that Blau does not see that the criterion is implicit in the imbalances and inequalities of power that he explores so incisively in the first part of his book. Such a criterion is suggested by the question that arises regarding any exchange relation: Are the values of the services exchanged between two or more parties equal? If not, one of the parties is exploiting the others.

In his comparative study of the exchange relations between lord and peasant, for example, Barrington Moore argues effectively that notions of "fairness" are totally inadequate and that the "subjective interpretation of exploitation [is] flagrantly self-contradictory. How can nine-tenths of the peasants' crop be no more and no less arbitrary an exaction than a third?"[10] Arguing in favor of an objective definition of exploitation, Moore suggests that

> the contributions of those who fight, rule, and pray must be obvious to the peasant, and the peasants' return payments must not be grossly out of proportion to the services received. Folk conceptions of justice, to put the argument in still another way, do have a rational and realistic basis; and

[10] Barrington Moore, Jr., *Social Origins of Dictatorship and Democracy* (Boston: Beacon Press, 1966), pp. 470–71.

arrangements that depart from this basis are likely to need deception and force the more they do depart.[11]

And, of course, it does not follow from this that the objectively exploited party necessarily grows absolutely poorer. The lord's relation to the "peasant community can become more exploitative without the peasants becoming any poorer, indeed even if their material situation improves. *This would happen wherever the lord's exactions increased and his contribution to the welfare or security of the village declined"* (italics added).[12]

Similarly, Alvin Gouldner has suggested that one can begin to develop an objective criterion by employing the concept of exploitation "to refer to certain transactions involving an exchange of things of unequal value."[13]

The recurrence of such transactions is most likely to take place where inequalities of power obtain. Although this seems implied in the analysis of imbalances of power that Blau makes early in his book, he never pursues this implication and instead presents an exclusively subjective view of exploitation as failure to meet standards of "fairness."

Where there is domination, the probability is great that there is also inequality in the exchange of goods and services. Under conditions of domination some are able to induce others to put into a relationship more than they get out of it. This is the principle that Blau appears to overlook but which Durkheim, for example, grasped firmly.

In *The Division of Labor in Society* Durkheim argued that every object of exchange has a "determined value which we might call its social value. It represents the quantity of useful labor which it contains. . . . Although this magnitude cannot be mathematically calculated it is nonetheless real."[14] According to this principle an *unjust* exchange is one in which "the price of the object bears no relation to the trouble it cost and the services it renders."[15]

Similarly, Durkheim continues, a contract is uncoerced and just "only if the services exchanged have an equivalent social value"; in "order that this equivalence be the rule for contracts it is necessary that the contracting parties be placed in conditions externally equal."[16]

Durkheim thus unequivocally affirms the principle of equality as a standard by which to assess the justice of an exchange relation. As applied to workers and other subordinates, this means that if they comply with the wishes of their superior "in order to live," it is an unjust contract despite the fact that they may subjectively have willed it. It is in this context that Durkheim asserts

[11] Ibid., p. 471.
[12] Ibid., p. 473n.
[13] Gouldner, "The Norm of Reciprocity," p. 166.
[14] Emile Durkheim, *The Division of Labor in Society* (New York: The Free Press, 1964), p. 382.
[15] Ibid., p. 383.
[16] Ibid.

that there "cannot be rich and poor at birth without there being unjust contracts."[1][7]

Explicitly employing the term exploitation in this connection, Durkheim goes on to observe that public morality increasingly "condemns every kind of leonine contract wherein one of the parties is exploited by the other because he is too weak to receive the just reward for his services. Public conscience demands, in an ever more pressing manner, an exact reciprocity in the services exchanged."[1][8]

We see, then, that Durkheim definitely recognized the desirability of developing objective criteria to determine whether a given relationship is exploitative or just.

THE ROLE OF VALUES IN COMPLEX STRUCTURES

For Blau there is a fundamental difference between micro- and macrostructures. The former develop out of the direct interpersonal interactions of their members, and these individual members constitute the component elements of a microstructure. The component elements of a macrostructure, in contrast, are not individuals but its constituent social structures. As most or all of the individuals of a society cannot interact directly, some mechanism is required to mediate "the structure of social relations among them. Value consensus provides the mediating mechanism" (253).

Blau emphasizes that an adequate analysis of macrosocial relations must give attention to patterns of power and stratification and how they are affected by mobility and opposition. In these terms legitimating values are only one dimension of macrostructures. Any analysis, therefore, which occupies itself solely with values is as one-sided and defective as an analysis that ignores them.

Common values tend to legitimate existing social relations and to stabilize them, thus contributing to the maintenance of social order. Elaborating Durkheim's thesis in much the same way as does Parsons, Blau argues that in the absence of moral norms serving as regulating mechanisms, exchange would not necessarily conduce to order. Exchange relations are predicated on some degree of mutual trust, which, in turn, requires the prohibition of force and fraud.

But values and norms also serve as media of exchange, thus widening "the compass of social interaction and the structure of social relations through social space and time" (263). When common values mediate and legitimate normative patterns, they are said to be institutionalized, and "perpetuated for generations, and sometimes for centuries if three conditions are met." These are: (1) the historical transmission of the formal organizing principles and arrangements, such as laws, corporate structures, and the dogma and ritual of religion; (2) the

[1][7] Ibid., p. 384.
[1][8] Ibid., p. 386.

transmission of the common legitimating values from one generation to another by means of socialization; and (3) the identification of the dominant groups in the society with the legitimating values and the lending of their "power to preserve the institutions that express them. Social institutions, therefore, have roots in the power structure and double roots in the past . . ." (281).

The merit of Blau's conception is that, unlike Parsons', it brings into relief the fact that if values and institutions are perpetuated, it is in great part because the dominant group is interested in their perpetuation. Blau also stresses a "counter-institutional component in the cultural heritage" as well as opposition to existing institutions. So, although Blau employs the concept of common values, he is careful to point out that "social solidarity in macrostructures is always problematical, because the particularistic values that unite ingroups create segregating boundaries between them in the larger collectivity" (285). He further distinguishes himself from the Parsonian view by facing the fact that in class-structured societies "the members of each social class [have] some common interests that differ from and often conflict with those of other classes" (287).

In short, Blau definitely does not subscribe either to the "unproblematic equilibrium" or to the "common value system" by which Parsons supposes he is accounting for social order. Instead he stresses that opposition ideals are divisive forces from the standpoint of the larger society, even while these ideals tend to solidify the groups and classes that hold them. In contrast with Parsons Blau highlights the conflicts of interests and values between classes and strata, between the central authority of an organization and its subordinate parts, between the dominant-official values of a community or society and those of opposition movements, and so forth. Indeed, opposition, for Blau, is "a regenerative force."

There "are also structural rigidities due to vested interests and powers, organizational commitments, and traditional institutions. These defy modification and adjustment except through social conflict and opposition" (301). And, while numerous crosscutting social ties prevent present-day liberal-democratic society from splitting into two hostile camps, "they do so . . . at a social cost that is paid by the most oppressed social classes who would benefit from radical changes in the *status quo*" (307–8).

SOME CONCLUDING REMARKS ON BLAU, HOMANS, AND PARSONS

As the title of his book indicates, Blau places power, domination, and conflict of interest at the center of his analysis; as a result his conception of social reality is a considerably more useful one than either Parsons' or Homans'. Blau's conception contrasts with that of Parsons, for whom the so-called "common value system" is a central "explanatory" principle, and for whom power is a generalized medium in the collective social interest. But Blau's work also contrasts with that of Homans.

Homans' equilibrium, though he calls it "practical," resembles Parsons' "common value system" in at least one respect. For neither in his theory nor in his interpretation of small-group studies does Homans take note of the power some acquire over others and the means they employ of exacting compliance; he also tends to dignify several forms of social pressure and coercion by uncritically labeling them as just. Abstracting his microworld of small-group relations from its larger context, Homans pushes out of sight the significance of the larger context of power and domination, such as business corporations and governmental bureaucracies, for the conduct of small groups of workers and other subordinates. We are told much about status competition among workers, their mutual envy, and the like, but nothing about their links with the institutional context of the larger society.

Blau, in contrast, keeps both the micro- and macrosocial levels before us, and he shows how at least a few basic principles are applicable to both. The control of services or resources for which there is no alternative source, he emphasizes throughout, is a source of power. If Other controls such resources and Person needs them, Person is obliged to comply with Other's wishes. Neither Parsons nor Homans give any systematic attention to this elementary but crucial fact.

If one asks why exchange relations endure, Parsons replies that the equilibrium is unproblematic so long as there is complementarity of expectations between the two parties, stressing, in addition, that they are bound together by common values. Homans, with a similar logic, would argue that the relation endures because both parties have a common interest in it, derive benefits from it, and regard it as "fair."

Insofar as Person has no alternative source for the service in question, he must remain in the relation; in this limited sense we might say he has an "interest" in it. But since Other controls the service, and has less need for Person than he for Other, it is nothing less than an obfuscation to say that both have common interests in the relation or that Person remains in it because he regards the exchange as fair. At the very least, "their interests conflict," as Blau notes, "concerning the ratio at which they exchange services" (315).

Perhaps Homans would not deny this. He would most probably conceptualize the matter quite differently, however. It is true, he might argue, that Other's advice is more valuable than Person's approval. But Other's ability to advise is made possible by the fact that his *investment* is greater than Person's. Is it not then fair and just that Other's profits be commensurately greater too?

In this way the concepts "investment," "cost," and "profit" are used to legitimate whatever occurs in prevailing relationships and at the same time to veil domination and exploitation. We need only ask a few questions to perceive the ambiguous and perhaps even ideological elements in these concepts. Does Homans employ them with a consistent and precise meaning? Does he have any objective criteria for determining what an individual's "investment" is in any given case? Is he justified in conceptualizing "investment" as the fruit of an individual's efforts alone, from which therefore he earns a profit?

Let us return once again to his paradigmatic dyad, Person-Other. Other furnishes Person with advice in return for his approval. Other is able to furnish this service, Homans would argue, because he has "invested" more of his own individual time, energy, and efforts in acquiring the knowledge and skill that enable him to advise. Yet this kind of argument is hardly less problematic on the interpersonal level than it is in the society at large: just as it is sociologically false to account for an individual's wealth and property by saying that he earned it exclusively through his own efforts, it is no less false to say that an individual's knowledge and skill are the fruit of his own "investments." In both cases one leaves out of account the fact that whether the wealth in investments takes the form of property, money, or knowledge, it is *social* in nature and origin. Innumerable others have contributed to its formation, and at a substantial cost to themselves. To fail to recognize this, as Homans does, is to subscribe to a highly individualistic but untenable conception of "investment." It is a kind of primitive, bourgeois, entrepreneurial "political economy" as applied to interpersonal relations—and applied as if it were a universal, suprahistorical, psychological law.

Homans himself recognizes that this type of objection may be raised against his conception of investment: "all the arguments about surplus value from John Ball to Karl Marx are one long attempt to prove that what employers count as investments ought not be so counted, and that they get more than their fair share of the returns of economic enterprise and exploit the workers."[19] But he brushes this aside and gives it no further consideration.

Finally, as we have already suggested, Homans presents his propositions on elementary social behavior as if they were independent psychological laws, as if his individual subjects were uninfluenced by the values and institutions of the larger society. He forgets that the behavior of his subjects cannot be accounted for in terms of their interpersonal relations alone; if they are possessive, acquisitive, competitive, and individualistic, it is not the result of a psychological law but rather of historically specific social institutions and values.

[19] Homans, *Social Behavior*, pp. 246–47.

III

CONFLICT THEORY

7

A Note on Coser's Functionalized Conflict

"Conflict theory" is a vague, omnibus term, as we see if we consider the list of its historical representatives: Ibn Khaldun, Machiavelli, Bodin, Hobbes, Hume, Ferguson, Smith, Malthus. The intellectual differences among these thinkers are at least as important as the similarities. And if we also include several varieties of Social Darwinism as well as the ideas of Gumplowicz, Ratzenhoffer, Sumner, and Small—as Don Martindale does in *The Nature and Types of Sociological Theory*[1] —it is not difficult to see that the heading covers several heterogeneous and even contradictory perspectives. Indeed, what do all of these have in common besides the term "conflict"?

Similarly, an examination of the work of contemporary "conflict theorists" will show that the differences are as significant and perhaps even outweigh whatever they might have in common. Surely this is true of, say, Lewis Coser, Ralf Dahrendorf, and C. Wright Mills. There is, in fact, no intellectual advantage to retaining the term "conflict theory"—particularly if it is intended as a viable alternative to functionalism.

For reasons which I try to make plain in my critical analysis of Dahrendorf's work, the now fashionable talk of "conflict theory" as opposed to "integration theory" tends to perpetuate a false theoretical dichotomy.

In the following pages I present a short critical discussion of the ideas of Coser and Dahrendorf, and from there proceed to what I regard as the affirmative section of Part III—a programmatic essay calling for the orientation of contemporary sociological thinking toward the classical tradition.

---

[1] See Don Martindale, *The Nature and Types of Sociological Theory* (Boston: Houghton Mifflin, 1960), pp. 127–207.

SOCIAL CONFLICT

The term "social conflict," at its most general level, embraces an array of phenomena from interpersonal disagreements and quarrels through class conflict and including, as well, international rivalry and war. Lewis Coser, in *The Functions of Social Conflict*, recognizes that there is no extant theory of social conflict that includes all these phenomena. Nor does he wish to construct such a general theory. Instead, he regards his work as "an effort to clarify the concept of *social conflict*" and "to consolidate conceptual schemes which are pertinent to data of social conflict."[2] His method is to elaborate and illustrate insights and ideas drawn from the writings of Georg Simmel.

Coser begins by defining social conflict as "a struggle over values and claims to scarce status, power and resources in which the aims of the opponents are to neutralize, injure or eliminate their rivals" (8). There is nothing essential to quarrel with in this definition. The statement of his main concern and its implications is another matter, however, for this statement reveals that Coser employs uncritically the problematic and ambiguous terms and assumptions of functionalism. "Our concern," writes Coser, "is mainly with the functions, rather than the dysfunctions, of social conflict, that is to say, with those consequences of social conflict which make for an increase rather than a decrease in the adaptation or adjustment of particular social relationships or groups" (8).

Social conflict, Coser tells us, has been severely neglected; insofar as sociologists have treated it, the emphasis has been on its "negative" side—how it undermines order, stability, and unity and, in short, "tears apart." Coser wants to restore the balance by underscoring the "positive" side of conflict—how it contributes to the maintenance and "adaptation" of social groups, relationships, and systems. The language of functionalism is employed here as if it were compatible with Coser's own definition of social conflict, although that definition focuses on opponents struggling over scarce values, each attempting to further his interests at the expense of the other. Yet in his interpretive comments and illustrations Coser speaks of conflict as "functional" (good) or "dysfunctional" (bad) for relationships and structures, including the social system as a whole.

If the conflict model, at its most general level, conceives of a society as a plurality of groups with conflicting values and interests, and if the model conceives of groups within the society as consisting of two or more individuals, then one can only determine—and even here not always or easily—whether specific actions benefit some more than others. One can never determine whether actions benefit the system as a whole; to speak as if one could is misleading.

---

[2] Lewis A. Coser, *The Functions of Social Conflict* (New York: The Free Press, 1956), p. 7. Page references to this book are hereafter cited in parentheses immediately following the quoted passage.

Take, for example, the family as a "system." If the husband and wife quarrel frequently and intensely and resolve their conflicts without divorce, all we can say about the particular system as a whole is that it persists and has not been destroyed. But whether the conflict is in any other sense either "functional" or "dysfunctional" (good or bad) for the system, we will never know and can never know. What we can learn about this conflict, given the perpetuation of the particular family, is, for instance, what its results have been for the husband, for the wife, and for the children: Has the husband's or wife's view prevailed or have they compromised? What price has each member of the family paid for maintaining the family intact? And so forth. In the case of larger social systems, consisting of several groups with different and conflicting interests, it is even more meaningless to speak of "functions" and "dysfunctions" for the total system.

By paraphrasing Simmel in functionalist terms, Coser often betrays the original. In the opening paragraph of Chapter 3, for instance, Simmel suggests that opposition to an associate "is often the only means for making life with actually unbearable people at least possible." He goes on to say that in the absence of such opposition, a group member might "take desperate steps" and "end the relation. . . ." Nowhere is it Simmel's point that the opposition is good for the relation; on the contrary, his unequivocal meaning is that opposition serves the *individual's* needs. Thus he writes: "Not only because of the fact that . . . oppression usually increases if it is suffered calmly and without protest, but also because opposition gives us inner satisfaction, distraction, relief. . . . Our opposition makes us feel that we are not completely victims of the circumstances" (39).

This concern with oppression and opposition and their consequences for the individual totally disappears from Coser's functionalized version of Simmel's penetrating insights. Indeed, it is in vain that one seeks in Simmel's formulation the ideas Coser attributes to him:

> "Simmel here asserts that the expression of hostility in conflict serves positive functions insofar as it permits the maintenance of the relationships under conditions of stress, thus preventing group dissolution through the withdrawal of hostile participants. Conflict is thus seen as performing group-maintaining functions insofar as it regulates systems of relationships . . ." (39).

It is much the same in the discussion of "safety-valve" institutions and the phenomenon of "scapegoating." Coser correctly suggests that "whereas conflict changes the terms of the interaction, mere expression of hostile feelings does not. Thus expression, as distinct from conflict, may be welcomed by the powers that be" (44). But this point is soon dulled by functionalist jargon: "an institution which serves to channel hostility and to prevent release against the original object, thereby maintaining the structure of the social system, may also have serious dysfunctions for either the social system or the actor, or both" (45–46).

The proposition that scapegoating may be welcomed by the "powers that be" clearly implies a relationship of domination and a conflict of interests. The dominant and powerful definitely gain from scapegoating. As for the oppressed, apart from venting their hostility and letting off steam, they gain nothing from scapegoating since it leaves the relation of domination intact and the power of their oppressors undiminished.

The traditional terms of power, domination, and conflict of interests express this idea lucidly and directly. Functionalist terms, in contrast, only obscure it, shifting attention away from a reality, domination, to a nonreality, a system's "adaptation." Take, for instance, these statements:

> conflict carried out directly against the object may prove to be less dysfunctional for the social system than channeling of aggressiveness through safety-valve institutions.
>
> Institutions which offer substitute channels for the release of aggressiveness may be dysfunctional for the social system in the same way as neurotic symptoms are dysfunctional for the personality system. (46)

Coser frequently dispenses with the functionalist terms and his exposition proceeds quite well without them. But they inevitably reappear—and most forcefully in his conclusion, where he informs us that he has been examining in this study the "conditions under which social conflict may contribute to the maintenance, adjustment or adaptation of social relationships and structures" (151). Continuing, he writes: "Internal social conflicts which concern goals, values or interests that do not contradict the basic assumptions upon which the relationship is founded tend to be positively functional for the social structures" (151).

We are never told precisely what it means to say that conflict is "positively functional for the social structure." If this phrase refers to an enhanced unity or cohesion that presumably results from conflict, we are not provided with any independent criterion of unity or cohesion. All that remains, therefore, is the *persistence* of the group. But then the statement becomes a tautology: the only way we have of knowing that the internal conflicts have not contradicted the basic assumptions of the relationship is that it persists. Persistence of the group is evidence that no basic contradiction exists; and evidence of no basic contradiction is found in group persistence.

Further, it would be untenable to argue that unity and cohesion are always better than disintegration. Whether sticking together is better for the group than the withdrawal of some or all of its members depends on a variety of circumstances, value judgments, and interests. Unity could be maintained under conditions that would not only endanger the interests of the group members but their very lives.

For all these reasons the functionalist formulation of Coser's conclusions is unsatisfactory. In his final statement, for example, Coser speaks of conflict as

> dysfunctional for a social structure in which there is no or insufficient toleration or institutionalization of conflict. The intensity of a conflict which threatens to "tear apart," which attacks the consensual basis of a social system, is related to the rigidity of the structure. What threatens the equilibrium of such a structure is not conflict as such, but the rigidity itself which permits hostilities to accumulate and be channeled along one major line of cleavage once they break out in conflict (157).

This veils reality in much the same way as does traditional functionalism. No amount of talk about dysfunctions for a social structure, or its rigidity, can lay bare the actual conflicts of interest within a group, organization, or society, or reveal the relationships of domination that characterize them.

The insights which Coser has derived from Simmel and supplemented from other sources are certainly not lacking in interest. Yet whenever these original ideas are translated into "functionalese," they gain nothing and lose their incisiveness.

8

Dahrendorf's Postcapitalist Society

Ralf Dahrendorf is among the best-known contemporary representatives of what has come to be called "conflict theory." Since the appearance of the English edition of his *Class and Class Conflict in Industrial Society*,[1] his name is that most frequently associated with the so-called conflict school.

In opposition to the prevalent view, which conceives of society in terms of "functional coordination, integration, and consensus," Dahrendorf has called for a reorientation of sociology toward "problems of change, conflict, and coercion in social structures, and especially in those of total societies" (xi).

Like so many of his predecessors in the history of Western sociology, Dahrendorf finds it necessary to come to terms with Marx; and like many sociologists before him, he conceives of his own undertaking as no less than an "empirical refutation and theoretical supersession" of Marx's theory (xii). By means of his critique of Marx, Dahrendorf desires "to render conflict theory applicable to the analysis of the political process both in totalitarian and in free societies of the present" (xiii).

Beginning his revision with an examination of Marx's two-class model of the capitalist system, Dahrendorf undertakes to complete the famous last chapter of the third volume of *Capital*. There, the reader will recall, Marx began what promised to be a most interesting discussion of social classes; but after only a page and a half the discussion comes to an abrupt and disappointing end with the words: "Here the manuscript breaks off." Using as his basis the many explicit and implicit statements on class that Marx made throughout his writings, Dahrendorf completes the chapter as he believes Marx might have had he lived to do so.

---

[1] Ralf Dahrendorf, *Class and Conflict in Industrial Society* (Stanford: Stanford University Press, 1959). Page references to this work will be cited in parentheses immediately following the quoted passage.

The main burden of Dahrendorf's version of the chapter is to demonstrate that Marx's conception of classes was so thoroughly embedded in nineteenth-century conditions as to preclude its application to the conditions of the twentieth century. Dahrendorf attempts to persuade the reader that Marx's "analyses are essentially based on the narrow, legal concept of property." For Marx, he argues, the real criterion of class was ownership and nonownership of the means of production in the strict and legalistic sense, and not the authority structure of the enterprise. Only by freeing class from this "narrow" definition will it become "applicable to all 'relations of production' " (21).

Marx did, of course, refer to "property relations" as the legal expression of what he called "relations of production." This is quite understandable, since in capitalism of the early nineteenth century the entrepreneur typically owned the means of production and, therefore held authority in the enterprise. But it is a mistake to take this to mean, as Dahrendorf apparently does, that Marx failed to grasp that *control* of production is the key to economic power. It is likewise a mistake to hold that Marx denied that control of the means of production, under capitalism, could be separated from ownership.

Dahrendorf tries to support his case by drawing attention to Marx's treatment, in the third volume of *Capital*, of joint-stock companies, which in Marx's time had already exhibited the tendency later described as the separation of ownership and control. This treatment, Dahrendorf believes, convincingly demonstrates that "for Marx, the relations of production as a determinant of class formation were also authority relations, but they were such only because in the first place they were property relations in the narrow sense of the distribution of controlling private ownership" (22).

A careful reading of Marx's discussion reveals that Dahrendorf has missed Marx's point. He quotes Marx as saying that the joint-stock company represents "the elimination of capital as private property within the capitalist mode of production itself" (22)—wishing thereby to suggest that for Marx the joint-stock company was halfway to the classless society. Throughout his own analysis Dahrendorf speaks of the separation of ownership and control, as well as other changes since Marx's time, as having given rise to a *postcapitalist* society. Marx's point, however, was that while ownership is increasingly divorced from management, the relations of production are no less capitalistic on that account.

Marx saw clearly that with the joint-stock company, profit became "mere compensation for owning capital that now is entirely divorced from the function in the actual process of reproduction, just as this function in the person of the manager is divorced from ownership of capital."[2] With the concentration of production and its expanding scale, it becomes increasingly impossible for single individuals to mobilize sufficient capital to enter production. Hence, capital assumes "the form of social capital (capital of directly associated individuals) as distinct from private capital, and its undertakings assume the form of social

[2] Karl Marx, *Capital* (Moscow: Foreign Languages Publishing House, 1962), 3:427.

undertakings as distinct from private undertakings." At this point and in this context Marx adds: "It is the abolition of capital as private property within the framework of capitalist production itself."[3] Clearly, what Marx means here is *not* that the joint-stock company abolishes capitalism partially or wholly; but rather that it indicates a progressively diminishing role in production for individual, private capitalists.

Marx goes further, noting that in stock companies the managerial function "is divorced from capital ownership."[4] This results in the "appropriation of social property by a few."[5] But there is no doubt that "the conversion to the form of stock still remains ensnared in the trammels of capitalism; hence, instead of overcoming the antithesis between the character of wealth as social and as private wealth, the stock companies merely develop it in a new form."[6]

It is plain, then, that Marx recognized the separation of ownership from management, i.e., the emergence of the manager as a paid "administrator of other people's capital" and the transformation "of the owner of capital into a mere owner . . ."[7] "The capitalist mode of production," Marx writes unequivocally, "has brought matters to a point where the work of supervision, entirely divorced from the ownership of capital, is always readily obtainable."[8]

But from this it does not follow, as it seems to for Dahrendorf, that the emergence of the stock company marks the beginning of a postcapitalist era. If these companies were "transitional" forms for Marx, it was only in the very restricted sense that stock companies, like cooperative factories, effectively demonstrated that the capitalist was becoming "redundant as a functionary in production." Despite all their shortcomings, cooperative factories nonetheless demonstrated that workers could associate and "use the means of production for the employment of their own labor."[9]

Therefore, far from abolishing capitalism or private property, the process that gave rise to stock companies simply reduced the number of those who dominated labor and exploited the social wealth. Since the institution of private property continued to prevail, and since economic power was concentrated in progressively fewer hands, and since, finally, the economic system continued to operate on capitalistic principles, Marx would have regarded as absurd the suggestion that the stock company was evidence of the supersession of capitalism.

Marx clearly recognized the tendency of the separation of ownership from control, although he did not go on to dissociate economic power and authority totally from property rights. Does this mean, however, that Marx had a "narrow" and "legalistic" conception of the relations of production?

---

[3] Ibid.
[4] Ibid., 3:428.
[5] Ibid., 3:430.
[6] Ibid., 3:430–31.
[7] Ibid., 3:427.
[8] Ibid., 3:379.
[9] Ibid., 3:431.

Dahrendorf believes it does, and that this is the chief defect of Marx's conception of class and class conflict. "Perhaps," he writes, "a Marx without the Marxian philosophy of history would have realized that power and authority are not tied to the legal title of property" (31). But this is gratuitous since, as we have seen, Marx had solid empirical grounds for tying economic power to property. Dahrendorf partially grants this himself, saying that Marx had some justification for holding that ownership and nonownership of the means of production objectively distinguished the two main classes of nineteenth-century, capitalist-industrial society. But he argues that structural changes since Marx's time have rendered his theoretical approach practically useless. Dahrendorf wants to substitute a theory of conflict and change that will be "applicable not merely to capitalist societies but to industrial societies in general" (36). The concept of capitalism, he contends, is too constricting. Capitalism, after all, signifies only one type of industrial society. There are factors associated with industrial production wherever industry appears. Those factors, "which cannot disappear . . . unless industry itself disappears, will be associated in this study with the concept of *industrial society*" (40). Dahrendorf's subject is therefore the conditions of class formation and conflict in any industrialized (or industrializing) society.

STRUCTURAL CHANGES SINCE MARX'S TIME

Let us examine Dahrendorf's contention that structural changes in capitalism have rendered Marx's analysis useless. One such change, which plainly fascinates Dahrendorf, is the separation of ownership from control. For some reason that he fails to provide, Dahrendorf calls this process the "decomposition of capital." He equates the decline of the family firm with the decline of capitalism, and accepts the much-touted theory of the wide dispersion of stock. He writes,

> Today, more than two-thirds of all companies in advanced industrial societies are joint-stock companies, and their property exceeds four-fifths of the total property in economic enterprises. The enterprise owned and run by an individual, or even a family, has long ceased to be the dominant pattern of economic organization. Moreover, the stock of companies is dispersed fairly widely. Three per cent of the adult population of the Federal Republic of Germany, and approximately eight per cent of that of the United States, own one or more shares of joint-stock companies. (42)

For Dahrendorf, the dominance of the corporation and the dispersion of stock constitute a total break with capitalism. This "radical view" Dahrendorf attributes to Marx himself, placing him in this camp alongside James Burnham and others, and wishing to persuade us that Marx regarded the emergence of the corporation as a managerial revolution, or the beginning of the end of capitalism.

A quite opposite view, however, which Dahrendorf dubs "conservative,"

> holds that the consequences of the apparent separation of ownership and control have been vastly overrated. It is argued that in fact owners and controllers, i.e., stockholders and managers, are a fairly homogeneous group. There are often direct connections between them, and where this is not the case, their outlook is sufficiently similar to justify insisting on the old assumptions of a homogeneous class of capitalists opposed to an equally homogeneous class of laborers. This view is not often heard in the West nowadays, although traces of it are evident in the work of C. Wright Mills. (43)

Dahrendorf acknowledges that property has not altogether "ceased to function as a basis of authority. The right of the manager to command and expect obedience accrues in part from the property rights delegated to him by the shareholders, acting either as a group or through an elected board of directors." But there is a "second, and often more important, basis of legitimacy for his authority, namely, some kind of consensus among those who are bound to obey his commands" (45).

Not only are delegated property rights of minor importance, but the incentives and motives of the corporation executives have ceased to be capitalistic: "Never has the imputation of a profit motive been further from the real motives of men than it is for modern bureaucratic managers" (46). Given these beliefs, it is not difficult to understand how Dahrendorf can state that "Capital—and thereby capitalism—has dissolved and given way, in the economic sphere, to a plurality of partly agreed, partly competing, and partly simply different groups" (47).

Alongside the presumed decomposition of capital there has occurred a decomposition of labor. The tendency Marx observed of factory labor becoming increasingly unskilled remained in effect only until the end of the nineteenth century; then the tendency was reversed. Dahrendorf cites Friedman, Geiger, Moore, and others, who agree that factory labor has undergone considerable stratification during the present century, resulting in at least three obvious categories: skilled, semiskilled, and unskilled. This implies a growing heterogeneity and even conflict of interests among industrial workers—so much so that, "as with the capitalist class, it has become doubtful whether speaking of the working class still makes much sense" (51).

At the same time the "new middle class" has become firmly a part of industrial society. Here Dahrendorf follows the numerous scholars who have documented the phenomenal growth of the white-collar work force. In preparation for his own theory of conflict, he convincingly argues that the heterogeneous grouping C. Wright Mills called an "occupational salad" may be divided into two quasi-classes: those who command and those who obey. "It seems to me that a fairly clear as well as significant line can be drawn between salaried employees who occupy positions that are part of a bureaucratic hierarchy and salaried employees in positions that are not" (55). The meaning of this line of demarcation will be taken up later. Meanwhile, however, there is no doubt that the growth of the new groupings of bureaucrats and white-collar workers is another significant structural change that has occurred since Marx's time.

Still other such changes that Dahrendorf reviews are social mobility, equality, and the institutionalization of class conflict.

Dahrendorf acknowledges that the mobility studies do not "stand up to a thorough methodological inspection" and that "we cannot . . . be sure about the so-called facts of the case" (58). Nevertheless, he assumes substantial and increasing upward mobility in industrial societies and assigns to the educational system a central role in the process. His impressionistic summary of the mobility data does not, however, inspire confidence. He writes:

> [all] we can infer from what patchy data we have is what anybody living in a modern society can observe for himself: in post-capitalist societies there is a great deal of movement, upwards and downwards as well as on one social level, between generations as well as within them, so that the individual who stays at his place of birth and in the occupation of his father throughout his life has become a rare exception. (59)

This enlightens us hardly at all. What do we learn from the assertion that some move up, some down, and some remain where they are? And what do we learn from the presumed fact that it is rare for a son to adopt the occupation of his father, unless we are told how far, and in what sense, the son has actually moved from the father's occupation? How do the father's and son's occupations compare in terms of the life-chances they make possible?

In a similarly uncritical way Dahrendorf discusses what he regards as the "remarkable spread of social equality in the past century . . ." (61). He writes, for instance, that "from the point of view of legal privileges and deprivations, every citizen of advanced industrial societies has an equal status . . ." And postcapitalist "society has developed a type of social structure that excludes both 'absolute' and many milder forms of privilege and deprivation" (62). "By the simultaneous rise of the real wages of workers and the taxation of top earnings, a redistribution of incomes has taken place . . ." (63).

It is undeniable that numerous structural changes have taken place since Marx died in 1883. But the important question is whether the changes have brought about a social system that warrants the term "postcapitalist."

Let us grant the transition from family firm to corporation; the stratification of the working class; the growth of the "new middle class"; the increase in mobility; the rise in real wages; and, finally, the institutionalization of class conflict. None of these either separately or together necessarily means what Dahrendorf so frequently asserts but never proves, that "most contemporary industrial societies have ceased to be capitalist societies" (67). He hastens, however, to remind us that this does not mean that power, domination, and conflict have ceased to exist. For in postcapitalist society no less than in capitalist society, there are those who control strategic resources and, therefore, command, and others who obey. Wherever there is authority, there are relations of domination and subordination.

But this, too, is not as realistic and incisive as at first it appears to be. For in place of a historically concrete analysis of a socioeconomic system with specific forms of exploitation, domination, and conflict, we are given an abstract, ahistorical postcapitalism in which men struggle for authority, pure and simple, wherever they happen to be—in industry, the church, the political party, or the social club. As for industrial conflicts per se, Dahrendorf views them as institutionalized, regulated, and insulated from the society at large.

THE TWO METATHEORIES OF SOCIETY

Dahrendorf has been a major participant in the discussion of the virtues of integration theory as opposed to those of conflict-coercion theory. He has insisted that one must distinguish two metatheories of society. One metatheory conceives of a social system as functionally integrated and attributes to values a fundamental role in maintaining the system in equilibrium; the other "views social structure as a form of organization held together by force and constraint and reaching continuously beyond itself in the sense of producing within itself the forces that maintain it in an unending process of change" (159).

Not everyone is aware, perhaps, that Dahrendorf has not placed himself squarely in the so-called conflict-coercion camp. "There are sociological problems," he writes, "for the explanation of which the integration theory of society provides adequate assumptions; there are other problems which can be explained only in terms of the coercion theory of society; there are, finally, problems for which both theories appear adequate" (159).

Dahrendorf is justified, I believe, in distinguishing two theoretical tendencies in contemporary sociology, and in noting that "in recent years, the integration theory of society has clearly dominated sociological thinking." He is right to disclose the extreme one-sidedness and, hence, inadequacy of the integration of functionalist theory. It is also sensible of him to refuse to choose between the metatheories, realizing that neither a theory based on values alone, nor one based exclusively on interest-conflicts, force, and coercion, could be adequate in itself.

Where, then, does Dahrendof err? He errs, I believe, in perpetuating a theoretical dichotomy, accepting *two* metatheories and considering both theories as valid for certain kinds of problems. The result is a state of affairs in which analytical dimensions are torn from a complex, multifaceted reality and placed in two separate piles: values here, interests there; integration here, conflict there; consensus here, coercion there, and so on. The acceptance of such a situation precludes the development of a single, unified theory.

Dahrendorf himself seems almost to recognize the shortcoming of his approach when he writes:

> However we look at social structure it always presents itself as composed of a moral and a factual, a normative and an institutional level or, in the doubtful terms of Marx, a superstructure and a substratum. The investigator is free to choose which of these levels he wants to emphasize more strongly—although he may be well-advised, in the interest of clarity as well as of comprehensiveness of his analysis, not to stress one of these levels to the exclusion of the other. (160)

This surely implies that a single theoretical approach, not two separate ones, is required for an adequate and comprehensive grasp of reality.

Indeed, Marx is an example par excellence of a theorist who sought to develop a unified theoretical approach. If he had subscribed to the "Dahrendorfian" formula, he would have developed two theories: one for the substructure and another for the superstructure. But Marx presented us with only one—and it was certainly not a conflict-coercion theory in Dahrendorf's sense.

While Marx recognized the interest conflicts of classes, and the relationships of exploitation and domination among them, he recognized equally that force and coercion were not the sole elements accounting for the successful domination of the subjected class. By now everyone knows how important ideology was to Marx's conceptual framework. Time and again he emphasized that the ruling ideas of a society in a given epoch are the ideas of the ruling class. The class that controls the means of material production also controls the means of mental production, and is thereby able to impose its values and ideas upon those who control neither. Marx was aware that values and ideas facilitate enormously the dominance of the ruling class and account in large measure for the "voluntary" submission of the subjected class, which internalizes in some degree the ruling class's definition of reality—"false consciousness," as Marx called it.

As this indicates, Marx was neither a conflict theorist nor an integration theorist. For he was as far from "value consensus" as he was from a perspective emphasizing force and coercion to the exclusion of ideas, beliefs, values, and norms.

Let us, however, return to Dahrendorf's discussion of the two metatheories. He summarizes the main tenets of the integration theory as follows:

1. Every society is a relatively persistent stable structure of elements.

2. Every society is a well-integrated structure of elements.

3. Every element in a society has a function, i.e., renders a contribution to its maintenance as a system.

4. Every functioning social structure is based on a consensus of values among its members. (161)

We have already explored at length in Part I of this book the problems, defects, and extreme one-sidedness of this approach. We shall not repeat the discussion here. But is the so-called coercion theory, as Dahrendorf conceives it, free of problems or any less one-sided? I think not. Here, according to Dahrendorf, are its basic tenets:

1. Every society is at every point subject to processes of change; social change is ubiquitous.

2. Every society displays at every point dissensus and conflict; social conflict is ubiquitous.

3. Every element in a society renders a contribution to its disintegration and change.

4. Every society is based on the coercion of some of its members by others. (162)

It is not very illuminating to assert that every society changes at every point without indicating the nature and extent of these changes. Similarly, the assumptions that dissent and conflict prevail at every point in society, or that every social element contributes to disintegration and change, tell us nothing about the quality of these conflicts and elements and fails to distinguish a quarrel among friends, for example, from class conflict.

Furthermore, is it true, as Dahrendorf asserts, that this theoretical approach can explain phenomena that the integration theory cannot? In attempting to substantiate this, he gives examples of two types of phenomena. The first example is the increasing tendency of industrial and commercial enterprises to add to their organizational structure the position of personnel manager. The second is the strike of construction workers in East Berlin of June 17, 1953 that led to a general uprising "against the Communist regime of East Germany" (161).

For Dahrendorf, functionalism is apparently capable of explaining the first phenomenon, while conflict theory is appropriate for explaining the second. In other words, we need two separate, partial, and one-sided theories, one for apparently stable and orderly phenomena and the other for conflict. Thus, in studying East German society, we would utilize functionalism before the June uprising and switch to coercion theory as soon as the rising occurred.

Clearly what is required for an understanding of the uprising is an understanding, among other things, of the history and nature of the East German regime, including the relations of the workers to the bureaucrats. To understand why the workers rose up in June requires that we understand why they did not rise up before. This is not the time or place to explore this event in detail; the point is to see what is wrong with Dahrendorf's prescription. What we need, again, is not what he prescribes—two separate theories to be used on different occasions—but *one unified and dialectical theory*.

The reader might object that this is precisely what Dahrendorf has advocated. After all, does he not explictly say: "We cannot conceive of society unless we realize the dialectics of stability and change, integration and conflict, function and motive force, consensus and coercion" (163)? And again: the two theoretical models "constitute complementary, rather than alternative, aspects of the structure of total societies as well as every element of this structure."

But in the very next sentence he adds: "We have to choose between them only for the explanation of specific problems; but in the conceptual arsenal of sociological analysis they exist side by side" (163). We are back again to *two* theories, lying "side by side," as if these corresponded to the actual elements of a bifurcated reality.

If Dahrendorf recognizes the desirability of a unified, dialectical theory, he nonetheless doubts that such a theory is possible. "Is there or can there be," he asks, "a general point of view that synthesizes the unsolved dialectics of integration and coercion?" And he replies: "So far as I can see, there is no such general model; as to its possibility, I have to reserve judgment. It seems at least conceivable that unification of theory is not feasible at a point which has puzzled thinkers ever since the beginning of Western philosophy" (164).

IMPERATIVELY COORDINATED ASSOCIATIONS

Dahrendorf views contemporary postcapitalist society as a plurality of relatively discreet "imperatively coordinated associations"—a cumbersome rendering of Max Weber's *Herrschaftsverband*, which I shall refer to hereafter as an association. "The state," writes Dahrendorf, "a church, an enterprise, but also a political party, a trade union, and a chess club are associations in this sense" (168). In all such associations a definite dichotomy exists between some who have authority and others who have none. Associations thus become the loci of domination and conflict.

We are now approaching closer to the core of Dahrendorf's own theory of the postcapitalist era. In opposition to the Marxian view, he argues that Marx's conception of the superimposition of wealth and power has lost whatever validity it may once have had. The state of affairs in which those who held economic power ruled politically and otherwise as well, Dahrendorf maintains, has definitely come to an end. Today, in the postcapitalist era, one finds, instead, a plurality of associations in which those who are at the top of some associations are at the bottom of others, and vice versa. Although Dahrendorf formulates this view somewhat cautiously, there can be little doubt that this is what he believes. He writes, for instance, that

> for the individual incumbent of roles, domination in one association does not necessarily involve domination in all others to which he belongs, and subjection, conversely, in one association does not mean subjection in all.

And again:

> Although empirically a certain correlation of the authority positions of individuals in different associations seems likely, it is by no means general and is in any case a matter of specific empirical conditions.

Finally,

> since domination in industry does not necessarily involve domination in the state, or a church, or other associations, total societies can present the picture of a plurality of competing dominant (and, conversely, subjected) aggregates. (171–72).

In Dahrendorf's postcapitalist plurality of associations, each association is composed of two opposing groups—one in authority and the other out. When their interests are merely latent, they are quasi-groups; when their interests become manifest, they are interest groups. In his words:

> In every imperatively coordinated association two quasi-groups united by common latent interests can be distinguished. Their orientations of interest are determined by possession of or exclusion from authority. From these quasi-groups, interest groups are recruited, the articulate programs of which defend or attack the legitimacy of existing authority structures. In any given association, two such groupings are in conflict (183–84).

But this sounds like a dogma—wherever there is authority, men will struggle for it. It is more in the nature of a psychological law than a sociological proposition. For it implies that conflicts are generated by *authority differences themselves*, rather than by oppression, exploitation, abuse of authority, and other substantive issues. In point of fact, it is from Pareto, Mosca, and Raymond Aron that Dahrendorf has derived this conception of things, as he himself explains. In the cases of Pareto and Mosca, their sociologies clearly presuppose a definite, inherent nature of man according to which he is selfish and power-seeking—not differing significantly from Dahrendorf's authority-seeking man.[10]

Yet Dahrendorf's conception of power and authority falls short of the insights of Pareto and Mosca. For both of these thinkers clearly discerned a governing elite or political class; whereas Dahrendorf dissolves the ruling class into a plurality of ruling groups, each confined to its own association: "Ruling groups are in the first place, no more than ruling groups within defined associations. In theory, there can be as many competing, conflicting, or coexisting dominating conflict groups in a society as there are associations" (197–98).

Dahrendorf himself finds the extreme pluralistic view—those at the top of some associations are at the bottom of others—not wholly satisfactory. For if one takes only industry, the state, and the church, "It is more probable that the workers of industry are at the same time mere members of the church and mere citizens of the state. One might expect that the dignitaries of the church are in some ways connected with the rulers of the state and possibly even with the owners or managers of industry" (214). This case would be closer to the superimposition pole of what he calls the "pluralism-superimposition scale." He insists repeatedly, however, that whether this is in fact a typical case is an empirical question.

To be sure! But does he mean to imply that an empirical investigation of "postcapitalist" social structure would be likely to reveal that workers occupy the command posts in industry? In the state? In the church? Or that while corporate executives control industry, the workers control the state? One rather doubts that Dahrendorf would seriously reply to these questions in the affirmative. Nevertheless, he sticks to his notion of a plurality of dichotomous associations in which the superordinate members of one are the subordinates of another.

For Dahrendorf, conflict is not only regulated but insulated as well. The conflicts in the sphere of industry, for example, do not ramify and affect other spheres of society; they remain confined. He writes: "It is one of the central theses of the present analyses that in post-capitalist society industry and society have, by contrast to capitalist society, been dissociated." And even more strongly: "Industry and industrial conflict are, in post-capitalist society, institutionally isolated, i.e., confined within the borders of their proper realm and robbed of their influence on other spheres of society" (268).

In this regard, T. B. Bottomore has remarked:

> Considered empirically . . . these propositions are more easily falsified than those of Marx which they are intended to replace; for numerous studies have shown that in the European industrial countries, and to a lesser

[10]For a critical analysis of the work of both of these thinkers, see my *Ideology and the Development of Sociological Theory* (Englewood Cliffs, N. J.: Prentice-Hall, 1968).

extent in the USA, the major political conflicts are closely and continuously associated with industrial conflicts, and express the divergent interests of the principal social classes.[11]

The fact is that Dahrendorf himself recognizes the powerful objections that can be raised against his thesis. He acknowledges that the structure of government in the "United States, Britain, France, Germany, and other countries would seem to sustain the thesis of C. W. Mills that the 'power elite' of post-capitalist societies is relatively uniform and dominated by the carriers of industrial authority" (271).

But Dahrendorf tries to save his thesis by arguing that it refers not to the actual state of affairs but to a "tendential reality." This "reality," according to him, is the one in which "there are as many discrete dominant and subjected classes in a society as there are associations. Here we assert that in post-capitalist society the rulers and the ruled of industry and society are tendentially discrete groups" (271). And later, he asserts: "Outside the enterprise, the manager may be a mere citizen, the worker a member of parliament; their industrial class position no longer determines their authority position in the political society" (276). If this is a tendency, it is a very weak one indeed.

As for the polity or the state, it has become in Dahrendorf's postcapitalist society just another association. Marx's and indeed even Weber's conceptions of the state are now obsolete. Why? Because

> Strictly speaking the association of the political state is an organization of *roles*. The empirical priority of its structure and dynamics cannot be derived from an assumption that it is, by definition or theory, more inclusive than other such organizations. What some social scientists refer to as the "polity" is a unit of social analysis strictly equivalent to an industrial enterprise, a church, or an army. (290)

This is a curious conception of the state. It implies that the state has no greater power or authority than any other association; and it denies the wide range of circumstances in which state authority supersedes all others. For Dahrendorf, however, the state remains a mere association. If anyone rules postcapitalist society, it is simply those who occupy the top positions of government in the executive, legislative, and judicial branches.

At the end of his work Dahrendorf tells us that he is interested in the differences between free and totalitarian societies, that he concurs "with the common belief that the struggle between free societies and totalitarian societies is the dominant issue of political conflict in our time" (318).

Unfortunately, however, his analysis is not likely to shed light on the workings of either type of society. For he sidesteps the central question of his

---

[11] T. B. Bottomore, *Classes in Modern Society* (New York: Pantheon Books, 1966), pp. 27–28.

work: Are the present-day industrial societies of the United States, Western Europe, and Japan actually postcapitalist, as he alleges? This question receives no systematic attention, insofar as the still dominant capitalistic principles and institutions of these societies are ignored. On the other hand, neither is there any examination of the totalitarian societies. As a result we are left with a vague rubric, "postcapitalist," which speaks to the essentials of neither type of social system.

9

Toward a Marx-Weber Model of Social and Historical Analysis

Among contemporary American sociologists C. Wright Mills best understood the significance of the critical encounter with Marxism, realizing that the debate with Marx's ghost had given rise to what he called the *classical tradition of sociological thinking*. This tradition, which included both Marxism and its critics, provided, he believed, an indispensable method for thinking about man, society, and history. In his words, "Classic Sociology contains an enormous variety of conception, value, and method, and its relevance to the life-ways of the individual and to the ways of history-making in our epoch is obvious and immediate. This is why it is central to contemporary cultural work, and among the most valuable legacies of Western civilization."[1]

In these terms, Mills was neither a Marxist nor a non-Marxist, but rather a "plain" Marxist, as he chose to call himself. With the term "plain," Mills sought to distinguish himself from those he had dubbed, respectively, as "vulgar" and "sophisticated" Marxists. The former have a dogmatic commitment to specific features of Marxian thought and "identify these . . . as the whole." The latter, on the other hand, refuse to acknowledge that Marx was wrong about anything. They try to make him sophisticated by incorporating into his system of thought "the whole tradition of sociology, before and after Marx."[2] For "sophisticated" Marxists,

> there is no "social science" of much worth; there is only marxist social science. Thus, they tend to stretch and to bend marxist ideas to fit new facts, and to confuse Marx's general model with specific theories. Even when Marx's terminology is obviously ambiguous and plainly inadequate

[1] C. Wright Mills, *Images of Man* (New York: George Braziller, 1960), p. 17.
[2] C. Wright Mills, *The Marxists* (New York: Dell Publishing Co., 1962), p. 98.

they are often reluctant to abandon it. At its best, this style of thinking is tedious and hampers analysis unnecessarily. At its worst, it becomes a substitute for reflection and inquiry, a sophisticated sloganeering.[3]

In contrast, Mills continues,

Plain Marxists (whether in agreement or in disagreement) work in Marx's own tradition. They understand Marx and many later marxists as well, to be firmly a part of the classic tradition of sociological thinking. They treat Marx like any great nineteenth-century figure, in a scholarly way; they treat each later phase of marxism as historically specific. They are generally agreed that Marx's work bears the trademarks of the nineteenth-century society, but that his general model and his ways of thinking are central to their own intellectual history and remain relevant to their attempts to grasp present-day social worlds. . . . In their work plain marxists have stressed the humanism of marxism, especially of the younger Marx, and the role of the superstructure in history; they have pointed out that to underemphasize the *interplay* of basis and superstructure in the making of history is to transform man into that abstraction for which Marx himself criticized Feuerbach. They have been "open" (as opposed to dogmatic) in their interpretations and their uses of Marxism. They have stressed that "economic determinism" is, after all, a matter of degree, and held that it is so used by Marx in his own writings, especially in his historical essays. They have emphasized the volition of men in the making of history—their freedom—in contrast to any Determinist Laws of History and, accordingly, the lack of individual responsibility.[4]

For Mills, then, "plain" Marxism is an integral part of the classic tradition of sociological thinking. It is a fundamental element of that tradition. Nevertheless, when taken alone without the later Marxian and non-Marxian developments of that tradition, it is inadequate for a comprehension of the social reality of the latter half of the twentieth century. After all, there is no getting around the fact that Marx died in 1883; we must accuse him of dying, as Mills says. And for this reason alone, if for no other, several aspects of his analysis are wrong. He did not live to see the developments which were to foil his expectations of the revolutionary transformation of capitalist society.

It is true that Marx has had no equals among his followers; nevertheless, Marxism did not end but rather began with him. It would be a great intellectual loss, Mills emphasizes, to remain ignorant of what the Marxists after Marx have done to develop and refine his theories and thereby to enrich the classic tradition. But it would be an equal loss to ignore the non-Marxian contributions

---

[3] Ibid.
[4] Ibid., p. 98–99.

to sociological thinking, those of academic social science in general and those of Marx's critics in particular.

Among the thinkers who shaped the classic tradition, not all were on the same level. Two of them, Mills believes, stood higher than all the rest: Karl Marx and Max Weber. "Were it necessary," he writes, "to limit ourselves to the works of two sociologists, these two would be my choice."[5]

Weber, in his view, is perhaps the greatest revisionist of Marx. What this means is not that Weber in any sense bested, refuted, or superseded Marx but that Weber's work is an important elaboration and "corrective" of Marx's framework. The respective conceptions of these two thinkers must *not* be viewed as antithetical but rather as complementary. The model of society that emerges with Weber's "corrective" is better than Marx's alone—although taken alone it is definitely superior to others.

Weber regarded Marx's methodological approach as one of fundamental importance and his own as supplementary to it. In no sense was Weber developing a method in opposition to Marx. Insofar as any refutation of Marxism was intended, it was of certain naive and mechanistic interpretations of Marx's theory held by some of his followers.[6]

There were of course several other thinkers of stature in what Mills calls the classic tradition, but I am inclined to agree that Marx and Weber are the most significant precisely because their respective paradigms are complementary. Their complementarity enables one to bring them together into one model constituting the sharpest analytical instrument available for thinking about the structure and process of modern society. What then are the main elements of the so-called Marx-Weber model?

Let us begin with the rudiments of Marx's paradigm. Clearly the most fundamental element is his master concept "mode of production," together with its analytical aspects, "productive forces" and "relations of production," or "property relations." Historically there have been several major modes of production, notably the primitive-communal, Asiatic, slave, feudal, capitalist, and socialist (although whether and in what measure the last of these modes actually prevails is problematic). The dialectical relationship between the developing productive forces and the prevailing property relations—the latter either facilitating the further development of those forces or thwarting them—provides a key to the understanding of the structure of societies and their historical changes.

The virtues of Marx's focus—which, as we shall see, was also Weber's—are still evident today. At a time when the advanced capitalist and noncapitalist industrial societies are experiencing an ecological crisis literally threatening the survival of their peoples, when Third World countries are searching for strategies

---

[5] Mills, *Images of Man*, p. 12.
[6] For a fuller discussion of Weber's relationship to Marx, see my *Ideology and the Development of Sociological Theory* (Englewood Cliffs, N. J.: Prentice-Hall, 1968).

of development and struggling to overcome the legacy of hundreds of years of direct and indirect domination—at such a time focusing on the mode of production is perhaps even more essential than it was in Marx's time. What could be more essential than an adequate analysis of today's productive forces and property relations and their effect on the people? What human costs do those who presently control the means of production exact from all of us? Has not the prevailing mode of production actually become a *mode of destruction*? These and similar questions should leave no doubt of the continuing validity of Marx's emphasis.

The concept "productive forces" refers to the direct producers; their skill, knowledge and experience; the tools and instruments with which they produce; and, finally, their cooperative relations in the work process. "Relations of production," in contrast, referred in Marx's time to ownership of the major means of production and other strategic resources. As we have seen in our earlier discussion of Dahrendorf, however, it is a mistake to suppose that Marx restricted his concept to ownership in a narrow legalistic sense. Surely in our time it would be foolish thus to restrict it. When studying "relations of production," the key question to ask is: Who controls the productive process? What legal and political forms does this control assume? We are thus led to an examination of the class structure of a society.

At the heart of Marx's analytical system, therefore, is a concern with property and power relations, or the stratification of a society into classes with conflicting interests. Classes, for Marx, are not arbitrary social divisions. Classes are historical categories referring to the conflicting positions men have occupied in the historically changing modes of production: master and slave, lord and serf, capitalist and worker. As the productive forces and relations of production change, so does the class structure of a society. In these terms Marx not only attempted to account theoretically for the transformation of one mode of production into another, but also for the significant changes taking place *within* a given mode of production.

To take the capitalist mode to which, of course, Marx gave the most systematic attention, a cursory review of Volume 1 of *Capital* will show in what minute detail he described the changing labor process from simple cooperation in early manufacturing to machine production—including the changes in the structure of the working class that this necessarily entailed.

It was one of Marx's central purposes in *Capital* to illuminate the powerful tendencies that effectively transformed the structure of society under capitalism. Marx emphasized that the capitalist mode of production was *revolutionary* compared with all previous modes; and that the capitalists as a class, in revolutionizing the means of production, would also revolutionize all other conditions of existence.

Less well known, perhaps, is that one of Marx's main theses in *Capital* was that competitive capitalism was giving way to another form; that capitalist accumulation necessarily brought with it the *concentration* and *centralization* of capital.

Marx's analysis demonstrated that capital accumulation assumes the form of a conflict among capitals, with some winning and others losing, the losers being either destroyed or absorbed by the victors. The growth of capital in one enterprise is facilitated by the fall of other enterprises. Owing to the increasing costs of investments in *constant* capital (means of production and raw materials) and the growth of individual capitals already in the field, fewer and fewer capitals are engaged in production. Hence capital is increasingly concentrated.

Capital accumulation and concentration, and the rising *organic composition of capital* (the ratio of constant to variable capital, the latter referring exclusively to wages or outlays for labor power) accompanying these processes, is also a battle of capitals using price competition as a major weapon. Under competitive capitalism, each capitalist tries to cheapen his commodities. Other factors being equal, his ability to do so depends on the productivity of labor, which, in turn, depends on the mass of means of production per worker—in short, on the scale of production.

The larger capitals defeat the smaller ones who seek to enter the less modern spheres of industry where smaller investments in means of production are required. The defeated smaller capitalists are numerous and weak. They enter spheres with lower organic compositions of capital and pay out more in variable capital. Running at great expense, they are not competitive and fail frequently. Some of their assets are absorbed by the bigger competitors, and others simply vanish.

This is the way Marx explained the structural changes in the economy and correspondingly in the class structure of the whole society, including the relations among the classes as well as their differentiation and stratification. This is the sense in which all of Marx's key concepts are historically fluid and specific; if one loses sight of this in applying his concepts, one has missed their essential quality.

As for Max's thesis itself, the point to bear in mind is that he demonstrated the unavoidable tendency under capitalism of an *increasing concentration of economic power*. The obverse side of this is the increasing separation of the producers from control over the process of production. It is to this thesis that Weber addresses himself, elaborating and revising it. But before considering Weber's elaboration, we need to take a glance at Weber's adoption of Marx's concepts.

WEBER ON CAPITALISM AND SOCIAL CLASSES

Weber concurs in all essential respects with Marx's characterization of capitalism. Although capitalistic forms existed in previous periods of history,

Weber agrees that capitalism as described by Marx is a modern phenomenon, and that it has become the dominant method of production since the middle of the nineteenth century.

What does modern capitalism presuppose? First of all, the appropriation of all physical means of production—land, apparatus, machinery, tools, etc., as disposable property of autonomous private industrial enterprises."[7] To lend support to his thesis that capitalism originally developed only in the West, and that capitalism became possible with the fundamental rationalization of all spheres of social life, Weber correctly stresses that modern capitalism presupposes rational capital accounting, rational technology, and rational law and administration. At the same time he emphasizes not only a free market but, what was more basic for Marx, "free labor."

"Persons must be present," writes Weber, "who are not only legally in the position, but are also economically compelled, to sell their labor on the market without restriction." And he continues:

> It is in contradiction to the essence of capitalism, and the development of capitalism is impossible, if such a propertyless stratum is absent, a class compelled to sell its labor services to live; and it is likewise impossible if only unfree labor is at hand. Rational capitalistic calculation is possible only on the basis of free labor; only where in consequence of the existence of workers who in the formal sense voluntarily, but actually under the compulsion of the whip of hunger, offer themselves, the costs of products may be unambiguously determined by agreement in advance.[8]

"Free labor," therefore—in the double sense of being free from slavery and other forms of forced servitude but also free (i.e., separated) from their means of production—is for Weber as for Marx a precondition of modern capitalism. For Weber, too, proletarians and capitalists—those who concentrate in their hands means of production, sources of power, and raw material—are the two major classes of modern industrial capitalism.

In *Economy and Society* Weber notes that "The unfinished last part of Karl Marx's *Capital* apparently was intended to deal with the issue of class unity in the face of skill differentials."[9] Weber's own highly sophisticated discussion of social classes may be regarded as an attempt to complete Marx's final chapter by pursuing the issues Marx raised.

Weber employs all of Marx's major concepts: class, class consciousness, class conflict, class interest, and so on. For Weber, the main social classes were:

[7] Max Weber, *General Economic History*, trans. Frank H. Knight (New York: Collier Books, 1961), p. 208.

[8] Ibid., pp. 208–9.

[9] Max Weber, *Economy and Society*, ed. Guenther Roth and Claus Wittich, 3 vols. (New York: Bedminster Press, 1968), 1:305.

(a) the working class as a whole—the more so, the more automated the work process becomes,

(b) the petty bourgeoisie

(c) the propertyless intelligentsia and specialists (technicians, various kinds of white-collar employees, civil servants—possibly with considerable social differences depending on the cost of their training),

(d) the classes privileged through property and education.[10]

Class consciousness most easily develops:

(a) against the immediate economic opponents (workers against entrepreneurs, but *not* against stockholders, who truly draw "unearned" incomes, and also *not* in the case of peasants confronting manorial lords),

(b) if large numbers of persons are in the same class situation,

(c) if it is technically easy to organize them, especially if they are concentrated at their place of work . . . ,

(d) if they are led toward readily understood goals, which are imposed and interpreted by men outside their class (intelligentsia).[11]

A careful reading of Weber's discussion of social class will show just how great was his convergence with Marx in this regard. Throughout he emphasizes that classes, like status groups and political parties, "are phenomena of the distribution of power . . ." Class situation is determined by the market situation. It is in this context that Weber defines "class": "We may speak of a "class" when (1) a number of people have in common a specific causal component of their life chances, insofar as (2) this component is represented exclusively by economic interests in the possession of goods and opportunities for income, and (3) is represented under the conditions of the commodity or labor markets."[12]

Today when, as we have seen, there are those who argue that property relations are of diminishing importance in the United States and Western Europe, it may be highly instructive to quote some of Weber's observations at length. For while his definition of class has received widespread attention in the social sciences, not so his remarks immediately following:

It is the most elemental economic fact that the way in which the disposition over material property is distributed among a plurality of people, meeting competitively in the market for the purpose of exchange, in itself creates specific life chances. According to the law of marginal utility, this mode of distribution excludes the non-owners from competing

---

[10] Ibid.

[11] Ibid.

[12] Max Weber, in *From Max Weber: Essays in Sociology,* trans. and ed. H. H. Gerth and C. Wright Mills (New York: Oxford University Press, 1958), p. 181.

for highly valued goods; this favors the owners and, in fact, gives to them a monopoly to acquire such goods. Other things being equal, the mode of distribution monopolizes the opportunities for profitable deals for all those who, provided with goods, do not necessarily have to exchange them. It increases, at least generally, their power in the price struggle with those who, being propertyless, have nothing to offer but their services . . . or goods constituted through their own labor, and who above all are compelled to get rid of these products in order barely to subsist. This mode of distribution gives to the propertied a monopoly on the possibility of transferring property from the sphere of use as a "fortune," to the sphere of "capital goods," that is, it gives them the entrepreneurial function and all chances to share directly or indirectly in returns on capital. All this holds true within the area in which pure market conditons prevail. "Property" and "lack of property" are, therefore, the basic categories of all class situations.[13]

This, as we see, is direct and unequivocal. It is not enough for Weber to speak in the abstract of groups and strata with conflicting interests and values, nor even of power and authority in the abstract. Property relations are a central and elemental economic fact.

THE ACCELERATED CONCENTRATION OF THE LATE NINETEENTH CENTURY

To return to Marx, it is true that he perceived and explained the inevitable tendency under capitalism of capital concentration. Nevertheless, the most dramatic effects of that process became evident only after his death, with the "second industrial revolution." This term refers to the technological changes of the late nineteenth and early twentieth centuries, which resulted in new sources of power and higher industrial productivity. Oil and electricity now joined coal; the gas engine and electric motor increasingly displaced steam as sources of industrial power; and steel became a basic industrial material.[14]

For our purposes, the important point is that this technical-industrial revolution substantially accelerated the concentration and centralization of capital. One reason for this was that the new technology in steel, aluminum, electricity, etc., was applied in highly expensive, large-scale capital equipment. The expanding costs of the immense minimum apparatus required to enter profitable production precluded anyone but the giant firms from developing new industries.

[13] Ibid., pp. 181–82.
[14] See Earnest Mandel, *Marxist Economic Theory*, trans. Brian Pearce, vol. 2. (New York and London: Monthly Review Press, 1968).

Further, this "second industrial revolution" developed most rapidly in the United States, Germany, Japan, and, to a lesser extent, Russia and Italy—"late-comers" to industrialization that were relatively unencumbered by the industrial plant and technology of the first stage of industrialization and hence were able to exploit the new developments to their utmost. This gave them a considerable advantage over the "first arrivals," England, France, and Belgium, and it was therefore among the "latecomers" that concentration of capital was most accentuated. Relatively few firms in each country acquired control of industries and large shares of the market at the expense of middle-sized and small producers. And, of course, with the high capital concentration and the domination of industries by a few giants, conditions became more favorable for the effective organization of monopoly control.

This is the process Max Weber witnessed in imperial Germany; but he also recognized that it was not confined to the economic sphere. There were several strategic areas of social life in which one could observe (1) the concentration of the means of power in the hands of small minorities, and (2) the consequent separation of the majority of men from those means. This was for Weber the inevitable corollary of advancing bureaucratization, or the formal rationalizing of social organization. For Marx and the Marxists the most essential question was: Who controls the means of production? For Weber it was necessary to ask in addition: Who disposes of the other strategic means of controlling and dominating men?

Weber does not deny the central importance of control over key economic resources, but he points out that this is not sufficient for an understanding of the structure of social power in general. He therefore generalizes Marx's theory and argues that control of the means of political administration, means of violence, means of scientific research, etc., are also major means of dominating men. He writes:

> Organized domination which calls for continuous administration, requires that human conduct be conditioned to obedience towards those masters who claim to be the bearers of legitimate power. On the other hand ... organized domination requires the control of those material goods which in a given case are necessary for the use of physical violence. Thus, organized domination requires control of the personal executive staff and the material implements of administration.[15]

Weber goes on to apply Marx's concept of "separation":

> To maintain a domination by force, certain material goods are required, just as with an economic organization. All states may be

---

[15] Max Weber, "Politics As a Vocation," in *From Max Weber*, p. 80.

> classified according to whether they rest on the principle that the staff of men themselves *own* the administrative means, or whether the staff is "separated" from these means of administration. This distinction holds in the same sense in which today we say that the salaried employee and the proletarian in the capitalistic enterprise are "separated" from the material means of production.[16]

In this way Weber suggests that Marx's "separation" of the worker from the means of production is only one aspect of a general social process. Men are increasingly separated from the means of power in several other strategic areas of social life—not only in the economic, political, and military spheres, but in the scientific as well.

> The large institutes of medicine or natural science are "state capitalist" enterprises, which cannot be managed without very considerable funds. Here we encounter the same condition that is found wherever capitalist enterprise comes into operation: the "separation of the worker from his means of production." The worker, that is, the assistant is dependent upon the implements that the state puts at his disposal; hence he is just as dependent upon the head of the institute as is the employee in a factory upon the management.[17]

The general process of "separation" is increasingly characteristic of modern society and is an integral aspect of what Weber describes as the bureaucratization of its social structure. Even scientists become wage-laborers dominated by those who control the means of scientific research.

If "separation" is one side of the coin, concentration of power is the other. Marx's concentration of the means of production Weber generalizes to other means of power, notably the administrative, military, and scientific.

> The bureaucratic structure goes hand in hand with the concentration of the material means of management in the hands of the master. This concentration occurs, for instance, in a well-known and typical fashion, in the development of big capitalist enterprises, which find their essential characteristics in this process. A corresponding process occurs in public organizations.
>
> .   .   .   .
>
> War in our time is a war of machines. And this makes magazines technically necessary, just as the dominance of the machine in industry promotes the concentration of the means of production and management.

.   .   .   .

[16] Ibid., p. 81.
[17] Max Weber, "Science as a Vocation," in *From Max Weber,* p. 131.

> In the same way as with army organizations, the bureaucratization of administration goes hand in hand with the concentration of the means of organization in other spheres.

.   .   .   .

> In the field of scientific research and instruction, the bureaucratization of the . . . research institutes of the universities is a function of the increasing demand for material means of management. . . . Through the concentration of such means in the hands of the privileged head of the institute, the mass of researchers and docents are separated from their "means of production," in the same way as the capitalist enterprise has separated the workers from theirs.[18]

Even as he draws our attention to the generality of this social process, Weber also stresses the primary role of capitalism in it. "Today," he writes, "it is primarily the capitalist market economy which demands that the official business of the administration be discharged precisely, unambiguously, continuously, and with as much speed as possible. Normally, the very large modern capitalist enterprises are themselves unequalled models of strict bureaucratic organization."[19]

The conception of society that emerges is clear: society is nothing if not a plurality of groups, strata, organizations, and classes with their respective interests and values—groups, strata, and classes, moreover, that do not simply exist side by side but whose relationships are characterized by competition, conflict, and patterns of domination. Further, these structures of domination are not merely hierarchical but dichotomous.

Long before Dahrendorf, Weber noted the class or quasi-class character of "imperatively coordinated associations"; but, in sharp contrast to Dahrendorf, he did not insulate these associations either from each other or from society as a whole. Weber does not regard a society in which economic power is concentrated in giant private corporations as "postcapitalist"; nor, finally, does he view the state as just another association.

Power, for Weber, refers to "the chance of a man or of a number of men to realize their own will in a communal action even against the resistance of others who are participating in the action."[20] What is clearly stressed here are the conflicting aims and interests of the participants. To have power means that one is able to struggle and overcome the resistance of others. Power permeates all social relations, but it is also concentrated in the hands of the state.

Quoting Trotsky at Brest-Litovsk, Weber writes: "Every state is founded on force." And "today," he continues, "the relation between the state and violence is an especially intimate one. . . . [A] state . . . (successfully) claims the

[18] Weber, *From Max Weber,* pp. 221–24.
[19] Ibid., p. 215.
[20] Ibid., p. 181.

monopoly of the legitimate use of physical force within a given territory."[21] The "state is a relation of men dominating men." Some command and others obey. Why do they obey? Not only, of course, because those who command control physical means of force; but also because the dominated may accept as justified the "basic legitimations of domination." Let us then note Weber's cautious formulation: the rulers *claim* legitimacy, which means that the ruled may or may not accept the claim, or accept it in varying degrees. Therefore the term "legitimation," for Weber, was a problematic concept, roughly equivalent to Marx's "ruling ideology," Sorel's "myths," Pareto's "derivations," and Mosca's "political formula." Weber thus assigns a definite role to values but one that illuminates rather than obscures social divisions, domination, force, and fraud.

Weber's general approach is also applicable to the relations of conflict and domination among states and societies. In a typically forthright analysis he explores the connection between capitalist interests and imperialism. Among the plurality of national and multinational states, "some, the Great Powers, usually ascribe to themselves and usurp an interest in political and economic processes over a wide orbit. Today such orbits encompass the whole surface of the planet." Great powers are frequently expansive, seeking to expand their territories "by the use or the threat of force." Yet this is not always the case. There are policy changes in this respect, "and in these changes economic factors play a weighty part." When, for instance, Britain sought to widen her orbit of influence, this "occurred, in part, through capitalist interests in expansion."[22]

It would, of course, be incorrect to say that Weber developed a full-blown theory of modern imperialism as did, for instance, Hobson and Lenin. Nevertheless, fragmentary though it may be, Weber's analysis is basically compatible with the Hobson-Lenin thesis. A few passages from Weber's discussion will bear this out:

> Today the polity as such is almost the sole agent to order war material and the engines of war. This enhances the capitalist nature of the process. Banks, which finance war loans, and today large sections of heavy industry are *quand même* economically interested in warfare; the direct suppliers of armor plates and guns are not the only ones so interested. A lost war, as well as a successful war, brings increased business to these banks and industries.
>
> The partners within a polity are politically and economically interested in the existence of large home factories for war engines.

.   .   .   .

[21] Weber, "Politics as a Vocation," p. 78.
[22] Weber, *From Max Weber*, pp. 161–62.

In general and at all times, imperialist capitalism, especially colonial booty capitalism based on direct force and compulsory labor, has offered by far the greatest opportunities for profit.

.   .   .   .

Increasing opportunities for profit abroad emerge again today, especially in territories that are "opened up" politically and economically, that is, brought into the specifically modern forms of public and private "enterprise." These opportunities spring from "public" contracts of arms; from railroad and other construction tasks carried out by the polity or by builders endowed with monopoly rights; from monopolist organizations for the collection of levies for trade and industry; from monopolist concessions; and government loans.

.   .   .   .

The safest way of guaranteeing these monopolized profit opportunities to the members of one's own polity is to occupy it or at least to subject the foreign political power in the form of a "protectorate" or some such arrangement. Therefore, this "imperialist" tendency increasingly displaces the "pacifist" tendency of expansion, which aims merely at "freedom of trade."

.   .   .   .

The universal revival of "imperialist" capitalism, which has always been the normal form in which capitalist interests have influenced politics, and the revival of political drives for expansion are thus not accidental. For the predictable future, the prognosis will have to be made in its favor.

.   .   .   .

Every successful imperialist policy of coercing the outside, normally—or at least at first—also strengthens the domestic "prestige" and therewith the power and influence of those classes, status groups, and parties, under whose leadership the success has been attained.[23]

Weber goes on to suggest that there are strong pacifist sympathies among the masses and particularly among the proletariat because it becomes more difficult to satisfy their social demands with the militarization of the economy. And yet experience shows that their pacific interests "very often and very easily fail." This is because they are more vulnerable to chauvinistic emotional appeals than other strata. Other classes and strata risk their property or power in the disorganization caused by war. Whereas the " 'masses' as such, at least in their subjective conception and in the extreme case, have nothing concrete to lose but

[23] Ibid., pp. 168–70.

their lives. The valuation and effect of this danger strongly fluctuates in their own minds. On the whole, it can easily be reduced to zero through emotional influence." In this way Weber illuminates conflict and domination both within and among national polities.

A somewhat similar interpretation of Weber—though one that does not relate him to Marx—has been put forth by Randall Collins. He correctly regards Weber's approach as historical-sociological, and he argues that for Weber

1. The basic unit of analysis is the *group*, or *organization*, viewed in relation to other organizations and groups with which it has contact.

2. and 3. The basic process that takes place in and among these units is the *struggle* of individuals and organizations to further their material and ideal interests.

4. The bases of stable coordination of human activities are *constellations of interests*, especially in solidary groups, and the *domination* of certain groups over others.

5. Political change is explained by the *struggle* for political advantage, both within and between states, made continual by the *instabilities and dilemmas* of legitimatizing principles and of arrangements of domination.[24]

Collins recommends this approach for use in comparative political sociology. It is an illuminating and potentially fruitful strategy and certainly superior to functionalism, with which he contrasts it.

Nevertheless, if such an approach is to yield truly significant intellectual results, it must go beyond the recognition of a plurality of groups and organizations with conflicting interests. This is only the beginning of wisdom. To advance beyond this it is necessary to recognize that some institutional spheres of society and their respective organizations play a more central role than others in determining the life chances and indeed the general fate of men. The advantage of what I have called the Marx-Weber model is that it keeps at the center of our attention the three most strategic institutional spheres of the present epoch: the *economic*, the *political*, and the *military*. For there can be no doubt that today and in the foreseeable future the most fateful question facing mankind is: Who controls the means of production, the means of political administration, and the means of violence?

[24] Randall Collins, "A Comparative Approach to Political Sociology," *State and Society: A Reader in Comparative Political Sociology*, ed. Reinhard Bendix (Boston: Little, Brown & Co., 1968), p. 67.

IV

PHENOMENOLOGY

10

Husserl and the Crisis of Science and Philosophy

We have now completed the task of critically scrutinizing three main currents of contemporary sociological theory: functionalism, exchange theory, and conflict-coercion theory. We have also arrived at a brief programmatic statement calling for the orientation of macrosocial theory along the lines suggested by the so-called Marx-Weber model. As I pointed out in the Preface, however, this model is predominantly structural.

It is therefore necessary to search for a social psychology that adequately illuminates the social interaction of acting-knowing subjects, and that is compatible with the Marx-Weber model. Our search will begin with phenomenology, a notoriously ambiguous concept that covers a bewildering variety of ideas.

Although the term "phenomenology" is used to label the philosophical method founded by Edmund Husserl, those who have referred to themselves as phenomenologists, or who are regarded as such by others, share no unified body of principles. Phenomenology is neither a "school" nor a "system." Even the term "movement" is employed by students of the history of phenomenology only with grave misgivings. Thus Herbert Spiegelberg, who calls his standard historical introduction *The Phenomenological Movement*, writes: "It would go too far to say that there are as many phenomenologies as there are phenomenologists. But it is certainly true that, on closer inspection, the varieties exceed the common features."[1]

Nor has the ambiguity of the label "phenomenology" diminished much since it was first introduced in the last decade of the nineteenth century. In 1945, Merleau-Ponty still found it necessary to begin one of his major works by asking: "What is phenomenology?" He adds, "It may seem strange that this

[1] Herbert Spiegelberg, *The Phenomenological Movement*, 2 vols. (The Hague: Martinus Nijhoff, 1960–69), 1:xxvii.

question has still to be asked half a century after the first works of Husserl. The fact remains that it has by no means been answered."[2]

And as recently as 1967 the material for a copious anthology of some 555 pages was also "chosen for the contribution it could make toward the answering of one vital question: What is phenomenology?" But the editor also hastens to inform the reader that "what phenomenology is, and in what areas of inquiry it has exercised an important influence, are questions so intricate and comprehensive in nature that no one-volume anthology . . . can provide the final word on the subject."[3]

We are therefore venturing into a philosophical realm, and a rather vague one at that. A brief critical exploration of that realm is nonetheless necessary since the roots of contemporary theoretical currents may be traced to Husserl's philosophy. My approach here is mainly analytical: I will ignore for the most part the historical aspects of the phenomenological "movement," focusing only on a few thinkers, and on those ideas that appear most pertinent to sociological theory.

PSYCHOLOGISM

All intellectual movements are probably best understood if one sees clearly not only what their adherents are arguing for but also what they are arguing against. Phenomenology is no exception, for Husserl began to shape the principles of his philosophy in the course of repudiating a prominent, perhaps even dominant, standpoint of Europe in the 1880s known as "psychologism."

Husserl began his scientific career in mathematics and physics, not philosophy, and soon came under the influence of the psychology of his day as represented by such men as Wilhelm Wundt, Carl Stumpf, and Franz Brentano. This influence together with that of Locke and Hume inclined him toward empiricism and psychologism. In his first book, *Philosophy of Arithmetic* (1891), he sought, accordingly, to derive fundamental arithmetical concepts from specific psychological acts. Empirical psychology, he argued, provides the epistemological basis of arithmetic. Criticism of his own book by Frege as well as Natorp's critique of Theodor Lipps' *Basic Facts of Mental Life* soon caused Husserl to abandon psychologism, however, and to develop a point of view in opposition to it.

What were the main characteristics of psychologism and how did Husserl's

[2] Maurice Merleau-Ponty, *Phenomenology of Perception*, trans. Colin Smith (London: Routledge & Kegan Paul, 1962), p. vii.

[3] Joseph J. Kockelmans, ed., *Phenomenology: The Philosophy of Edmund Husserl and Its Interpretation* (Garden City, N. Y.: Doubleday Anchor Books, 1967), p. 5.

phenomenological psychology differ? Psychologism imitates the physical sciences and adheres to the doctrines of "naturalism" and "objectivism," according to which only the physical is real. The reality of the ideal is denied or it is "naturalized" by regarding it as a physical reality. Dominated by this point of view, psychology becomes a combination of psychophysical and physiological investigations, quantitative and experimental, to determine the relation between objective stimuli and subjective responses.

For Husserl such a psychology is inadequate because it deals only with external facts arrived at by observation and experiment, and ignores consciousness and meaning. Although this psychology appears methodologically scientific, Husserl argued, and has in fact illuminated certain important psychophysical processes, it nevertheless remains quite limited and even impotent if the object is to achieve an understanding of consciousness. As naive naturalists the practitioners of this method model their experimental science after physics, erroneously presuming that one method is sufficient to comprehend both the physical and the conscious realms. But as naive empiricists they make another error as well, which implies that their method is actually unscientific. They effect their observations and experiments by means of assumptions and concepts that enter into their conclusions and for which objectivity and scientific validity are claimed. Yet these assumptions and concepts are left unexamined. They make no effort to assess their validity for either the subjects or the psychologists.

Although the term had not yet been invented, the reader will recognize that psychologism of the 1800s was the forebear of "behaviorism," the tenets of which were very similar. Behaviorism also insisted on:

1. *Objectivism:* objective techniques for obtaining data. The corollary was, in Watson's words, to "bury subjective subject matter."

2. *S-R Orientation:* all psychological propositions are to be stated in stimulus-response terms.

3. *Peripheralism:* phenomena traditionally classed as "mental" are reduced to objective, S-R terms.

4. *Emphasis on learning and on some form of S-R associationism as the basic laws of learning:* sensory and perceptual problems are replaced by an emphasis on learning as an objective field of study. For Watson the basic laws of learning came to be based on *conditioned reflex* principles.

5. *Environmentalism:* the term environment referred to one's surroundings in the crude physical sense.[4]

Husserl began his critique of the behaviorism of his time in his *Logische Untersuchengen* (1900) and developed it further in the essay "Philosophy as

[4] This summary description is based on Sigmund Koch, "Psychology and Emerging Conceptions of Knowledge as Unitary," in *Behaviorism and Phenomenology*, ed. T. W. Wann (Chicago: University of Chicago Press, 1964), pp. 7–38.

Rigorous Science" (1911).[5] The essay is quite important for an understanding of Husserl's philosophical aim, implicit in its title. His position is neither antiscientific nor antipsychological; rather, he seeks to break out of the misleading and deceptive tradition that dominated empirical psychology since the eighteenth century and to develop an adequate and scientifically rigorous method that "follows the nature of the things to be investigated and not our prejudices and preconceptions" (102). The very term "nature" is appropriate only in reference to the "spatiotemporal world of bodies." Only with reference to the external corporeal world does it make sense to speak of substance, real properties, and causality. At this stage of his thinking, therefore, Husserl follows Hume and Kant, concluding that causality belongs only in the realm of nature. (In his later work, however, one catches him speaking of motivation as a form of "spiritual causality.") The psychical realm, in contrast, is fundamentally different, for here appearance and being are not distinguished. The psychical "is precisely phenomenon and not nature." Husserl continues:

> A phenomenon, then, is no "substantial" unity; it has no "real properties," it knows no real parts, no real changes, and no causality; all these words are here understood in the sense proper to natural science. To attribute a nature to phenomena, to investigate their real component parts, their causal connections—that is pure absurdity, no better than if one wanted to ask about the causal properties, connections, etc., of numbers. It is the absurdity of naturalizing something whose essence excludes the kind of being that nature has. (107)

Thus Husserl fashions a rather rigid dichotomy between the natural and the psychical, the latter appearing as an absolute flow or stream of consciousness. This stream or flow is nonetheless a unity of consciousness, having nothing to do with space, time, substantiality, or causality but rather possessing its own peculiar forms and its own inner "time" that "no chronometers measure." Understanding this realm of consciousness therefore requires that one overcome the "naturalistic attitude," the tendency to adulterate the psychical by assimilating it to the natural. One must develop an appropriate method that will facilitate a strictly immanent investigation of consciousness—of which more later.

Philosophy as a rigorous science could yield such a method. In fact, it could also yield *certitude*, which was among Husserl's highest values. But what have positive science and the naturalistic attitude yielded? Far from certitude, they have resulted in a philosophical crisis in which relativity and skepticism

---

[5] Edmund Husserl, "Philosophy as Rigorous Science," in *Phenomenology and the Crisis of Philosophy*, trans. Quentin Lauer (New York: Harper Torchbooks, 1965). Page references to this volume (which also includes the essay "Philosophy and the Crisis of European Man") will be cited in parentheses immediately following the quoted passage.

prevail. Finding this state of affairs disconcerting in the extreme, Husserl puts forth his own phenomenological method in the hope that it will lead to the reconstruction of philosophy on the foundations of necessary and absolutely certain truths.

HISTORICISM AND WELTANSCHAUUNG PHILOSOPHY

If psychologism's "naturalism" threatened from one side, historicism threatened from the other. Husserl acknowledges that Wilhelm Dilthey was among the first to see clearly the basic errors of naturalism and objectivism. But Dilthey, according to Husserl, in his *Weltanschauung* philosophy went to the extreme of viewing all truths as relative to historical epochs; in this view, the variety of competing and conflicting philosophical systems that emerged in the course of historical development destroyed once and for all the possibility of accepting the absolute and universal validity of any single philosophy.

In his quest for certainty Husserl could not but object to this point of view, as he interpreted it (it is doubtful that Dilthey was the thoroughgoing relativist Husserl makes him out to be). Husserl grants the historical character of science—that scientific views change and that what once was proved true is later recognized as false. But does this mean that scientific propositions lack a lasting validity? He rejects the implications of an affirmative reply to this question. "It is easy to see," he writes, "that historicism, if consistently carried through, carries over into extreme sceptical subjectivism. The ideas of truth, theory, and science would then, like all ideas, lose their absolute validity" (125). With the loss of unqualified validity would be lost also the principle of contradiction and even of logic in general. It would not occur to historicists to suggest that mathematical truth is relative to historical development. "How, then, is it to be the historian's task to decide as to the truth of given philosophical systems and above all, as to the very possibility of a philosophical science that is valid in itself?" (126).

In this way, Husserl sought to advance toward his philosophic aim. By exposing the defects of historicism and *Weltanschauung* philosophy, he hoped to prevent truth from dissolving into historically relative ideologies. His point was not that there was no room for a world outlook but that the line between ideology and science had to be clear. Otherwise, the scientific impulse would be weakened and with it the pursuit of valid knowledge and truth.

In a spirit anticipating Max Weber's *Wissenschaft als Beruf* ("Science as a Vocation"), Husserl writes that "science is one value among other equally justified values." But one must never lose sight of the essential difference between science and *Weltanschauung*; for "just as both have their distinct sources of value, so they also have their distinct functions, their distinct manners of working and teaching" (143).

HUSSERL'S PHENOMENOLOGICAL METHOD

What inevitably strikes the student of Husserl's work is its basically programmatic character. Spiegelberg, for instance, has noted the "striking disproportion between programmatic announcements of epochal discoveries to be made within the 'infinite horizons' opened up by his new methods, and the long-deferred and never complete fulfillment of such promises . . . "[6] And Kockelmans has similarly observed that "it is not easy to express Husserl's idea of phenomenology. The reason lies in the fact that hitherto only a relatively small part of his writings have been published, and most of these publications are more concerned with picturing an ideal program than with its execution."[7]

For Husserl the most important task is to develop a rigorous method that would enable the philosopher as scientist to get at the "things themselves." From the time of Locke, the empiricists, with their naturalistic attitude, mistakenly believed that they grasped reality, or things, directly, naively, and "immediately." Their inductive method, they thought, allowed for a direct contact with reality, unmediated by concepts. Knowledge was simply the cumulative recording of sensory impressions of reality, as it is, on a "mind" blank at birth. Mind, according to this view, was a relatively passive receptacle, a categoryless entity, playing no significantly active, organizing role in the development of knowledge. Husserl rejects this—as did Kant long before him—as naive. The empiricists failed to recognize that their knowledge was mediated by concepts.

Husserl is, however, equally opposed to the Kantian view. Kant's contribution was revolutionary because he recognized the creative and constitutive qualities of mind and hence the subjective dimension of all knowledge. Like Kant, Husserl seeks the criterion of knowledge in the act of cognition. But more than this he cannot accept, rejecting resolutely Kant's a priori categories that forever hid the "things in themselves" from the knowing subject; and rejecting as well the Kantian dualism of the phenomenal and noumenal.

The really important task, as Husserl sees it, is to transcend both traditions by means of a radically new method that would facilitate an original intuition of the things themselves and a return to the immediate and original data of consciousness. Neither induction nor deduction but solely intuition of the primordial phenomena will yield valid knowledge undistorted by the presuppositions of the other sciences.[8] In these terms Husserl's philosophical ideal is a philosophy without presuppositions, an ideal that can be approached by the method he calls "reduction."

Positive scientists, whether they are aware of it or not, provide us with an abstract and artificial structure of the world but not the world of our original

---

[6] Spiegelberg, *The Phenomenological Movement*, 1:90.

[7] Kockelmans, *Phenomenology*, p. 25.

[8] Husserl, *Phenomenology*, pp. 98–122. See also Spiegelberg, *The Phenomenological Movement*, 1:73f. and 1:124f; and Kockelmans, *Phenomenology*, p. 24f.

experience. To break out of the artificial world of the positive sciences and to get at the world of our immediately experienced life (what Husserl later calls the *Lebenswelt*), one needs to employ the method of "reduction" and to grasp a fundamental property of consciousness, namely, *intentionality* (a concept he took over from his teacher, Franz Brentano, but markedly transformed). Consciousness always directs itself towards that which it is not. It is the essence of consciousness to form meanings and to constitute its own objects.

THE TRANSCENDENTAL-PHENOMENOLOGICAL REDUCTION

Following Descartes, but again introducing modifications, Husserl wants to begin his philosophizing with radical doubt. One begins by calling into question everything previously taken for granted. This requires a different attitude (*Einstellung*) toward the world, looking at it with "new eyes." In his *Cartesian Meditations*[9] Husserl refers to this attitude as one in which one denies validity to the "natural belief in the existence of what" one experiences. One "invalidates," "inhibits," "disqualifies," all previously taken positions regarding the experienced objects. Finally, to quote Husserl's best-known phrase, one "brackets the objective world." Drawing his metaphor from mathematics, where one places an expression in brackets with a plus or minus sign before it, Husserl suggests that by bracketing the objective world one "gives it a different value."[10] The "reduction" enables the phenomenologist to transform himself into a disinterested or disengaged observer.

With this change of practical attitude the object of experience becomes "phenomenon." We recognize the claim to reality the object makes upon us but we temporarily suspend any judgment as to the validity of the claim. What remains is world as pure or mere phenomenon.

"Reduction" also leads to the discovery of what Husserl calls the "transcendental ego." This is the "I" that ultimately decides sense and validity. In the process of intending objects other than itself it becomes aware of itself; it changes the world into mere phenomenon. The "I" becomes conscious of itself changing the world, but does not itself change. The "I" is pure ego, totally devoid of content and consisting of different forms of relatedness. In carrying out the "reduction" one does not reject or turn away from experienced reality; one simply suspends judgment about the reality and validity of the experience. Richard Schmitt has explained this rather well: "The world before the

---

[9] Edmund Husserl, *Cartesianische Meditationen*, ed. S. Strasser, Husserliana, vol. 1 (The Hague: Martinus Nijhoff, 1950), pp. 59–60.
[10] Edmund Husserl, *Ideen zu einer reinen Phänomenologie und phänomenologischen Philosophie*, ed. Walter Biemel, Husserliana vol. 3 (The Hague: Martinus Nijhoff, 1950), p. 174.

transcendental-phenomenological reduction and the world which I have transformed into 'mere phenomenon' do not differ in content, but in the way in which I am related to each of them."[11]

In light of the foregoing discussion we can begin to make some sense of Husserl's terminology. He calls the transcendental-phenomenological reduction "transcendental" because in the process the ego discovers itself, and discovers also that it is only for itself that anything exists or has meaning. He calls it "phenomenological" because the world is thereby transformed into mere phenomenon. Finally, he calls it "reduction" because the process presumably "leads back" (from the Latin *reducere*) to intentionality, the ultimate source of the meaning of the experienced world.

To make these concepts more meaningful, we might try to express them in plainer English and to provide a few homely illustrations of their applicability. Schmitt sums up phenomenology as a "reflective enterprise," and distinguishes thinking from reflecting. But, as we shall later see, this is only one interpretation, a "sociological" one, that reads into Husserl's method more than is actually there.

Let us suppose that a child has been punished for disobeying his parents and sent to his room. There he cries for a while, perhaps thinking about how he has been wronged, and thinking too that his parents do not love him. The child regards the experience wholly from his own standpoint; he thinks about his own ideas and feelings, his own unhappiness. So far he is thinking but not reflecting; for he does not ask himself whether his punishment was justified or whether his world is in fact as he sees it. His angry and miserable state has prevented him from "standing back" and "detaching" himself from the situation; he continues to view it in one perspective.

As his emotions subside, however, he begins to *reflect*. Now his attitude is one of critical detachment; he recapitulates events, but this time from his parents' point of view, thus perceiving himself and the entire situation in a different light. Reflection is not only a matter of a different perspective; it is more inclusive than mere thinking. For reflection brings to light new facts that previously remained hidden or seemed irrelevant.

Likewise, a "true believer" in any given ideology or belief system views the world from a single perspective. He is singlemindedly devoted to certain ideals and may even find evidence for the justice of his commitment. He is thinking but not reflecting. Indeed, he senses a danger in reflection, for it involves questioning his previously unquestioned assumptions and adopting other perspectives toward the existing situation. This might cool his ardor and even detach him from his aims.

The point of Husserl's "reduction," according to this interpretation, is to go beyond thinking and accomplish reflection in the sense described above.

----

[11] See his "Phenomenological Reduction," in Kockelmans, *Phenomenology*, p. 61. In the present clarification of Husserl's obscure-sounding terms I rely heavily on Schmitt's convincing interpretation.

Everyman has a definite intentionality toward the objects of his thought He is "interested" in these objects so that the objects in turn "impose" a definite reality and validity upon him. Husserl calls this the "natural attitude," an unquestioning acceptance of the experienced. But what is good for Everyman is not good for the philosopher as rigorous scientist. The latter, in pursuit of valid and certain knowledge. must perform the "*epoché*"–the suspension of belief in the objects of experience. He must suspend his interest, or disinterest himself. This requires abandoning the natural and adopting a "neutral attitude."[12] The *epoché*, then, does not mean that one rejects or denies the world or one's experiences, but rather that one begins to question them.

From the *epoché* one enters the first phase of the "reduction"–as illustrated by our reflecting child. Only in the reflecting phase does one distinguish the real experience from the prereflective distorted one. Reflection also brings other gains. So long as one is "interested," one's thought is highly selective: one notices only certain facts and ignores others. However, with reflection, everything one previously "knew" becomes questionable, while facts that were unnoticed or regarded as insignificant now emerge clearly and demand description and examination. Phenomenological reduction is therefore a *descriptive* discipline. Since in reduction (reflection) we question the world and do not as yet know what the world or situation in question is really like, there is nothing to explain yet.

As the knowing acting self, in the process of reduction, takes on the disinterested attitude, the experience under examination acquires a different meaning and additional dimensions. Here Husserl's "reduction" results in a mental posture not unlike the one Max Weber described in his concepts *Wertfreiheit* and the accompanying *Wertbeziehung*–"objectivity" and the approximation of this ideal in science and scholarship.

Husserl's "reduction" thus moves in two directions, toward the *noesis* (the act directed to an intentional object), and toward the *noema* (the object of a *noetic* act);[13] or, toward the knowing self as well as toward the world as intentional object. To amplify, Husserl's so-called noetic analysis is this: one examines the *object* of one's intentional consciousness in relation to oneself when one tries to distinguish the genuine phenomenon from the mere assumptions or presuppositions about it; and one examines one's *consciousness* in relation to the object by scrutinizing the wishes, feelings, and beliefs that entered into the experience of the object that one is now reflecting upon. Husserl's conception of the intentionality of consciousness is that subject and object are inseparable and interactive and that each can only be understood in light of the other. Every object is object for some subject; and every subject has some part of the world as its intentional object.[14]

Finally the ego itself is revealed in the process of noetic analysis. As the

[12] Husserl, *Ideen*, p. 264f.

[13] Spiegelberg, *The Phenomenological Movement*, 2:721.

[14] Husserl, *Cartesianische Meditationen*, p. 99f.

object reveals itself as object-for-a-subject, i.e., whose validity and meaning flow from the subject, and as the subject shows itself as subject-of-this-object, i.e., as the "constituting" subject, the reflecting ego makes itself felt but remains nonetheless anonymous, eluding description.

For Husserl, the intentionality of consciousness and noetic analysis hold out the possibility of "overcoming" the one-sidedness of perspectives. All perspectives are partial and one-sided. In perceiving a house, for example, one actually sees only one side, one "profile" at a time. Learning more about the object requires that one adopt a variety of new perspectives—which, however, always remain partial. Yet eventually one experiences the many profiles as profiles of a particular house, and as a single object. The reason for this is, according to Husserl, that each separate act of perception *intends* more than a single profile, that is, other profiles as well as the whole house. This intended meaning of the whole, which transcends the separate profiles, and is grasped in the perceiving act, is Husserl's noema. Each perception thus becomes a phase of a total meaningful process in which the manifold perceptions yield a single unified object.

In this way the partiality or one-sidedness of the separate perspectives is overcome. This results not from the temporal sequence of perceptive acts, but from the fact that they harmonize—they complement and confirm one another. Perception carries with it more than perception. Strictly speaking, when one looks at a house, one perceives only one side of it. Yet that perception has a meaning that is not actually perceived, but that contributes to the noema.

Thus for Husserl every noema has a core that refers meaningfully to an "internal horizon"—aspects of the whole not immediately given. Of course, the more familiar we are with the perceived object, the more evident is the "internal horizon" that the core suggests. Husserl also reminds us that every object also has its "external horizon"—the context or background of the perceived object. Clearly, concepts, ideas, and even other acting subjects may also be regarded as having a core, and internal and external horizons.

THE LEBENSWELT

Husserl's early writings give the impression of an idealistic, even solipsistic method in which a single pure consciousness contemplates itself, even reaching beneath the cultural and historical levels of experience. In his later writings, he turns his attention to *intersubjectivity*, but in a strange and limited sense.

To understand Husserl's *Lebenswelt*, one must always bear in mind that the term refers not to the actually existing life-world, but rather to the world in whose existence one suspends belief—beginning with the *epoché* and continuing with the "reduction." "Life-world" refers exclusively to one's consciousness of the world. All elements and structures of reflection are objects of experience; it is these *ideal* entities of the experienced world, *Lebenswelt*, which one grasps. Men live simultaneously in the "real" world of social institutions, imagination, art, and so on; but Husserl focuses on these *only* in the form of categorial structures and processes in men's consciousness. He also refers to these processes as intuitions, which rest, in turn, on perceptual intuitions. Perception is consciousness's primary contact with the world and all other elements of consciousness rest on perception.[15]

Descending from the categorial or "predicative" structures, one soon discovers the underlying "prepredicative" stratum of experience. "This," James M. Edie explains, "is the foundational, prereflexive field of pure experience in which the world is constituted as a world *for* consciousness. The primary task of phenomenology is to return to this world as the matrix of all the derived constructions of thought. Experience precedes any thought about experience."[16]

When one begins to reflect on this "reduced" world, one soon discovers that it is not one's private world but a world of meaning and value that has been intersubjectively constituted and to which one has unconsciously contributed.[17] One now finds a world of experienced others, of fellow men, of subjectivities, all endowed with the same conscious activities as oneself. The world one experiences after completing the reduction to pure consciousness is an intersubjective world, accessible in principle to Everyman.

How does Husserl see the phenomenological process ultimately revealing an intersubjective world in consciousness? In the process of reduction I first eliminate everything mediately and immediately pertaining to the subjectivity of others and arrive at my own being as a self-sphere. This is the primordial sphere, my most private world. Within this sphere, I most easily distinguish an object I call my body. By the process of "appresentative pairing" an "other" appears, first also as a body, then as a mind. I soon constitute the other as an ego other than myself but who mirrors myself in his self-sphere. The other is an alter ego. He is like me but not a mere duplicate. From my viewpoint, his "here" is my "there," and vice versa. We therefore get different aspects of our common world, which, however, would be the same if we exchanged places.

Yet all this is taking place in "reduced" pure consciousness. This intersubjectivity exists purely in the reflecting ego and is "constituted purely from the sources of my intentionality, but in such a manner that it is the *same* transcendental intersubjectivity in every single human being . . . in his intentional experience."[18]

There are severe ambiguities and perhaps even contradictions in Husserl's

[15] See James M. Edie, "Transcendental Phenomenology and Existentialism," in Kockelmans, *Phenomenology*, pp. 237–51.
    [16] Ibid., pp. 248–49.
    [17] Alfred Schütz, *The Problem of Social Reality*, Collected Papers, vol. 1 (The Hague: Martinus Nijhoff, 1967), 123.
    [18] Ibid., p. 126.

conception of the phenomenological reduction. On the one hand, phenomenology is supposed to become a way of digging down to the so-called preconscious structure of experience having a universal validity; on the other hand, it is at least *implicit* in Husserl's view that the structures are neither innate nor fixed. After all, the concept of *intentional* consciousness implies that the structures are open, historically and culturally meaningful products of the subject's lived existence. One is never sure when reading Husserl, nor do his interpreters agree, whether the perceptual experience towards which the phenomenological reduction aims is primordial, fundamental, and absolute; or whether it is historical and cultural, therefore having only temporary or relative validity.

Although he stresses throughout that consciousness is always "consciousness of," it may not be going too far to say that Husserl never advances in his studies beyond the isolated, pure consciousness contemplating itself. For Husserl's so-called *Lebenswelt* never becomes the actual life-world of men. Exclusively concerned with "immanent seeing" as he is, he develops a philosophical method that effectively severs and isolates consciousness from being—from the actual social interaction and existence of men.

As a thinker, Husserl appears to have forgotten that it is one's actual involvement with being that is the ultimate source of thought, reflection, consciousness, and knowledge; that the enrichment and validation of knowledge depend on encounters with other people who are also involved in being. For all these reasons, Husserl falls short of his own philosophical objective.

We know that Husserl was profoundly influenced by William James's *Principles of Psychology* and that James's concepts "stream of thought," "fringes," and "intersubjectivity" contributed significantly to Husserl's thinking.[19] But Husserl missed other concepts in James that would have enabled him to transcend pure consciousness explicitly—such concepts as the "social self," "subuniverses," the "me," and so on. These concepts, as we shall see in Part V, became the essential elements with which George Herbert Mead and his followers developed a social psychology superior in its insights to anything Husserl's method ever yielded. The sociological dimension in Husserl is quite weak, perhaps nonexistent. We shall now turn to Max Scheler, the co-founder of the phenomenological movement, who addressed himself to this dimension explicitly and systematically.

[19] See Spiegelberg, *Phenomenology*, p. 111f.

11

Max Scheler

If Husserl's aim was to overcome the philosophical crisis of his time, Max Scheler's was to overcome what he regarded as the more general social, economic, and political crisis. The root cause of the crisis Scheler saw in what he called the "overthrow of values." The Christian value system had been undermined and even largely replaced by a bourgeois ethic; on this, other scholars, like Weber, Sombart, and Troeltsch, were also agreed. The bourgeois outlook stressed business rationality, acquisitiveness, utility, quantitative criteria for evaluating men, and the like. There was no going back to the precapitalist morality, but moral regeneration was nonetheless a necessity.

The new values had to be sought, Scheler felt, in a form of Christian socialism and a revitalization of Christian ethics. This would revive humility and reverence and at the same time combat the false bourgeois values resulting from *ressentiment*—a spirit that denigrated the qualitatively superior, all that was out of one's reach, and glorified everything within it. Phenomenology, Scheler believed, could provide the key to the reconstruction of ethics he so strongly desired.

Scheler was equally interested in another aspect of the crisis. The great disunity of Europe during and after World War I particularly pained him. Not only was Europe as a whole torn by war and national conflicts, his own Germany was rent by religious, political, and class conflict. As a Catholic, Scheler retained for a long while a powerful faith in Catholicism as the only great spiritual force that could both unite the people of Europe and regenerate their values. Particularly in Germany a new sense of solidarity would emerge from the moral conversion of all Germans to the common Catholic faith. Brotherhood and mutual understanding would replace general discord. In the 1920s, however, for a variety of personal as well as political reasons, Scheler began to lose hope that Catholicism would serve as a unifying force in

Germany.[1] He now turned from religion to science, and more specifically to social science as the panacea. Sociology might, he felt, illuminate the causes of the prevailing social and political cleavages. To serve his analysis, Scheler began to develop the subdiscipline of *Wissensoziologie*, the "sociology of knowledge."

Like Husserl, Scheler gives systematic attention to the question of perspectives, or perspectival knowledge; but unlike Husserl, he applies this important idea mainly to the social and cultural world. Perspectives, for Scheler, refer to one's *Standort*, one's social position, and the corresponding point of view. All social perspectives are one-sided and partial; and all social knowledge is necessarily perspectival. Therefore, social knowledge from any given perspective is partially truth and partially knowledge.

At a time when fascists, communists, social democrats, liberals, conservatives, Protestants and Catholics vied with one another for the allegiance of the German people, Scheler sought the resolution of the struggle in the sociology of knowledge and in an appeal to the political elite. Like Mannheim after him, Scheler believed that intellectuals could attain a relative detachment from political and other ideological struggles. Unattached to any specific class, the "free-floating" intellectual could explore and disclose the social sources of the various political ideologies and recognize the partial truth in each. The intellectual's task was also to lead the various groups and strata to an awareness of their ideologies. Political leaders were to be educated to recognize their own ideological prejudices as well as the validity of other points of view, and would incline them to respond more favorably to the valid demands of each group. The sociology of knowledge, for Scheler, was no mere academic discipline.

These introductory remarks might seem to suggest that Scheler was a thoroughgoing relativist regarding social knowledge and its validity. In common with Husserl, however, Scheler insisted throughout his work on absolute and certain criteria of validity. He worked out and clarified his approach to this problem—again, somewhat like Husserl—in relation to *Lebensphilosophie* and to *Weltanschauung* philosophy in general.

Lebensphilosophie, as the term indicates, was a philosophy of life. As such it repudiated both the irrelevance of German idealist philosophy to men's lives and its separation of existence from values. The new philosophy stressed that the philosopher's task is not to deal endlessly with concepts about life but to grasp life intuitively. The representatives of the new doctrine shared many characteristics with the romantic-conservative revolt of the early nineteenth century: both demoted reason and elevated the irrational; both looked to religion as the key to life, meaning, and order; both were antidemocratic, upholding the ideal of a society based on precapitalist, aristocratic principles.

Although Scheler had once been sympathetic to several of these ideas, he now found them unappealing, for they flew in the face of his recently formed view of the role of science. He now wholeheartedly adopted Max Weber's

[1] For these biographical details I have relied on John R. Staude's fine study, *Max Scheler, 1874–1928: An Intellectual Portrait* (New York: The Free Press, 1967).

position as he had made it known in his famous 1918 lecture "Science as a Vocation." Scheler agreed that the only appropriate posture for the scientist was "objectivity." He agreed that science, in Weber's words, "could not answer questions of the *value* of culture and its individual contents" nor the "question of how one should act in the cultural community and in political associations." Science could never teach values for life. Retracting his earlier antirationalist antimodernist position, Scheler turned to the principles of the Enlightenment.[2]

WELTANSCHAUUNG PHILOSOPHY

With the bewildering array of ideologies in Weimar Germany, it is perhaps little to be wondered at that the classification and analysis of *Weltanschauungen* came to be regarded as an important philosophical task. Dilthey, Weber, and other representatives of the new philosophical relativism argued that all philosophical systems reflect a limited number of world outlooks. A thinker's output can only be understood in relation to his biographical situation and as a manifestation of a specific world outlook. Intellectual and philosophical systems therefore have no absolute truth but only the partial truth grasped by the thinker from his particular standpoint.

For Scheler, this extreme relativism is totally unacceptable. He accepts the idea that there are certain basic world outlooks but criticizes Dilthey on a number of counts. Dilthey's *Weltanschauungen* are artificial, intellectual constructs that fail to grasp authentically the underlying cultural mentalities of the group or people in question.[3] These relatively natural mentalities develop organically and gradually and are self-evident to the culture's participants. Dilthey's classification is also parochial insofar as he considers only European intellectual systems. Finally, and most importantly, Scheler attacks Dilthey's relativism. Transcending all relatively natural world outlooks, there exists a constant, absolute, unchanging *Weltanschauung* that remains untouched by social conditions and historical change. This is the source of absolute validity the essence of which could be grasped phenomenologically—though not without great difficulty.

In this way Scheler sought to employ sociology and yet safeguard what he regarded as the realm of absolute validity. As social scientist he saw his task as descriptive and analytical; but in his role as philosopher, he saw it within his power and responsibility to assess the validity of *Weltanschauungen*. The realm of absolute truth is never wholly grasped by any one people; only fragments of this realm are reflected in the actual development of a culture. Each society has its unique objective conditions so that its participants have unique experiences, different from those of another society. These experiences shape the whole

---

[2] Ibid., p. 152.

[3] See Max Scheler, *Schriften zur Soziologie und Weltanschauungslehre*, Collected Works, vol. 6 (Bern and Munich: Francke Verlag, 1963) pp. 13–26.

cognitive and conceptual structure of a people, resulting in different and even contradictory "natural" world outlooks. This does not mean that the differing outlooks are false. Indeed, Scheler maintains that they could all be true—but, of course, only partially so. All view the same ultimate reality but each from his own vantage point. The validity of knowledge and its social origins are two separate issues.[4]

Just as the carriers of different *Weltanschauungen* view the world from different angles, they each partake differently of the absolute, metaphysical realm of validity. Scheler insists on the practicability of working back from the particular and concrete truths to the realm of absolute truth in which they partake. This realm, with its absolute hierarchy of values (a vestige of his abandoned Catholicism), remains a key article of faith throughout the development of Scheler's own peculiar conception of the social determination of ideas.

SOCIOLOGY OF KNOWLEDGE: COMTE AND DURKHEIM

Scheler believed that his own *Wissensoziologie* corrected fundamental errors in the work of the pioneers in this area—Comte, Marx and Durkheim. According to Scheler, Comte and his followers believed naively that religion and metaphysics would be superseded once and for all by science and positive philosophy. Scheler unmasks Comte's positivism[5] as an ideology that glorified the interests and achievements of bourgeois capitalism. Accordingly, Comte uncritically accepted the bourgeois prejudice that scientific and technical-industrial knowledge was most valuable while other forms of knowing, such as the religious and the metaphysical, were increasingly obsolete. This is Comte's well-known law of progress, from the theological age to the metaphysical age and from there to the highest and ultimate stage—the scientific-positive polity.

Scheler finds this doctrine objectionable, even offensive, arguing that Comte failed to recognize the independent validity of religious and metaphysical knowledge; along with scientific knowledge, they are permanent attributes of social life. The distinct forms of knowing are characteristic of types of men: the religious type seeks contact with the divine, the metaphysician speculates, and the scientist employs strict rules of logic and observation.

Moreover, Comte was wrong to posit cumulative progress for all types of knowledge. Only scientific-technical knowledge may be regarded as cumulative and progressive in the sense of later discoveries superseding earlier. The other types of knowledge have an enduring validity and are not rendered passé by

[4] Max Scheler, *Die Wissenformen und die Gesellschaft,* Collected Works, vol. 8 (Bern and Munich: Francke Verlag, 1960), p. 26. In addition, I have relied on Staude's exposition in *Max Scheler,* p. 158f.
[5] Scheler, *Schriften zur Soziologie,* p. 29f.

social change. Every people in every epoch makes cultural contributions that retain their validity despite the historical changes that a society undergoes.

On the other hand, Scheler accepts the notion of stages from Comte. In fact, he also discerns three main stages in history, but they are fundamentally different from Comte's:

> 1. A phase in which *blood relationships* of every kind and the institutions that rationally govern them . . . form the *independent* variable of events, and blood relationships determine even the *organizational form* of groups; that is they determine the *scope* of what can happen from other causes of a real sort, for example political and economic.
> 2. A phase in which this causal primacy—understood in the same limited sense of the determination of scope—passes over to the factors of *political* power, in the first place to the efficacy of the *state*.
> 3. A phase in which *economy* receives the causal primacy and the "economic factors" determine real events, though for intellectual history they merely open and close the sluice gates of the spirit.[6]

These stages are the manifestations of an immanent tendency that would be even more evident than it is were it not for its disturbance by external influences. Each stage is governed by what Scheler calls *Realfaktoren*, i.e., the *"racial,"* the *political*, and the *economic*. The racial was the first such factor that determined the structure of society and also selected the appropriate spiritual elements. The sense of Scheler's term "race" may best be inferred from his example of India, where the origins of the caste system, he suggests, may be traced to the conquest of the original dark-colored population by the light-skinned Aryans. This real factor also regulated the "sluice gates," accepting and rejecting the spiritual elements contributing to the peculiarly Brahmanic form of religion and culture.

The dominance of the racial or blood factor was evident in Europe when kinship was the main principle of social organization. This was eventually supplanted by the second stage, during which the state emerges as the center of power, subjecting racially different groups to its rule. For centuries the political factor enjoyed hegemony and subordinated others.

Only in the third and final stage does the economic factor acquire causal priority. This is the age of capitalism, the only age in respect to which one may justifiably speak of the dominance of a positive, scientific view (as did Comte) and of the determining influence of the mode of material production or of the economic system (as did Marx). Here, particularly, Scheler's thesis is polemical, directed against both Comte and Marx, whom he sees as committing the error of elevating to a universal status a principle that applies only to a definite stage.

Scheler also acknowledges that the succession of *Realfaktoren* may be regarded as "progress," but only in a very limited sense. Men in the modern age

[6] Scheler, *Die Wissenformen*, pp. 44–45. Quoted and translated by Staude, *Max Scheler*, p. 175.

are not better, for they have not achieved greater goodness or beauty. The only respect in which they have surpassed their forebears is in the mastery of natural forces, but this does not necessarily bring with it, as the positivists believed, moral, artistic, or other advantages. Modern culture, Scheler maintains, is neither better nor deeper but simply broader, in that it possesses greater spiritual potentialities than ever before. The epoch in which the predominantly economic factor prevails is also the age when the "sluice gates" open widest and thus inhibit the spiritual potential least. Spiritual culture is not more valuable or greater in this period but rather richer, more variegated. At the same time men's consciousness has a potentially greater influence on the course of historical developments.[7]

In these terms we can see why Scheler had also to reject Durkheim's positivistic sociology of knowledge. For Durkheim, the most fundamental categories of thought, e.g., time, space, class, number, cause, substance, force—in short, the entire cognitive structure of men's minds—are all derived from the structure of society. The contents of minds, *collective representations,* also depend on their underlying social structures. Indeed, Durkheim dissolves the sacred and divine so that they become merely social. God and society are one, for Durkheim, because what people call God is actually the symbolic manifestation of the powers of society. Each man is right in believing that there exists a power greater than himself, for this is the "moral power upon which he depends and from which he receives all that is best in himself: this power exists, it is society."[8]

This view, which rejects the independent validity of religious and metaphysical experience and knowledge, is unacceptable to Scheler. Scheler finds both Comte's and Durkheim's theories offensive because their positivistic method obscured from their view a certain kind of experiential knowledge that only the phenomenological method can yield. Both Comte and Durkheim failed to grasp the intentionality of religious acts and beliefs. One does not really grasp the authentic meaning of these acts unless one sees that they are directed to God, not society. Grasped essentially, religion can never be reduced to the social.[9]

SCHELER AND MARX

We saw earlier that Scheler's real factors include "blood," political power, and the economy, each enjoying hegemony in a definite epoch. It follows from this that Marx's so-called "materialist conception of history" and particularly

[7] Scheler, *Die Wissenformen*, p. 51.
[8] Emile Durkheim, *The Elementary Forms of the Religious Life* (New York: The Free Press, 1964), p. 225.
[9] Scheler, *Schriften zur Soziologie*, p. 30.

the great determining influence he assigns to economic interests and developments, applies only to capitalism, not to previous epochs. Scheler thus accepts the partial validity of Marx's theory but charges him with having elevated it to the rank of a universal law, valid for all times and places. (And Staude appears to accept Scheler's interpretation of Marx uncritically, for he writes that Marx erroneously "assumed the *independent variable* to be one and the same throughout history").[10]

This interpretation indicates that Scheler was not a careful student of Marx, for Marx most definitely was not laying down a general or universal historical law when he spoke of developing productive forces coming in conflict with existing relations of production, or when he described the process of primitive accumulation and capitalist development. Marx emphasized throughout the historically specific character of his laws, intending his generalizations to apply not to all societies and all periods but to Western Europe and particularly England in a definite era.

In *Capital*, in the chapter "The So-called Primitive Accumulation," Marx writes: "Although we come across the first beginnings of capitalist production as early as the fourteenth or fifteenth century, sporadically, in certain towns of the Mediterranean, the capitalistic era dates from the sixteenth century. . . . The history of this expropriation, in different countries, assumes different aspects, and runs through its various phases in different orders of succession, and at different periods. In England alone, which we take as our example, has it the classic form."[11]

Further evidence that Marx intended his conception to be understood as historically specific may be found in his correspondence. Marx quite forcefully dissociated himself from the attempt to transform his emphasis, which was accurate under certain historical circumstances, into a universal principle. In a letter to Mikhailovsky, Marx rejects the latter's attempt to present his sketch of the origins of capitalism in Western Europe as if it were a suprahistorical theory "of the general path every people is fated to tread, whatever the historical circumstances in which it finds itself. . . . But I beg his pardon. (He is both honoring and shaming me too much.)"[12] Similarly, in another letter, clarifying what he meant by "historical inevitability," Marx writes: "Hence the 'historical inevitability' of this movement [the genesis and development of capitalism] is *expressly* limited to the countries of Western Europe."[13]

To return to Scheler's own conception, his so-called real factors determine only the possible forms mental production might take, not the actual forms. The actualization of possibilities depends on the selection of ideas by the ruling interests or perspectives—that is, by the ruling class or elite.[14] It is not in terms

[10] Staude, *Max Scheler*, p. 176.
[11] Karl Marx, *Capital* (Moscow: Foreign Languages Publishing House, 1954), 1:715–16.
[12] Karl Marx and Frederick Engels, *Selected Correspondence* (Moscow: Foreign Languages Publishing House, 1953), p. 379.
[13] Ibid., p. 412.
[14] Scheler, *Die Wissenformen*, p. 58.

of interests alone, however, that ruling groups select ideas, but also on the basis of instinctual drives. Only when ideas are combined with interests and drives can they become effective; failing this, ideas remain impotent and unrealized.

Scheler thus agrees with Marx that social being determines social consciousness, but in his scheme *ideal* and *real* factors codetermine thought and knowledge. As Staude aptly observes, this attempt "to integrate idealistic and Marxist interpretations revealed Scheler's heritage; he insisted on preserving the 'eternal essences' of his phenomenological period. These essences were independent of social determination; they were ideal factors in that they were supposed to exist according to their own laws. On the other hand, they could only be realized when men perceived them, and the perception of the ideal realm was determined by the 'ruling perspective of social interests.' "[15]

Thus, as a number of Scheler's critics have noted, his formulation, if taken literally, presents us with an unbridgeable dualism. For Scheler never makes clear how his substructure, which is powerful but blind, can select ideas that are in and of themselves radically separated from being and hence impotent. It is ironic that Scheler, for whom the preservation of the absolute validity of ideas was a paramount goal, reduces mental productions to mere epiphenomena.

KNOWLEDGE AND IDEOLOGY

Throughout his *Die Wissenformen* Scheler seeks to establish and preserve the distinction between valid knowledge and ideology. Here, too, he sees himself refuting what he regards as a Marxian premise that all thought is ideological—though his criticism is more applicable to some of Marx's disciples than to Marx himself.

That one's class position influences one's thinking, Scheler readily acknowledges; he argues, however, that only objects of thinking and certain basic propensities are so influenced, not content. The lower classes, for example, allegedly emphasize becoming, and hold a generally mechanistic, materialistic, pragmatic, and optimistic world-view; while the upper classes stress being, and hold a more teleological, spiritualistic, and pessimistic outlook. These general propensities, of which men are most often unconscious, the intellectual has the special responsibility of bringing to light. The main instrument through which he can accomplish this is the sociology of knowledge: only by becoming aware of the class-determined forms and inclinations that shape one's thought can one free oneself from such influences and thereby achieve objectivity—a sine qua non of the pursuit of truth.

In this respect, if we disregard his tenacious belief in metaphysical transcendental truth, Scheler's approach to the problem of acquiring valid knowledge is not unlike that of Edmund Husserl, Max Weber, and Karl

[15] Staude, *Max Scheler*, p. 174.

Mannheim. Husserl, we will recall, put forward his method of phenomenological reduction precisely in order to attain certain and valid knowledge. The ideal could be most closely approximated through reflection, as opposed to uncritical thinking. In reflection, one "stands back" and disengages oneself from the situation. Recognizing one's own interests and commitment, one "overcomes" them by mentally neutralizing them and by adopting the perspectives of the relevant others. In this way one not only looks at the world from a different angle but also gains additional knowledge—new facts and dimensions of the situation. As for Weber, we have already seen in several other connections that Weber's conception of "ethical neutrality" and "objectivity" is not one in which scientific man becomes an Olympian god, raising himself above society and its conflicts of interests and values. Objectivity is rather an attitude or posture most befitting the social role of scientist or scholar, an ideal towards which one should strive. Only by becoming aware of the value and interest relevance that certain problems, issues, or ideas have for the scholar (*Wertbeziehung*) could one begin to "free" oneself from the influence of those values and interests. By neutralizing them, one achieves a degree of *Wertfreiheit*. For Weber, as for Husserl and Scheler, this process also entailed the adopting of a variety of perspectives with respect to the situation in question.

Karl Mannheim, who, one should add, was influenced by all three of these thinkers, also made a significant effort to preserve the boundary between valid knowledge and mere ideology. His concept of "relational" knowledge, his insistence that the social determination of knowledge and its validity are two separate questions, and, finally, the special role he assigned to "relatively unattached intellectuals," all attest to that effort.

It may now be instructive to return to Scheler's allegation that for Marx all social thought was ideology—the implication being that Marx was uninterested in knowledge or truth. In fact, Marx's conception of class ideologies or class-interested perspectives no more precluded valid knowledge than did Weber's, Mannheim's, Husserl's, or Scheler's.

That Marx believed he could distinguish between scientific knowledge and mere ideology, and that the distinction was important, is indisputable. In *Capital*, his chief work, for example, it is clear that he thinks of himself as engaging in scientific analysis. To understand the "laws of motion" of the capitalist system it is necessary both to overcome the inadequacies of classical political economy and to expose its ideological elements. In Marx's view, English political economy achieved a high degree of objectivity, but only for the period when the conflict between capital and labor was as yet undeveloped. Ricardo, he states, was the last great representative of that tradition, for after him the class struggle became more intense in both France and England and

> took on more and more outspoken and threatening forms. It sounded the knell of scientific bourgeois economy. *It was thenceforth no longer a question whether this theorem or that was true, but whether it was useful*

> *to capital or harmful, expedient or inexpedient, politically dangerous or not. In place of disinterested inquirers, there were hired prizefighters; in place of genuine scientific research, the bad conscience and the evil intent of apologetic.*[16]

Thus Marx decries the increasingly ideological character of postclassical political economy.

The above-quoted passage merely states unequivocally what the careful reader of *Capital* could never doubt: that Marx's intention is scientific, not ideological. His choice of words, which contrasts "genuine scientific research" with "evil intent of apologetic," is indicative. Equally interesting for our purposes is Marx's use of the phrase "disinterested inquirers" as opposed to "hired prizefighters"; it suggests that the pursuit of truth requires some disinterestedness. Before the class struggle had reached a severe pitch, Marx is saying, political economists could disinterest themselves more easily; however, with the intensification of class conflict, such a stance became more and more difficult until scientific analysis was replaced with class-interested thinking, or ideology.

One might therefore ask whether Marx regarded himself in *Capital*, say, as a "disinterested inquirer," and in what sense. If, as he believed, political economy had degenerated from a science into an ideology, largely as a result of the uncurbed domination of thought by class values and interests, then at least one methological conclusion clearly followed: science could be rescued from ideology only by curbing those class interests and values and systematically excluding their influence from one's analysis. Marx thus saw that he had to lay bare the extremely partial, one-sided, and justificatory nature of the prevailing doctrines while simultaneously developing an alternative analysis. By peeling away the old categories, indeed by seeing through them, he could begin to view the phenomena in question through "new eyes."

Nothing in Marx's work or method suggests that he would have opposed in principle the subjecting of his own system to the same critical treatment he gave others. Nor was Marx's "disinterestedness" one-directional. As we know, he methodically detached himself not only from what he saw as bourgeois ideology and error, but also from a variety of socialist analyses and programs which he deemed ideological and erroneous.

As for Scheler's own methodological advocacy of disengagement, it is not clear from what he disinterested and disengaged himself. His sociology of knowledge was rather consciously designed as a manipulative instrument of the ruling elite. Thanks to Scheler's doctrine, the elite would see the partial truth in all the major social perspectives, and incorporate them in a social program that would win the allegiance of all social classes—thus presumably conducing to the social order and unity Scheler so strongly craved.

---

[16] Marx, *Capital*, 1:15, italics added.

SCHELER'S PHILOSOPHICAL ANTHROPOLOGY

In Scheler's last work, *Man's Place in Nature,*[17] we encounter many themes familiar from his earlier writings that Scheler intended as the grounding for his "philosophical anthropology." Scheler retains, in this essay, his intense metaphysical interests and deals in mainly philosophical terms with the question he has set for himself: In what does the uniqueness of man consist? Answering this question, he fashions his own phenomenological conception of man.

Scheler opens his work by noting that there is a sense in which one may justifiably speak of a psychophysical life not only in man but also in animals and even in plants. The differences, of course, are fundamental, and an exploration of these differences can help to clarify the uniqueness of man's psychophysical being.

For Scheler, the most rudimentary form of "psychic" life is found in plants and is manifest in drives and impulses that direct the organism's vital processes. In these terms plants have a "psychic" function but, to the best of our knowledge, have no consciousness or sensation. Plants lack an "inner life in any sense" (9).

Plants have no *center*, as do animals, to which to report their organic states. They are uniquely oriented only to the outside—a condition Scheler calls "ecstatic," to denote that their state is beyond reason and self-control. Lacking also the communicative ability of animals, plants can neither free themselves from the immediate environment nor pioneer and follow by "setting an example and imitating" (12). Thus plants have a "psychic" function that regulates their relations with both the inorganic environment and the animate world of insects and birds, but no inner life, no nerve center, no communication.

In contrast, all animals, including man, share what Scheler calls the "first stage of inner life," that is, vital feelings, drives, or impulses. These are at work whether the organism is asleep or awake and account at least partially for the attention given to external stimuli: "Even the simplest sensation," writes Scheler, "is not merely the response to a stimulus, but always the function of a drive-motivated attention" (13). This vital feeling inevitably experiences *resistance* and it is through this primary experience that the organism feels "reality."

The second stage, Scheler suggests, becomes evident with instinctual behavior. Recognizing the vagueness of the concept "instinct," he provides a rather precise definition:

1. Instincts facilitate the nourishment and reproduction of the organism in question or of another organism, as in the case of the mother providing for the child.

2. Instinctual behavior manifests "a definite unchanging rhythm" (15).

---

[17] Max Scheler, *Man's Place in Nature*, trans. with an introduction by Hans Meyerhoff (New York: Noonday Press, 1969). Page references to this book will be cited in parentheses immediately following the quoted passage.

The rhythmic pattern is not acquired through learning or habit but is nonetheless directed to present and even future needs and states (e.g., provision of food for the winter) "as if" the organism actually anticipated the future.

3. Instinctual behavior ultimately serves not only the individual members of the species but contributes to the survival of the species itself. Instinctual behavior is typical of the species, a response to "typically recurrent situations which are significant for the life of the species . . . " (16). Hence the "rigidity" of instincts that continue to guide well when specific environmental factors have changed, but that display error, confusion, and disturbance when the *structure* of a typical environmental pattern changes.

4. Instinctual behavior is "innate and hereditary" in that individual members of the species inherit not only a general capacity but "specific modes of behavior" (17). Scheler goes on to remind us that innateness need not mean that the instinct is already present at birth; it may be coordinated with definite stages of growth and development.

5. Finally, instinct is "complete from the outset." What Scheler means here is that the hunting instinct, for example, is inherited, "but not the skill to do so successfully." Instincts, in short, determine and control the organism and whatever habits or learning the organism acquires do not change the basic workings of the instinct.

Out of instinctual behavior there emerge the higher third and fourth forms of psychic life, the "habitual" and the "intelligent." The habitual is characterized by trial and error and "associative memory." Here the organism has a certain capacity for spontaneous behavior, which eventually results in the "fixing" of patterns yielding gratification. This can come about either by means of "self-training" or, when man intervenes, by "conditioned training." Imitation and reproductive memory also make "tradition" possible among animals at this stage, although, of course, this must be sharply distinguished from the kind of tradition characteristic of man. In the case of herds and packs and other social forms of animal life, "the herd learns from the example set by the pioneers and passes its knowledge on to coming generations" (26).

The fourth stage of psychic life, called "practical intelligence," enables the organism to solve concrete problems not encountered earlier in its life history and to make choices, whether these be among material things or among fellow members of the species. Intelligence involves the ability to use both experience and "anticipatory representation" to cope with new situations. With the term "practical intelligence," Scheler wants to underscore that this stage involves a genuine act of discovery, the result of neither instinct or habit on the one hand, nor the conscious reflection unique to man, on the other. Animals at this stage, then, can choose, and can intervene spontaneously in their drives even to the point of deferring gratification; in their affects they are even closer to man, for they show "the capacity for generosity, help, reconciliation, friendship, and similar phenomena" (34).

THE UNIQUENESS OF MAN

Having laid the groundwork for distinguishing man from all other animals, Scheler presents his own view of man, which he develops in opposition to two others. The one denies intelligence and choice to animals, seeing these attributes as uniquely human; while the other, Darwinism in particular, sees only a quantitative difference between man and other animals. For Scheler, both positions are wrong: the second view denies the uniqueness of man, while the first locates it in the wrong place.

With man a new quality emerges that does not belong to the merely psychic and vital functions. Therefore this quality cannot be comprehended by psychology and biology. Humanity is based on a new principle that not only transcends "life" but is even "opposed to life as such, even to life in man" (36). The new principle Scheler calls "spirit"—which includes what the Greeks called reason

> but which, in addition to conceptual thought, also includes the intuition of essences and a class of voluntary and emotional acts such as kindness, love, remorse, reverence, wonder, bliss, despair and free decision. The center of action in which spirit appears within a finite mode of being we call "person" in sharp contrast to all functional vital centers which, from an inner perspective, may be called "psychic centers" (36–37).

Spirit, Scheler emphasizes, has achieved a qualitatively new emancipation from both its own biological drives and the external environment. Scheler's favorite expression in this regard is that spirit is "free from the environment," and "open to the world" (37). The animal always remains "ecstatically" immersed in nature, either his own or the external one. This Scheler illustrates diagrammatically:

A (animal) $\rightleftharpoons$ E (environment)

In contrast, spirit's "liberation" from the cycle is unique and takes the form of

M (man) $\rightleftharpoons$ W (world) ──────→ ──────→

The animal lives in the environment; but man is able to detach himself so that he transforms the "environment" into the "world" and into "objects." The animal remains bound by nature; while man and only man has the capacity for a "world openness," "self-consciousness," and "objectification." Man has the ability to objectify not only external natural forces, but also his own psychic and physical states to the point where they oppose life. "It is for this reason that this being [spirit] can also throw his life away freely" (40). Scheler's concept of "spirit" and particularly its center, which he calls "person," and which achieves self-consciousness, is parallel to what James and Mead called the "social self." "Person," for Scheler, "must be envisaged as the center of acts raised beyond the interaction and contrast between organism and environment" (42). Similarly, Scheler's concepts of "objectification" and "self-consciousness" parallel conceptualization, symbolization, and the reflexive self—as well as Marx's conception of alienation, as we shall see in a later context.

Only man, Scheler argues, creates "categories of thing and substance" (43). The ape recognizes a "thing" only in certain forms directly related to his drives; indeed, the whole banana, which he readily recognizes, frightens him when it is half-peeled. Man, in contrast, can coordinate all his senses and conceptual ability and thus grasp that his seeing, hearing, smelling, etc., refer to "a unity belonging to one and the same concrete object" (43).

Equally important is the related ability in man to intuit space and time, and then to employ these as abstract categories with which to order the things about him. Man is able, in short, to liberate himself from "the concrete actuality of [his] immediate present" (45). He alone is able to transcend both his organic nature and the spatiotemporal world and to make everything, including himself, "into an object of knowledge" (46).

Finally, Scheler suggests, man is capable of objectifying everything except spirit. For spirit "is pure actuality. It has being only in and through the execution of its acts. The center of spirit, the person, is not an object or a substantial kind of being, but a continuously self-executing, ordered structure of acts" (47). Moreover, the essential characteristic of the form of being we call person is that *it can never become an object either to itself or to others.* This requires explanation.

Since the very being and only being of a "person" is the actual process of his action, he cannot simultaneously act and treat himself as an object. The "person" in these terms can capture his acts only after they have been completed. Through reflection he can, after the fact, treat his acts as psychic objects, but not during the process of the action itself. The same logic applies to interaction among persons. We communicate with other persons and understand them "only by participating in, or by entering into, their free acts, through the kind of 'understanding' possible in an attitude of empathic love, the very opposite of objectification . . . " (48). This important idea we shall encounter again in Mead's distinction between two dimensions of the social self, the "I" and the "Me."

"Persons" are therefore the dynamic spiritual centers, the pure acting subjects, of man's intersubjective world. The "world" is intersubjective, not objective, since it is not an already finished world of being and ideas that we discover existing independently of our actions, but, quite to the contrary, "a genuine co-creation" of the world. And although Scheler retains his transcendental bias, adding that this co-creation is "coordinated with the eternal logos, the eternal love and the eternal will," his conception of spirit, person, and intersubjectivity can stand independently of that bias. For he emphasizes that man's characteristic capacity to distinguish existence from essence, his capacity for apriori knowledge is no "permanent structure of reason, as Kant believed. On the contrary, this structure is always subject to historical change" (51).

SPIRIT AS ANTI-LIFE

Another important idea in Scheler, not altogether original with him, is that man is the only being who can say "No!" Spirit can deny and even destroy life. Scheler recognized what many present-day social psychologists and sociologists deny or ignore—namely, that man's spiritual (sociocultural) being inevitably entails an ascetic attitude toward his vital drives and a repression of them. He agreed with Freud that spirit takes its energy from repressed drives, which it sublimates into spiritual activity. But he differed with Freud in one important respect.

In Scheler's *Wissensoziologie* he insists on two essential characteristics of spirit: its autonomy and its impotence. This view he developed in opposition to both the classical Judeao-Christian and Greek traditions, on the one hand, and the materialist tradition, on the other. For the classic tradition spirit was not only autonomous but active and powerful: the more spiritual the being, the more powerful it was, the hierarchy culminating in the purely spiritual and omnipotent God. The materialists, in contrast,—the exponents of what Scheler calls the "negative theory," lumping together Epicurus, Hobbes, Machiavelli, La Mettrie, Schopenhauer, Marx, and Freud—deny all autonomy to the spirit.

Scheler rejects both theories and maintains, instead, that spirit is autonomous but also impotent. Concentrating his fire on Freud, Scheler argues that Freud attributes all of man's culturally creative activities to his capacity for repression, a view that denies spiritual autonomy. Rather, Scheler argues, repression does not create the spirit itself, which always exists in the form of pure powerless intentionality. Repression simply provides the energy for spiritual activity that spirit in and of itself does not possess.

Thus, while Scheler recognizes that the process of civilizing, socializing, or humanizing exacts a substantial toll from the vital organism, he also clings tenaciously to his older idea of an autonomous powerless spirit deriving its energy from powerful but blind "real factors," in this case repressed vital urges. His insistence on this dichotomous view of spirit and matter appears to be a corollary of his conception of history, in which elites (spirit) become powerful only by harnessing the energy of the masses (matter).

For Scheler the "person" is neither a spatial nor a temporal entity but rather pure intentionality, whose being nevertheless intersects with life. In this respect he approaches an important idea but falls short of developing it as effectively and systematically as did George Herbert Mead.

12

The Phenomenological Dimension in Max Weber

Weber's conception of sociology, as is known, may be viewed as an effort to mediate between the two opposing intellectual standpoints that prevailed in Germany in his time. The adherents of the first position, greatly impressed with the successes of the physical sciences, maintained that their methods would also lead to great advances in the study of man and society. The adherents of the second view insisted, in contrast, that what was really important about man—his spirit, mind, culture, and history—could never be grasped through natural science techniques, for these are superficial and deal only with the external aspects of man.

Psychologism, positivism, and later behaviorism were the principal manifestations of the first standpoint, in opposition to which Husserl and Scheler, as we have seen, developed their respective phenomenological approaches. *Weltanschauungsphilosophie* and historicism were examples of the second standpoint, with which the names of Dilthey, Windelband, and Rickert are associated. These thinkers stressed that the uniqueness of the human spirit requires special methods to enable one to grasp it authentically. Only sympathetic intuition and a concern with meaning can yield an adequate understanding of culture and history.

For Max Weber, understanding the sociocultural world does indeed demand specific methods with which to grasp the motives and meanings of men's acts. In these terms, sociology is a science that concerns itself with interpreting and sympathetically understanding human actions. Sociological explanations have therefore to be adequate at the level of meaning. This does not mean, however, Weber emphasizes, that sociology should or must abandon the quest for causal connections among social phenomena. A concern with causal explanation and generalization is common to all sciences, Weber maintains, and ought to be a major concern of the social sciences as well. In this way Weber seeks to salvage what is important in the two opposing standpoints.

The human condition is such that no science truly comes to terms with it that ignores either meaning or causality. Sociology is therefore to be a science that comes equally to grips with the subjective meanings men attribute to their actions and with the objective causes and consequences of these actions—bearing in mind that meaning itself is a causal component of action. Hence, Weber's well-known definition of action as " 'social' insofar as its subjective meaning takes account of the behavior of others and is thereby oriented in its course."[1] Ideally, sociology has therefore to provide explanations adequate on two levels: on the level on meaning and on the level of causality.

The term "subjective" as Weber employs it in his definition is important. For it distinguishes him at once both from those who ignore meaning in the study of man and from those who believe in objectively valid and true meanings. Whether ethics, aesthetics, or other branches of culture, their validity and truth are not determined for Weber, as they are for Scheler, by metaphysical transcendental standards. For Weber, "subjective" refers to the meaning the actors themselves attribute to their acts, which meaning the sociologist should strive to understand.

Weber's social world is therefore an intersubjective one, as it is for the phenomenologists. Empathy, sympathy, intuition, and intentionality are all essential, Weber holds, "for clarity and verifiable accuracy of insight and comprehension (*Evidenz*)" (5). Since action ranges from the highly rational to the highly emotional, verifiable understanding may be rationally analytical, emotionally empathetic, or artistically appreciative. Weber is accordingly amenable to employing intuitive techniques involving one in identification with the actors in question and in sympathetic participation in their emotions. This is a form of understanding appropriate to the situation.

But understanding may also be appropriately cold and analytical, as when one follows mathematical or other logical reasoning, or when one observes the scientist carrying out the steps of an experiment. In these cases the meaning of the actions is grasped with relative ease and clarity. Similarly, the conduct of men in the economic world is rendered understandable when one knows what ends they are pursuing and with what means. This Weber calls rational action, and it constitutes one of the four major ideal-types of action that he regards as analytically useful.

When we, as outside observers, know men's goals and purposes, we can assess the efficacy of the means they employ to achieve those purposes. We may even be able to perceive the "costs" of their pursuing some ends instead of others. The ideal-typical form of this rational mentality Weber calls *zweck-rationales Handeln*, or rational-purposeful action. As a general orientation it is

[1] Max Weber, *Economy and Society*, ed. Guenther Roth and Claus Wittich, 3 vols. (New York: Bedminster Press, 1968), 1:4. Page references to this work are hereafter cited in parentheses immediately following the quoted passage.

based on the assumption that in specified circumstances humans behave in predictable ways. The rational model of action also enables us to understand nonrational actions, conceived as departures from the ideal type.

By asking what would be the most rational course of action for an actor in a specific situation; and by knowing his aims and the actual means he is employing; and, finally, by observing the consequences of his actions, we can: assess the degree to which the actor has departed from the rational norms; determine what the consequences might have been had the actor not departed from the norms; and, finally, determine whether and in what measure the nonrational actions contributed to the outcome. This ideal-type thus becomes a valuable analytical device by means of which we might provide explanations of actions that are both meaningfully and causally adequate.

There is, however, another form of rationality, which Weber calls *wertrationales Handeln* (value-rational action). In this type the actor has an overwhelming commitment to ultimate ends or values, which he pursues relentlessly without regard for the cost that such a singleminded pursuit entails. Understanding such action is easier the more similar such ultimate ends are to one's own. In the study of such conduct we must be particularly careful to prevent our own values from intruding, for they could cause us to dismiss exceedingly zealous acts, whether religious, political, or whatever, as irrational fanaticism.

This form of rationality shades into the emotional or, in Weber's terms, into *affectual* action. This type is also an important heuristic aid in grasping the variety and complexity of human actions. For the affectual as for the value-rational, empathy and sympathetic intuition may be essential; and such empathy is less difficult the "more we ourselves are susceptible to such emotional reactions as anxiety, anger, ambition, envy, jealousy, love, enthusiasm, pride, vengefulness, loyalty, devotion," and the like (6). And even if we, as observers, are not subject to these emotions with the same intensity as the actors themselves, we can gain "a significant degree of emotional understanding of their meaning and can interpret intellectually their influence on the course of action and the selection of means" (6).

Weber's fourth and final pure type of action that can be grasped in terms of the subjective meaning of the actor, he calls *traditional* action. Certain definite ways and practices have become so ingrained and habitual that they may not be meaningfully oriented actions at all. This type would therefore include actions ranging from the self-conscious but habitual, to the quasi-automatic repetitive responses to customary stimuli. Traditionalism in the widest sense includes the "great bulk of everyday action" (25), the realm of phenomena on which Alfred Schütz centered attention (as we shall see in Chapter 13).

It should be clear, then, that Weber's concept of understanding is *not* to be equated strictly with sympathetic intuition. It is a wide concept, ranging from the rationally analytical at one end to the intuitive-empathic on the other. The social world is an intersubjective world of meaning; the social world is the process of meaningful and symbolic interaction among living, acting men.

Under no circumstances, Weber emphasizes, should the concept "intersubjectivity" be taken to mean that the relationships among men have no objective consequences for them. For these relationships do, of course, affect the quality of their being, their "life-chances," even whether they shall live or die. The intersubjective world assumes, in certain historical circumstances, an "objective" quality so that men act and follow patterns "as if" these patterns were totally independent of men's will, "as if" the patterns were iron inexorable laws. To understand this phenomenon one must study history, economics, social stratification, relations of power and domination, etc., as in fact Weber did.

Weber also stresses that his definition of social action should not be taken erroneously to mean that the sociologist may safely ignore things apparently devoid of meaning, whether these be human or nonhuman. There are conditions and events that have no meaning as either means or ends of action, but that nonetheless stimulate, favor, or hinder action. These conditions have sociological relevance insofar as they are phenomena to which human beings orient themselves. Because such phenomena are data for the social actors, they must also be taken into account by the sociologist.

Finally, a concern with the actors' subjective meanings must not be construed to imply that the actors are always conscious of their intentions and purposes. Weber's typology of action explicitly allows for a considerable range of awareness within the conscious-unconscious dichotomy. Nor, certainly, should a concern with meaning lead one to ignore the fact that the actors' actions entail consequences that they did not intend and of which they are unaware. Indeed, in this area the social scientist may make a most important contribution; he alone may be equipped to see what the direct participants do not see—the drama working itself out beyond their gaze.

13

The Intersubjective World of Everyday Life: The Ideas of Alfred Schütz

In his major work, *The Meaningful Structure of the Social World*, Alfred Schütz sought to trace some of the main concepts of social science to their roots in the fundamental characteristics of consciousness, pointing thereby to a connection between Weber's *verstehende Soziologie* and Husserl's transcendental phenomenology. Among Schütz's central concerns, however, here as well as in his other writings, are a critique of naturalism, a critical reflection on conscious life, and an understanding of signs, symbols, and ideas. The influence of Husserl is evident throughout, notably his theory of intentionality and his conceptions of intersubjectivity and *Lebenswelt*.

The social world of everyday life, Schütz tells us, is always an intersubjective one. This is the world I share with my fellowmen, with others, who also experience and interpret it. My world is therefore never wholly private; even in my consciousness I find evidence of others, evidence that my unique biographical situation is not wholly the product of my own actions. Each of us is born into a historically given world that is simultaneously natural and sociocultural. The world existed before I came into it and will continue to exist long after I am gone. Each of us is an element in the life situation of others, just as they are in ours. I act upon them and they act upon me, and we all experience our common world in a similar fashion. Our experience of this everyday world is a common-sense one, for each of us takes for granted that our fellow men exist, that they have a conscious life, that we can communicate with them, and, finally, that they live in the same natural, historically given, sociocultural world as we do.[1]

---

[1] Alfred Schütz, *The Problem of Social Reality,* Collected Papers, vol. 1 (The Hague: Martinus Nijhoff, 1967). Page references will be cited in parentheses immediately following the quoted passage.

KNOWLEDGE OF OTHERS

Schütz spells out the essentials of the common-sense, taken-for-granted, everyday world—an elaboration of Husserl's *Lebenswelt*. He employs as well Husserl's notion of appresentation to explain how we come to know others and communicate with them. Only the other's body is presented to me, not his mind. His conscious life is appresented, not presented. My consciousness receives indications of his conscious life and experiences mainly by visual perception of his body, his actions, and the actions of others upon him. These well-ordered indications Husserl calls a system of appresentations, which, in turn, he regards as the source of sign systems and, ultimately, of language. In short, we grasp the physical body of the other as expressing his "spiritual I"—a concept roughly equivalent to Scheler's "person" and the symbolic interactionists' "self." It is towards this "I" and its motivational meaning that each of us directs his actions. When we say, for example, that we are in empathy with an other, it is the same as saying we have grasped his meaning through appresentation.

This process is not unlike the one in which we find meaning in any cultural object, whether this be a book, a tool, a house, or what-have-you. When I read a book it is clearly not to the book as material object that I orient myself, but to its meaning. It is the spiritual meaning of the object that we appresentationally apperceive and not its actual appearance. We constitute the object in accordance with the meaning it has for us. Similarly, in face-to-face interaction it is not the words merely as external sounds that we hear as we listen to someone talking, but rather words as vehicles of meaning that enable us to comprehend him.

RECIPROCITY OF PERSPECTIVES

When Schütz speaks of the microworld of "face-to-face" interaction, he also uses terms like "world within my actual reach" and "world within my manipulatory zone." The concepts, if not the actual words, are also employed by William James and George Herbert Mead.

This microworld, the sector that comes within my actual reach and becomes my Here, is not the same as that which comes within your reach; that is, your Here is my There. True, our worlds may overlap, so that some things and events may be within the manipulatory zone of both of us. Yet the objects and events will appear differently from our respective standpoints as to their "direction, distance, perspective, adumbration, etc. ... " (315). The common-sense, taken-for-granted attitude we share is that we could exchange places and that if we did so each would then see the world just as the other did previously.

Of course, this applies not only to spatial but also to sociocultural perspectives. The biographical situation of each of us is unique. It follows that our purposes and systems of relevances must differ. Nevertheless, both of us assume that despite our private purposes and systems, "we" interpret our common world in an "identical" manner. The typifying constructs we share (words, symbols, and concepts) enable us to go beyond our private worlds into a common one.

Schütz reminds us, however, that the thesis of "interchangeability of standpoints" is an idealization—even in the relatively simple microworld. For although it is true that we can often reciprocally exchange our standpoints and, hence, our perspectives, at least for practical purposes, there is also some inevitable transcendence of each other's worlds. Even the members of the most intimate dyad share only a limited sector of their unique biographies. Each enters the relationship with only a fragment of his personality, that is, by assuming a specific role. Their respective systems of relevance, resulting from their biographically unique situations, can never be totally congruent; Ego can never make Alter's system of relevance really his own, he can merely understand it (317). For all these reasons you and I transcend each other's worlds. There is, however, still another form of transcendence that becomes evident with the "We-relation." This phenomenon, says Schütz, belongs to the realm of meaning transcending everyday life and can only be grasped symbolically.

MULTIPLE REALITIES

Here Schütz modifies William James's notion of "subuniverse." James had suggested that anything that excites or stimulates our interest impresses us as real, and that the impression remains with us so long as it is uncontradicted. We experience many different kinds of realities or "subuniverses," the most important of which are the world of physical things, the world of science, of ideal relations, of "idols of the tribe," of the supernatural, of individual opinion, and, finally, "sheer madness and vagary" (207). Given his psychological interests, however, James did not pursue the social implications of these differing orders of reality; this is precisely what Schütz wishes to do.

Men's interests in the world of everyday life are eminently practical, not theoretical. In their "natural attitude" they are governed by pragmatic motives—they strive to control, dominate, or change the world so as to realize their projects and purposes. Schütz calls the practical everyday "world of working" the paramount reality (226), for this is the area of social life in which men treat the world as a field to be dominated, and strive to overcome the resistance of objects and others to their life plans. This is the reality we are all most interested in; but not all aspects of this paramount world are equally relevant to our life projects. We select from the world within our actual or potential reach those objects that we believe will serve our interests and the realization of our projects.

In this paramount reality our hopes, fears, and wants impel us to act, to plan, to resist obstacles, to realize our projects. But the anxieties of everyday life spring from our most basic existential experience: our knowledge and our fear of death. Each one of us knows he will die and fears dying before he has fulfilled his hopes and realized his plans. This, Schütz says, is our "fundamental anxiety." Anxiety is an essential element of our social experience in the world of our working, daily lives. This world, its objects, and its typical patterns we take for granted until proof to the contrary asserts itself. We believe we experience things as they really are so long as we have no good reason to believe otherwise. This is man's "natural attitude" in his paramount reality.

In this connection Schütz borrows two terms from Husserl, but reverses their meaning. The *epoché*, for Husserl, we recall, was the first phase of the "reduction" in which one suspended belief in reality, overcoming the natural attitude by means of radical doubt. Everyman, for Schutz, in his natural attitude also employs a type of *epoché*, but what he suspends is not belief in the existing world but doubt. "What he puts in brackets," writes Schütz, "is the doubt that the world and its objects might be otherwise than it appears to him. We propose to call this . . . the *epoché of the natural attitude*" (229).

The paramount reality is the paramount world of meaning, but there are also many other "finite provinces of meaning." Schütz prefers this term to James's "subuniverses" to emphasize that it is men who intersubjectively give an accent of reality to things, that it is the meaning of their experiences and "not the ontological structure of the objects which constitutes reality" (230). The phrase "finite provinces of meaning" is a way of describing the flow of man's daily life through a variety of meaningful experiences and the corresponding flow of his consciousness.

From the paramount reality he may shift to the world of phantoms: daydreams, jokes, play, and the like (234). Here he leaves behind his will to master the world and his pragmatic motives. He becomes an imagining self who plays any role and projects himself into any world he chooses. He has freedom of discretion, says Schütz—a specific freedom he lacks in both the paramount reality and the "world of Dreams" (240). In the latter, events appear inexorable as the dreamer is powerless to influence what is happening. Neither does he have purposes or projects, for his life is wholly within the "inner *durée*" (a term he borrows from Henri Bergson) whose flow he controls not at all.

Finally, there is the world of scientific theory, which Schütz deliberately defines narrowly as activity aiming toward the observation and understanding of the world but not toward its mastery. The practical and meliorative motives are not, strictly speaking, "an element of the process of scientific theorizing itself" (246).

We see that the "finite provinces of meaning" are not separate states with definite boundaries. They are simply the names one gives to the range of meaningful experiences one has in conscious and unconscious life. Ultimately, all of these experiences are communicable to one's fellow man in language and in action.

With this all-too-brief introduction to Schütz's rudimentary concepts, we can turn to a problem area that he regarded as most important: What are the implications of a common-sense, taken-for-granted, everyday world for concept formation, methodology, and theory construction in the social sciences? It is in this area in particular that his efforts to connect *verstehende Soziologie* and phenomenology become evident. Schütz's aim is (1) to clarify the relation of the common-sense world to the scientific, and (2) to delineate the special character of the social sciences.

COMMON SENSE AND SCIENTIFIC CONCEPTS

Philosophers generally agree that all perception, even the simplest, is never purely sensory but rather involves imagination and concepts. Seeing, hearing, touching, etc., are always mediated and accompanied by thinking or conscious activity. This is true of both the common-sense world of everyday life and science. It is an error, then, to assume that we see the world immediately and directly. What we see is not at all the so-called "concrete" or "actual" world. For the most rudimentary common-sense perception involves highly complex abstractions. What we see is never just a "thing," "out there," "as it is." It is rather a thought object constituted by our consciousness. He who fails to bear this in mind, be he Everyman or Scientist, commits what Alfred North Whitehead called the "fallacy of misplaced concreteness."

All knowing, then, is mediated by intellectual constructs, for it involves generalization, idealization, and abstraction. In these terms, the so-called "facts" that are sometimes described as "speaking for themselves" never do so but are always the product of selection and interpretation. Facts always carry meaning and are inevitably selected, interpreted, abstract facts. Our knowledge is necessarily perspectival and we therefore grasp only aspects of reality, but never the "whole," "concrete" reality. These epistemological assumptions hold for all knowing.

With the advent and increasing institutionalization of science, the aspects of reality science centers on diverge from those of everyday life. The history of science is also the history of a widening gulf between its thought objects and those of common sense. Indeed, the latter are soon totally superseded by scientific concepts—a development that has different implications for the physical and the social sciences.

Ideally it is the natural scientist himself who selects his problem and decides what aspects of reality to study. The facts are not preselected or preinterpreted by the subjects of his inquiry, since meaning is not intrinsic to nature. Nor, obviously, do the facts or events have meaning for the mindless objects he studies.

The social scientist, in contrast, studies a world that has already been preselected and preinterpreted by the living, thinking, acting subjects within it. Men orient themselves and cope with the everyday world by means of common-sense constructs and thought objects. Inevitably, then, the social scientist's constructs refer not to a mindless, meaningless world, but to a socially constructed world of meaning. This means, writes Schütz, that "the constructs used by the social scientist are, so to speak, constructs of the second degree, namely constructs of the constructs made by the actors on the social scene, whose behavior the scientist observes and tries to explain in accordance with the procedural rules of his science" (6).

For Schütz, the natural and social worlds are therefore structured differently. From this, however, he does not conclude that a social science is impossible or that it is based on fundamentally different rules of procedure. He dissociates himself both from those who deny the possibility of a social science and from those who have opted for a behaviorist method that ignores or radically departs from the common-sense concepts men employ in their everyday lives. For Schütz, the social sciences present special difficulties that may be overcome through specific methodological devices. In this respect he follows Weber, but supplements Weber's typology of action with phenomenological insights.

THE TYPICALITY OF EVERYDAY EXPERIENCE

"The individual's common-sense knowledge of the world," writes Schütz, "is a system of constructs of its typicality" (7). The world of each of us has always been preexperienced and preinterpreted, so that our knowledge of the world is always based on the experience of predecessors as well as our own experience and that of our contemporaries. This becomes our taken-for-granted, unquestioned, "though at any time questionable stock of knowledge at hand" (7). Furthermore, the preexperiences we inherit are *typical*: We experience the world not as unique objects and events but as typical ones—dog, cat, man, tree, etc., are such typical and general concepts that only man employs to apprehend reality. Yet, as Schütz emphasizes, we need not always think in types. Rover, my dog, my friend, is surely also an animal and mammal. But, "I am, without a special motive, not induced to look at Rover as a mammal, an animal, an object of the outer world, although I know that he is all this too."

What happens here as elsewhere is that I select only certain aspects of the type that are of interest and relevance to me, and ignore the other aspects. The key terms are "interest" and "relevance." You and I occupy different positions in the sociocultural world and, accordingly, our interests and systems of relevance differ. Despite our differing locations, however, "we" tend to assume that (1) our standpoints are interchangeable, and that (2) our systems of relevance are congruent "for all practical purposes." All who are included in the "we" take these assumptions for granted and idealize them.

With these assumptions knowledge no longer appears as "yours," or "mine," or "theirs," that is, knowledge from the respective standpoints of our biographically unique situations. Rather, it appears as "everyone's knowledge," "objective and anonymous" knowledge, independent of our standpoints and situations. Indeed, much of our knowledge of everyday life consists of such commonly accepted, practical, and efficient ways of coping with the environment. This knowledge, being intersubjective and social, serves us all (within a particular in-group) rather well; for it teaches us typical means for achieving typical ends in typical situations.

Included in such typical knowledge is the type of expertise that others possess and I do not, but which I might require. Inasmuch as actual knowledge varies from individual to individual, I need to know when, how, and whom to consult—e.g., doctors, lawyers, plumbers, etc.—in typical circumstances. In everyday life, then, men employ typical common-sense constructs and relate to one another as exemplars of types. They take into account the typicality of actions, projects, and motives and orient themselves accordingly.

We typify our actions and those of others when we see them in definite social roles. In defining the role of another I define my own role. In our projects we also plan for situations with a high degree of typicality. We assume that by acting again as we did earlier in similar circumstances, we will achieve similar results; and that if we know in advance how and in what degree the future state will deviate from earlier circumstances, this can be taken into account and planned for. But motives are also important for an understanding of actions and projects.

"IN-ORDER-TO" MOTIVES AND "BECAUSE" MOTIVES

"In-order-to" motives clearly refer to a future state that an actor wishes to bring about by his actions. "Because" motives, on the other hand, refer to the past. They determine, in some sense and in some measure, that the actor act as he does or did. In the course of his action, the actor is only conscious of his "in-order-to" motives but not his "because" motives. The latter he becomes aware of only after he has completed the act or its initial phases. This awareness is acquired ex post facto, by means of reflection. "But then," Schütz reminds us, "the actor is not acting any more; he is an observer of himself" (22).

In social interaction—for example, questioning and answering—the "in-order-to" motives of one actor become the "because" motives of the other. We know that typically our questions will cause the other to answer and to provide the information or object we need. In some cases, the motives are simple and obvious. When I say, "May I have the salt?" my "in-order-to" motive is quite evident to my partner in dialogue across the table. Other cases, on the other hand, are complex. I ask an apparently simple question: "Where is the ink?" but my ultimate purpose—in Schütz's example, applying for a fellowship—may be known only to myself. All that my partner knows is that I wanted some ink. To go beyond this proximate motive to my ultimate one, he would need to construct it on the basis of additional observation and information.

This simple example is used by Schütz to illustrate, first, that it is by no means certain we will truly understand each other in everyday life, and that there is only a chance for such understanding; second, that we increase this probability by grasping "the meaning the action has for the actor" (24). To grasp the other's meaning in everyday life, Schütz argues, Everyman implicitly constructs "course-of-action types." In these terms neither the search for subjective meaning nor the construction of typologies of action are peculiar to the methods of the social sciences. The important issue is the relation between the common-sense types and the social science types.

COMMON SENSE AND SOCIAL SCIENCE

All sciences, the physical as well as the social, employ abstractions and study typical, not unique events. The social sciences are justified in doing so since Everyman in everyday life also employs abstractions and orients himself in terms of typical facts, events, and experiences. What is it, then, that makes the social sciences different and what is it that imposes special obligations upon them? For Schütz, the special problem and responsibility of the social sciences is "to develop methodological devices for attaining objective and verifiable knowledge of a subjective meaning structure" (36). This requires a special posture on the social scientist's part as well as systematic attention to the relation of the typical constructs of common sense to those of social science.

In common with Husserl, Scheler, and Weber, among others, Schütz advocates that the social scientist be a "disinterested" observer. One need not be a social scientist, however, to be a disinterested observer. In everyday life Everyman often finds himself observing others in their interaction, but without his being a party to their interaction, and without his being involved in their motives. In such cases he is not directly interested in the interaction or its outcome. In this sense he is detached and disinterested. This permits him to see both more and less than the actors themselves. For he sees them only from the outside and does not really know their motives and meanings. Since he is observing them from the outside, if he wishes to gain an understanding of their transaction, he must relate it to other similar ones in typically similar situations, and thereby construct the participants' motives from the limited and fragmentary sector of their actions that he has observed.

Because the observer's interest in this situation is different from that of the actors themselves, and because his purpose in seeking understanding is also different, his constructs also differ from theirs. There is no guarantee but only a likelihood that Everyman as a disinterested observer will truly understand the participants' acts. The more typical, standardized, and institutionalized the pattern, the greater is the likelihood. Thus disinterested observation and the interpretation of subjective meaning by means of typical constructs is by no means the exclusive province of social science. On the contrary, all of us find ourselves in situations in everyday life where we act as disinterested observers trying to infer the subjective meanings of others by means of common-sense, typical constructs.

The social scientist is therefore a special case of disinterested observation. He, too, presumably, has no vital or practical interest in the situation he observes, only a cognitive or theoretical one. He is uninvolved in the hopes and fears of the participants and shares none of their anxiety about the outcome of their actions. He is, in short, "detached." To be sure, the social scientist always remains a participant in the social world and is therefore always interested, involved, or engaged in some aspect of it. In a society consisting of classes, strata, groups, and associations, there can be no doubt that he will inevitably favor the values and interests of some and oppose those of others. Schütz would therefore agree that the social scientist is never absolutely detached.

So, in terms quite similar to Husserl's "reduction," Scheler's and Mannheim's "disinterestedness" and "relatively unattached intellectuals," and Weber's "value-neutrality" (achieved by a clear awareness of one's interests and values and their relevance for an intellectual problem, issue, or inquiry), Schütz also emphasizes that disinterestedness is a matter of *attitude*. It is an ideal posture towards which the social scientist should strive. Approximating this posture requires that one apply what Schütz's phenomenological predecessors prescribed: one reflects on one's position, situation, and experiences in the social world and the values and interests resulting from them. One "brackets" one's biographical situation in everyday life, together with its system of relevances, and adopts in their place the interests, systems of relevance, and values of the scientist qua scientist, the disinterested observer par excellence. Again, however, it should be clear that this is an attitude that everyone occasionally adopts in some degree and that some sophisticated persons, though nonscientists, frequently adopt in everyday life. Important differences nonetheless remain between the nonscientific constructs of common sense and those of science.

If one temporarily ignores, as does Schütz, the sociology-of-knowledge problems involved, then the difference may be summed up as the deliberateness, self-consciousness, and methodicalness with which the social scientist assumes his disinterested posture. He brackets, systematically and self-consciously, his biographically determined situation, his "Here" in the everyday world, and "considers his position within it and the system of relevances attached thereto as irrelevant for his scientific undertaking" (39). In addition, of course, since science is an organized, institutionalized, formalized activity, it has its own corpus of knowledge and rules of procedure that differ from Everyman's in everyday life. It is this difference that for Schütz constitutes a possible source of "danger"—for it means that social scientists may be studying and describing not the "real" social world and its meaning but rather their own marionettes and the scripts they have written for them.

THE CONSTRUCTS AND MODELS OF SOCIAL SCIENCE

Exploring this source of danger, Schütz reviews the social scientists' typical procedure. To explain certain observed actions he constructs ideal-typical courses of action along with the accompanying hypothetical actors, whom he endows with equally hypothetical consciousness. All this he does as it relates to his specific scientific problem. Fictitious motives are thus ascribed to fictious actors engaged in fictitious situations.

Clearly, these creatures of the scientist have no real "biographical situation in the social world of everyday life." It is not they who define their situation but their creator, who "has created these puppets or homunculi to manipulate them for his purpose" (41). These homunculi have no life, no anxiety, no freedom, and no consciousness; they cannot under any circumstances act otherwise than was predestined by their creator. Nonetheless, the fact that the social scientist has set the stage, assigned the roles, and written the scripts does not mean that this lifeless puppet show cannot illuminate the real social world. On the contrary, these abstract, fictitious, and "rational" models are indispensable in thinking about real men and their actions; if properly constructed they do in fact provide an understanding of social reality.

There are no simple or precise recipes for the construction of these models. Instead, what Schütz suggests in this regard are some general and programmatic postulates. These are intended to guide the social scientist in the construction of models that will enable him to deal objectively with human actions and their subjective meaning. At the same time the postulates alert the scientist to the danger in constructing models that depart so far from the common-sense thought objects of everyday life that they are inconsistent with them. Finally, it should go without saying that the postulates are in no sense intended to replace the basic canons of scientific procedure, but to complement them. Schütz lists three postulates:

1. *"The postulate of logical consistency."* The scientist's system of constructs should have the utmost clarity and distinctness as well as full compatibility with formal logical principles. It is this formal logical character that distinguishes scientific from common-sense thinking (43).

2. *"The postulate of subjective interpretation."* This underlies Weber's conception of the main task of sociology: the scientist's concepts and models

should enable him to refer human action and its consequences to the subjective meanings of the actors involved.

3. *"The postulate of adequacy."* This postulate enjoins the scientist to strive for consistency between his constructs and those of common-sense experience of the social reality. In Schütz's words: "Each term in a scientific model of human action must be constructed in such a way that a human act performed within the life-world by an individual actor in the way indicated by the typical construct would be understandable for the actor himself as well as for his fellow men in terms of common-sense interpretation of everyday life" (44).

The second and third postulates, we see, represent Schütz's effort to connect Weber's emphasis on *Verstehen* with Husserl's phenomenology as applied to the *Lebenswelt.* His general efforts are directed to the development of a scientific method that would yield valid propositions about subjectively oriented action—but at the same time propositions in which real, social-world actors would be able to recognize themselves.

So Schütz's approach, like Weber's, is concerned with subjective meaning, but not in the sense that has too often been supposed. Neither Weber nor Schütz ever advocated, as some still claim today, a method of understanding that employed a "private, uncontrollable, and unverifiable intuition," or any such nonsense (56). For both thinkers *Verstehen* is "subjective" only in the sense that the purpose of the method is to determine what meaning the action has for the actor as opposed to his partner or a disinterested observer.

Schütz's main aim is to remind us that *Verstehen* is also a common-sense method of everyday life that yields public, controllable, and verifiable truths. It is a method with which men make numerous predictions with a probability approaching unity—as for instance when they mail a properly stamped and addressed letter, "knowing" that it will most probably reach its destination. Men in their daily lives understand and organize their experiences of the social world; and if social scientists fail to grasp the general principles according to which men do so, they have failed in their most important task.

Schütz's work is mainly programmatic; apart from the ideas summarized here, there is remarkably little development or application of the method he advocates. Moreover, we must raise several critical points regarding his effort.

Schütz's program tends to abstract the so-called everyday world from the larger social universe, and to treat that world as relatively self-enclosed and unproblematic. As a result, we learn nothing about how Everyman's daily existence is shaped by the structure of the larger society in which he lives and works. Further, we get the impression that Everyman's assessment of his everyday reality is unerring, though most of the examples of his uncanny control of his fate are trivial ones, like that of mailing a letter and "knowing" it will get to its destination.

There is, then, a sense in which Schütz not only abstracts the everyday world but idealizes it as well; throughout his work is the implication that Everyman's common-sense, taken-for-granted assumptions about his everyday world are always tried, tested, and valid. Schütz can only support this conception of things by severing the everyday world from the larger institutional context and by focusing consistently on relatively unproblematic transactions.

The problem lies in the way Schütz has conceived the everyday world and the social scientist's relation to that world. What Schütz has done, we recall, is to invert Husserl's definition of the *epoché*. For Husserl it involved the suspension of belief and was to be a step in the process of critical reflection that would bring one closer to the truth. For Schütz, in contrast, the *epoché* refers to Everyman's suspension of doubt, which he maintains in his common-sense, taken-for-granted reality until that reality compels him to act otherwise.

Yet it is only a very limited and routinized sector of everyday life that is as unproblematic as Schütz would have us believe. If, instead of defining the everyday reality as Schütz does, we were to define it in a way that would allow for its penetration by the social forces resulting from the larger society's institutional arrangements, we would begin to see how problematic everyday realities are and how inappropriate the suspension of doubt may be. In Schütz's scheme, however, Everyman is basically uncritical. He lives and works in an unproblematic world whose meaning and validity he grasps readily and unerringly. The scientist, if he follows Schütz's methodological injunction, need only grasp the meaning of Everyman's acts as Everyman himself understands that meaning. The unavoidable result of following this injunction would be description in the most superficial sense.

The real problem with Schütz's scheme is that it provides us with no independent means of assessing the validity of Everyman's judgments about his existential conditions and his interpretations of his relations with his fellow men. We shall clarify this criticism further in our discussion of ethnomethodology.

14

Garfinkel's Ethnomethodology

Harold Garfinkel and his associates have been engaged for some years in research rooted in the phenomenological tradition. Although Garfinkel acknowledges the influence of several thinkers, including Weber, Mannheim, and the "awesome" work of Talcott Parsons, it is evident that Schütz is the major and most immediate source of what Garfinkel has chosen to call ethnomethodology.

At the opening of his *Studies in Ethnomethodology*, Garfinkel replies to the question, "What is ethnomethodology?" by explaining that the studies collected in this volume "seek to treat practical activities, practical circumstances, and practical sociological reasoning as topics of empirical study, and by paying to the most commonplace activities of daily life the attention usually accorded extraordinary events, seek to learn about them in their own right."[1] Ethnomethodology is, clearly, a form of phenomenology and deserves attention as a version of that tradition.

Garfinkel's main efforts have been directed toward the *empirical* study of everyday, commonplace activities and phenomena. In common with other phenomenologists Garfinkel is concerned with meaning and how it is intersubjectively conveyed. His several researches, reported in Chapter 2 of *Studies in Ethnomethodology*, attempt to demonstrate (1) that commonplace everyday conversations convey a good deal more meaning than is carried immediately by the words themselves; (2) that such conversations presuppose a common meaningful context; (3) that the common understanding accompanying or resulting from the conversation consists of an ongoing process of intersubjective interpretation; and, finally, (4) that everyday exchanges and affairs have a

---

[1] Harold Garfinkel, *Studies in Ethnomethodology* (Englewood Cliffs, N. J.: Prentice-Hall, 1967), p. 1. © 1967; reprinted by permission of Prentice-Hall, Inc., Englewood Cliffs, N.J. Page references to this work are hereafter cited in parentheses immediately following the quoted passage.

methodical, planful, and, hence, "rational" character, so that one gets the sense or meaning of another's utterance by grasping the "rule" according to which it was made.

Following Schütz, Garfinkel argues that the apprehension of meaning is more than a mere matching of "substantive matters." "To see the 'sense' of what is said," Garfinkel writes, "is to accord to what was said its character 'as a rule.' . . . The appropriate image of a common understanding is therefore an operation rather than a common intersection of overlapping sets" (30).

How does one get at these implicit "rules," at the planful character or "routine grounds of everyday activities"? How does one discover and make explicit what for Everyman is so taken for granted that he may not take notice of it? How, in short, may one make the commonplace visible? "Procedurally," Garfinkel replies, "it is my preference to start with familiar scenes and ask what can be done to make trouble" (37). One "makes trouble" by estranging oneself deliberately and temporarily from the common-sense, taken-for-granted, everyday activities; in the particular research in question one treats as altogether problematical what others assume is "common, reasonable, understandable, plain talk" (41).

This is the methodological point of Garfinkel's requiring his student-experimenters to demand of their subjects an explanation of the obvious. When a subject, for example, says he had a flat tire, he is astounded by the question, "What do you mean, you had a flat tire?" When a woman's husband remarks that he is tired, she asks, "How are you tired? Physically, mentally, or just bored?" To which he replies, "I don't know, I guess physically, mainly." And she continues to badger him with like questions until he tells her, finally, to "drop dead!" (42f).

Similarly, when Garfinkel requires his student-experimenters to view the activities in their own homes as if "they were boarders in the household" (45), this deliberate and methodical estrangement is supposed to yield insights not otherwise attainable—bringing the unnoticed routine grounds of everyday life into view.

The value of these experiments for both the subject and the experimenter is, however, highly questionable. Garfinkel himself candidly acknowledges that the subjects found their experience unamusing, and "only rarely . . . instructive as the student argued it was supposed to have been" (48–49). And indeed nowhere are we told explicitly what Everyman or the social scientist might learn from these experiments, or what Garfinkel and his associates in fact concluded from them. Could this be because the conclusions tend to confirm what everyone knows?

Are the conclusions any more illuminating that Garfinkel cautiously and tentatively draws from a staged interview between a fake medical school representative and a fake applicant? Twenty-eight premedical students individually participated in a three-hour experimental interview, during which time they provided the "medical school representative" with answers to questions such as the following: "What kind of man are the medical schools looking for? What should a good candidate do in the interview? What should he avoid?" (58). When each student had given his opinions, he was informed that the official interview had been completed and "was asked if he would care to hear a recording of the actual interview. All students wanted very much to hear the recording" (58).

The recording was the staged one between the fake representative and the fake applicant; the latter was portrayed throughout as boorish, ignorant, vulgar, boastful, evasive, etc. When the students gave their predictable evaluations of the "applicant," the "medical school representative" provided information relating to the applicant's academic record and personal character that deliberately contradicted the students' evaluations.

> For example, if the student said that the applicant must have come from a lower class family, he was told that the applicant's father was vice president of a firm that manufactured pneumatic doors for trains and buses. Was the applicant ignorant? Then he had excelled in courses like the Poetry of Milton and Dramas of Shakespeare. If the student said the applicant did not know how to get along with people, then the applicant had worked as a voluntary solicitor for Sydenham Hospital in New York City and had raised $32,000 from 30 "big givers" (59).

Under these circumstances, students became curious about "what 'the others' thought of the applicant" and whether he had gained admission. Each student was then informed that the applicant had indeed been accepted and that he was living up to the high promises predicted by the "interviewer" and six psychiatrists. Finally, each student was also told that twenty-eight out of the thirty other students agreed entirely with the "interviewer" while the "remaining two had been slightly uncertain but at the first bit of information about the 'applicant's' outstanding characterological fitness had seen him just as the others had. . . . Following this the student was invited to listen to the record a second time, after which he was asked to assess the applicant again" (59). Twenty-five of the twenty-eight students were successfully deceived (60). And twenty-two of them "expressed marked relief—ten of them with explosive expressions—when the deception was [eventually] disclosed. Unanimously they said that the news of the deception permitted them to return to their former views" (64).

What does Garfinkel make of all this? The students' views before and after deception are examples of highly motivated compliance with certain expectancies and attitudes of daily life; they are the "natural facts of life" to which the members of the relevant social world subscribe. Given a shaking up, a calling into question of those "natural facts"—as was done in this case by confronting the students with contradictory and incongruous materials—the individuals experience confusion and anxiety. But Garfinkel desires an even more precisely formulated proposition, so he states that "under the breach of the expectancies of everyday life, given the conditions for the optimal production of disturbance, persons should shift in exhibited confusion in an amount that is coordinate with the original extent of their grasp of the 'natural facts of life' " (65).

Surely the first part of the proposition comes as no news: when one's expectations are breached or disturbed, confusion and maybe even anxiety result. As for the second part of the proposition—alleging that after the disturbance one will find a coordinate relationship between the "shift in exhibited confusion" and the "original . . . grasp of the 'natural facts of life' "—it comes as something of a surprise that Garfinkel should present his findings in the form he does. Before the incongruent material was introduced, he writes, "the extent of students' subscription to a common moral order of facts of premedical school life and the students' anxiety correlated −.026. After the incongruous material had been introduced and unsuccessfully normalized and before the deception was revealed, the correlation was .751" (65).

It is surprising because neither the proposition nor the statistics add to our understanding. Nowhere is there a definition of the proposition's key variables, let alone precise measures of them. Garfinkel himself cautions the reader that "because assessment procedures were extremely crude, because of serious errors in design and procedure, and because of the *post hoc* argument, these results do no more than illustrate what I am talking about. Under no circumstances should they be considered as findings" (65). Then why the correlations?

SOCIOLOGICAL MAN AS A "CULTURAL DOPE"

More significant is Garfinkel's attempt to illustrate empirically the extent to which sociological "models of man in society portray him as a judgmental dope" (67). Following Schütz, Garfinkel argues that sociologists have insufficiently taken into account that their types are standardized expectations, fictions that may obscure the degree to which people actively create and sustain their standard patterns of conduct. This often results in a misunderstanding of "the nature and conditions of stable actions" (67). Garfinkel's critique of the sociological "cultural dope" is similar to Schütz's critique of sociological homunculi or puppets. Sociological man is either a dope or a puppet because he invariably complies with legitimized and official patterns of culture: he bucks no trends, remains set in his ways, makes no real choices, and, indeed, lacks common sense. Garfinkel's experiment brings out clearly—at least in one area of social life—the difference between the "dope" and the real person in society.

The point of the experiment was to determine the consequences of bucking the "institutionalized one-price rule," which, according to Talcott Parsons, was essential to the institution of contract. The internalization of this rule, Garfinkel reasoned, should have generated shame, fear, or anxiety in both the student-experimenters and the salesperson when the former, in carrying out their assignments, bargained "for standard priced merchandise" (68–69). The results suggested that students felt fear and anxiety most in anticipation of the experiment and when they approached the salesperson for the first time. In the course of the experience, however, anxiety declined, and "most of the students who bargained in two or more trials reported that by the third episode they were enjoying the assignment" (69).

A more important finding, however, is that "many students reported that they had learned to their 'surprise' that one could bargain in standard priced settings with some realistic chance of an advantageous outcome, and planned to do so in the future, particularly for costly merchandise" (69).

From this Garfinkel makes the significant inference that when a person in society adheres to rules this is not necessarily a sign or result of his value commitment. Rather it may be "the anticipatory anxiety that prevents him from permitting a situation to develop, let alone confronting a situation, in which he has the alternative of acting or not with respect to a rule . . . " (70).

Fear and anxiety often prevent people from testing rules, learning about them, and changing them. Hence, professional as well as lay knowledge of institutions is often inadequate or false since it attributes to rules a character that has never been tested. "Indeed, the more important the rule, the greater is the likelihood that knowledge is based on avoided tests" (70). Insofar as the sociologist ignores this—that fear, anxiety, and ignorance, not positive value-commitments, often account for compliance—he makes real persons in society into judgmental dopes.

This experiment (and the principle it illustrates) has more implications than Garfinkel explicitly draws out; it has critical and even revolutionary implications in that it points directly to the potential flexibility, contingency, and changeability of institutions. It brings out clearly that institutions often regarded as necessary are merely those whose necessity has not been tested.

Another implication relates directly to our earlier criticism of Schütz's conception. Too often Schütz and some of his followers give the impression that they regard so-called common-sense, everyday, taken-for-granted knowledge as adequate and valid, with nothing more to be said about it. Everyman's pragmatic common-sense knowledge enables him to cope with the problems of daily life and get by; ergo, it must be valid knowledge. But this is too uncritical a view of Everyman's pragmatic knowledge. No doubt such knowledge is adequate for many practical purposes, but more likely than not it also involves a degree of submission, compliance, and resignation to certain social arrangements that fear and anxiety discourage the individual from testing and challenging. Garfinkel's findings in this experiment seem to imply this.

Those findings also suggest what Schütz failed to make explicit: that while the sociologist can learn about and from his subjects—for example, that they have anxiety and fear of testing certain rules and why—he can also teach them. He can teach them to judge more realistically whether their fears of such tests are justified, and to assess more accurately the probable consequences of complying or testing. If we think of social science as an intellectual instrument with which to further human freedom, and if we go beyond the one-price rule and apply the logic of Garfinkel's experiment to all social, economic, and political institutions, then the importance of a dialogue between social scientist and layman appears quite evident. The term "dialogue" is appropriate here because it describes perfectly the dialogical relation that ought to obtain between the social scientist and the people. The knowledge they have enabled him to acquire should in some manner find its way back to them so that they might benefit from it. Dialogue in these terms is a conversation that avoids two equally undesirable errors: capitulating uncritically to Everyman's view of reality; or presuming that the social scientist always knows better.

Surely this is compatible with Garfinkel's programmatic aim of achieving a better understanding of common-sense activities and knowledge by treating them as problematic phenomena.

V

SYMBOLIC INTERACTION

15

The Social Psychology of Erving Goffman

Erving Goffman is among the best-known social psychologists writing today. In *The Presentation of Self in Everyday Life* his guiding principles, he tells us, "are dramaturgical ones" and his perspective "that of the theatrical performance. . . . "[1] His work thus falls somewhere between the symbolic interactionist and phenomenological traditions.

In *The Presentation of Self* he is mainly concerned with documenting what he calls "expressions given off," that is, expressions of "the more theatrical and contextual kind, the non-verbal, presumably unintentional kind, whether this communication be purposely engineered or not" (4). We infer meanings and obtain impressions from the acts of others, often relying more for our impressions on their actions than on their words. Facial expressions, gestures, and the rapidity and quality of actions may convey true feelings more accurately than verbal behavior. As one speaks, one also communicates in a nonverbal way, and many of us attend to the latter as a check upon the authenticity of the former. We use one stream of communication (the nonverbal) to test the second (the verbal).

Of course, as one becomes aware that others regard nonverbal behavior as less controllable than verbal, one can use this information deliberately to manage and manipulate the impressions one makes. As others are also sophisticated in this way, they attempt to detect some nuance that the individual has not successfully managed to control. In this way, social interaction becomes a kind of information game in which each individual tries to manage his impressions while seeking to penetrate those of others in order to grasp their true feelings and intentions.

[1] Erving Goffman, *The Presentation of Self in Everyday Life* (New York: Doubleday Anchor Books, 1959), p. xi. Page references to this work are hereafter cited in parentheses immediately following the quoted passage.

In everyday life this contest proceeds sub rosa and does not typically disrupt social relations. Each participating actor suppresses his true feelings and communicates a view of the situation that he senses the others will find acceptable. The "smooth working of society" is thus facilitated by a "veneer of consensus" behind which each participant hides his true feelings. To maintain this modus vivendi each actor projects an image of himself as well as a definition of the situation that he feels the others will accept. Striving to avoid embarrassment by protecting the images they project, actors employ strategies and tactics. Goffman calls these "defensive practices" when the actor seeks to save his own image and "protective practices" when he seeks to protect the images or definition projected by another. In short, Goffman is concerned in this study with the techniques of impression management—with the dramaturgical problems of presenting oneself and one's actions to others. He is interested in "performances" or "encounters," or in the reciprocal influence of persons when in one another's presence.

In his performance an actor may deceive himself as to his true motives or he may cynically deceive others. These are the extremes within which performance motives range. Performances involve a mixture of belief and cynicism. The "front" is that part of the performance that an actor employs "in a general and fixed fashion to define the situation for those who observe the performance" (22). And, as we might expect, the dramaturgical perspective also implies that the actions take place in a given "setting" involving scenery and props. The setting refers to "the scenic parts of expressive equipment" while the "personal front" refers to the expressive equipment the actor takes with him wherever he goes—e.g., "insignia of office or rank; clothing; sex, age, and social characteristics; size and looks; posture; speech patterns; facial expressions; bodily gestures; and the like" (24). Typically we expect and find a consistency "among setting, appearance, and manner" (25).

In their performances actors tend to guide themselves by what they regard as the official values of society. Of course this may involve the actor in situations where a conflict of values forces him to subordinate some to others. An actor puts his best foot forward, presenting an idealized version of himself and underplaying those aspects of self that appear incompatible with that version. The actor thus presents what he would like others to regard as the "essential" self but at the same time must come to terms with the fact that different groups and situations demand that he show a different self to each of the groups. In order therefore to maintain his fostered impression, the actor strives to segregate his audiences to enable him to play the right part for the right audience. Our performances must pass strict tests "of aptness, fitness, propriety, and decorum" (55).

Following Kenneth Burke, Goffman seeks to grasp and analyze performances not in mechanical terms such as, say, "equilibrium," but rather with poetic-artistic metaphors. This type of metaphor "prepares us for the fact that a single note off key can disrupt the tone of an entire performance" (52). The impressions we seek to foster by our performances are delicate and fragile and "can be shattered by very minor mishaps" (56).

Here as elsewhere, Goffman seems to allow for the "I," the impulsive, active, creative self. His formulation in this connection is interesting: "The expressive coherence that is required in performance points out a crucial discrepancy between our all-too-human selves and our socialized selves. As human beings we are presumably creatures of variable impulse with moods and energies that change from one moment to the next" (56). As characters playing to an audience, however, we undergo a "certain bureaucratization of the spirit" (56) and a definite "social discipline" (57). Thus Goffman points to the impulsive side of man (an important concept we shall explore at length in the chapter on George Herbert Mead) but quickly resolves whatever little tension it implies in favor of society. He cites Durkheim in this context and appears to follow his one-sided social determinism. Only later, in his other works, notably in *Asylums*, does Goffman pursue somewhat the implications of what he calls the "discrepancy" between the human self and the social self. In *The Presentation of Self*, however, he leaves unexplored the significance of a sentence he quotes from Jean Paul Sartre's *Being and Nothingness*: "There are indeed many precautions to imprison a man in what he is, as if we lived in perpetual fear that he might escape from it, that he might break away and suddenly elude his condition."

When a number of actors cooperate to stage a routine, Goffman states, the set of individuals is a "performance team" (79). Whether husband and wife, executive and secretary, fellow workers, doctor and nurse, and so on, teammates depend on each other to present and maintain a given definition of the situation. It follows that a single team member "has the power to give the show away or to disrupt it by inappropriate conduct" (82). Performance teams do not necessarily coincide with the authority structure of a group or organization. Some performances require cooperation within a status or rank, as when parents resolve never to side with their children against each other, or when officers never disagree in the presence of their men. Other performances, however, require cooperation across statuses, as when an officer aligns himself with his men to put on a successful show for his superior officers.

Furthermore, dramaturgical dominance may not coincide with the actual structure of power in a given situation. For example, during the World War I British sergeants of working-class background taught "their new lieutenants to take a dramatically expressive role at the head of the platoon and to die quickly in a prominent dramatic position as befits public-school men. The sergeants themselves took their modest place at the rear of the platoon and tended to live to train still other lieutenants" (102). A performance team is therefore a grouping in relation to specific interaction situations and does not necessarily coincide with the grouping's structure of authority. We are all members of such teams, so we are all conspirators in this sense, collaborating to conceal certain facts from our audiences.

To conceal successfully it follows that some of our performances and their preparation require *regions*, or places set off in some "degree by barriers to perception" (106). The "front region" is where the team members actually present their performance to the intended audience. In contrast, a "back region" Goffman defines "as a place ... where the impression fostered by the performance is knowingly contradicted as a matter of course" (112). As an illustration he cites Simone de Beauvoir's description of women's backstage activities when the male audience is absent. Backstage, the woman "is getting her costume together, preparing her make-up, laying out her tactics; she is lingering in dressing-gown and slippers in the wings before making her entrance on the stage ... "[2]

But "backstage" can refer to any of those regions of social establishments that are generally off limits to the audience. Performers wear their masks in the front region and take them off backstage. An interesting time to observe impression management, therefore, is when the performers leave the back region and come upon the stage or when they return "therefrom, for at these moments one can detect a wonderful putting on and taking off of character" (121).

The separation of front and back regions may be found throughout our society. In the home, in social establishments, in residential areas, and elsewhere, there exist regions where appearances are meticulously maintained; and regions in which the front is dropped, and mask and costume removed. To the front and back regions Goffman adds a third, "the outside." Conforming with the common-sense view, this refers to the goings-on literally outside the walls of the establishment or building in which the performance is taking place.

If "performance team" implies cooperation, it also implies collusion and conspiracy. Every team therefore has either "dark," "strategic," or "inside" secrets. Dark secrets are concealed because if revealed, they would blatantly contradict the image the team is striving to maintain. Strategic secrets are concealed because they entail the plans for future actions a team has vis-á-vis its opposition. There are, finally, inside secrets, which an individual shares simply by being a member of a group. Knowledge of these separates the "inside dopester" from those not "in the know" (142). These "secrets" are never perfectly kept because the "congruence among function, information possessed, and accessible regions is seldom complete" (145). This Goffman explains by means of "discrepant roles."

Among the more obvious of the "discrepent roles" is the "informer." Posing as a member of the team, he gains access to the back region and gives away the information so gained to the audience. On the other hand, there is the "shill," who pretends he is a member of the audience but is actually "in league with the performers" (146). The "shill," "claque," "stick," and "shillaber" we associate with the entertainment business and most often with "non-respectable

---

[2] Simone de Beauvoir, *The Second Sex*, trans. H. M. Parshley (New York: Knopf, 1953), p. 543; cited in Goffman, *The Presentation of Self*, p. 113.

performances," but the concepts can be applied appropriately to everyday encounters.

Another agent of the audience protects its interests by checking up on the standards of the performers. Sometimes he gives them fair warning but sometimes he does not, as is the case with the "spotter" who is "understandably disliked" (147). Then there is the "professional shopper—the Gimbels' man in Macy's and the Macy's man in Gimbels; he is the fashion spy and the foreigner at national air meets" (149). In addition, there are mediators, "non-persons," such as servants, and finally various types of service specialists who have gained privileged information about the performers. The doctor, lawyer, psychoanalyst, and priest are just a few examples of such specialists, who are committed by their professional ethic "not to give away a show whose secrets" their duties have enabled them to acquire (153–154).

"COMMUNICATION OUT OF CHARACTER"

There are times when performers and performance teams engage in communications that are sharply at variance with the impression they want officially to maintain during interaction with the audience. Goffman considers four such types of interaction. The first two he calls "treatment of the absent" and "staging talk," situations in which the performers backstage evaluate their performance and talk about themselves and generally derogate, criticize, and ridicule the audience. This backstage activity, Goffman suggests, enhances the mutual regard of the performers, as well as the solidarity of the team, "compensating, perhaps, for the loss of self-respect that may occur when the audience must be accorded accommodative face-to-face treatment" (171). The contrast between the team's backstage attitude and its face-to-face treatment of it should not be regarded as hypocrisy, pure and simple. The teams's backstage activity serves to bolster its morale; its frontstage activity is dictated by the mutual interest it has with the audience.

The third type, "team collusion," typically occurs in the audience's presence but without its awareness that the definition of the situation is not quite what it appears to be. Team members engage in collusive communications without undermining the impressions they have been fostering for the audience. Finally, there are what Goffman calls "realigning actions." In this case performers go somewhat beyond the safe means of communicating their discontent but without openly threatening either the smoothness of the performance or the team's relation with the audience.

All four types point to the need all team performers have not only for backstage relaxation but for collusive communication in the very presence of their audience. Yet smoothness of performance is not unproblematic. Performances are frequently interrupted or thrown off key and it is precisely such events that "the techniques of impression management function to avoid" (208).

Examples of events that cause either embarrassment or dissonance are unintended gestures, unanticipated intrusions, and faux pas. But complete disruption of the working consensus between team and audience may also occur, and this as a result of a deliberate "scene." In everyday life no less than in theater both the team and the audience have an interest in minimizing such minor and major disruptions. Both therefore develop techniques to reduce the likelihood of their occurence. Some of these techniques the performers employ to save their show. These are called "defensive practices," and include: (1) dramaturgical loyalty (teammates' mutual obligations to safeguard performance secrets); (2) dramaturgical discipline (the obligation to learn one's part well, and to avoid unintended gestures, faux pas, etc.); and (3) dramaturgical circumspection (the need for prudence and forethought in deciding how best to present the performance).

On the other side are the measures the audience employs to help the performers save their show. These "protective practices" correspond with the respective defense practices of the performers. The audience is generally tactful and discreet and does not go backstage uninvited; nor does it pay attention to performances which, though occurring in its presence, are clearly not intended for its eyes or ears. Tact is the key word here. The audience tactfully cooperates with the performers in checking conduct that might create "scenes." Anything short of a scene the audience pretends not to notice.

In order for the audience to assist the performers in this way the performers must not behave in a manner that makes audience assistance impossible. Cooperation requires "tact regarding tact." Performers must be sensitive to the various cues the audience gives that the show is proceeding in an unacceptable fashion and ought soon to be modified to prevent embarrassment or worse. If a performer chooses to indulge himself in a misrepresentation of reality he must avail himself of the appropriate etiquette. "In telling an untruth, the performer is enjoined to retain a shadow of jest in his voice so that, should he be caught out, he can disavow any claim to seriousness and say that he was only joking" (234).

In *The Presentation of Self* Goffman tells us he is studying "social establishments" as relatively closed systems from the standpoint of impression management or the dramaturgical perspective. It would be closer to the truth, however, to say that he has studied not social establishments but "situations" abstracted from their institutional or organizational contexts. We are provided with numerous illustrations of everyday encounters in a variety of situations, but no attempt is made to specify typical encounters in typical social establishments. The result is some interesting *aperçus* but not really an understanding of the structure of everyday life.

Is there not more at stake in everyday life than merely avoiding embarrassment and "off-key" performances? If one wishes to investigate these questions, and if one is concerned, as Goffman is, with the structure and texture of everyday life and not merely "with aspects of theater that creep into" it, then one must study everyday encounters in definite institutional contexts, taking into account their power and authority structures.

Goffman argues that social establishments may be studied from many vantage points and that his "dramaturgical approach may constitute a fifth perspective to be added to the technical, political, structural, and cultural perspectives" (240). But as we all know, some perspectives are methodologically superior to others in that they reveal certain strategic dimensions of reality that the others obscure. One cannot simply lay several perspectives side by side. That Goffman himself recognizes this becomes evident in his *Asylums*, where he subordinates the dramaturgical point of view to the political-structural.

ASYLUMS

Every perspective is determined by the social standpoint and hence, the interests and values of the "observer." Whether he is aware of it or not, his interests tend to coincide with those of some groups more than others as he studies any socially stratified association. The more conscious he is of his own interests and those of the groups he is studying, and the more aware he is that he favors one group over another, the more candid will be his account and the more intelligent will be his all-important decision as to what constitutes the most strategic perspective from which to investigate the social reality in question.

In *Asylums* Goffman guides himself by these principles. He wishes "to learn about the social world of the hospital inmate, as this world is subjectively experienced by him."[3] And he acknowledges immediately that to describe this world faithfully "is necessarily to present a partisan view." It is the partisan view of the inmate that Goffman presents, and he justifies this by arguing that this places the imbalance "on the right side of the scale, since almost all professional literature on mental patients is written from the point of view of the psychiatrists, and he, socially speaking, is on the other side" (x).

In contrast to *The Presentation of Self*, Goffman here centers attention not on abstract unanchored situations but on situations determined by a definite social and political structure. Hence *Asylums* acquires a critical dimension relatively absent from his first book. The mental hospital, the prison, and the concentration camp are examples of what Goffman calls the "total institution"—"a place of residence and work where a large number of like-situated individuals, cut off from the wider society for an appreciable period of time, together lead an enclosed, formally administered round of life" (xiii).

[3] Erving Goffman, *Asylums* (Garden City, N. Y.: Doubleday Anchor Books, 1961), p. ix. Page references to this work are hereafter cited in parentheses immediately following the quoted passage.

In total institutions large numbers of individuals are forced to conduct all their life activities in one place and under a single authority. Inmates or members of such institutions march through life "in the immediate company of a batch of similar others" (6). They are under strict surveillance and control, so that each inmate is where he is supposed to be at any given moment and those in power know the whereabouts of all.

Total institutions have a quasi-class character, for there is a basic cleavage between the inmates and the supervisory staff, the latter feeling "superior and righteous," the former, "inferior, weak, blameworthy, and guilty." Interaction and mobility between the two strata are severely restricted while "social distance is typically great and often formally prescribed" (7). Two antagonistic quasi-classes are in evidence, and power is firmly in the hands of one that dominates the other. Neither stratum has any illusion about who rules this association, and both recognize that the institution is ruled in the interests of the staff, not the inmates.

From the moment the inmate enters the institution, he is systematically subjected to a "series of abasements, degradations, humiliations, and profanations of self" (14). Soon "disculturation" results: the inmate is rendered increasingly unfit for the outside world and trained for the new one in which he is destined to remain for a lengthy period, perhaps forever. Inmates thus suffer "civil death" in that they lose their most precious civil rights, acquiring in their place only the meager "rights" that are paternalistically granted from above. When inmates resist this "resocialization," or defy authority, they are severely punished until they yield.

In this "resocialization" the inmate may be stripped of his name, his personal articles, clothing, and supplies, and stripped even of the appearance he had on the outside. He is mortified and degraded by consistently having to obey, and to adopt humiliating physical postures and humilating verbal responses to his superiors. Throughout he is subjected to "forced social relationships," forced associations with others. In short, concludes Goffman, the total institution is an extreme form of social relationship in which some men, in degrading others, degrade themselves and thereby the whole species.

THE STAFF

Total institutions—or, more correctly, their rulers and ideological spokesmen—present the institution to the outside public as a rational and effective instrument serving the avowed and approved goals of public policy. Actually, however, total institutions "seem to function merely as storage dumps for inmates . . . " (74). The staff continually faces the fact that it has interests of its own and interests in "institutional efficiency" that are seldom, if ever, reconcilable with conduct governed by standards of humanity. The staff is therefore confronted by "some of the classic dilemmas that must be faced by those who govern men" (77).

The interpretive scheme that the governors impose on the inmate is such that his very presence there becomes prima facie evidence that he belongs there. "A man in a political prison must be traitorous; a man in a prison must be a lawbreaker; a man in a mental hospital must be sick. If not traitorous, criminal or sick, why else would he be there?" (84). The staff therefore seeks and finds a crime to fit the punishment. In this and in other ways, those who rule seem to justify the prevailing arrangements and hence their power and practices.

Occasionally the governors allow institutional ceremonies to take place in which inmates profane the staff—whether "through a sly article, a satirical sketch, or overfamiliarity during a dance . . . " (109). Clearly, this does not mean that the rulers have actually relinquished power. Their very toleration of these ceremonies is a sign of the strength of their "state." Nevertheless, the ceremonies do demonstrate "that the difference in character between the two groupings is not inevitable and unalterable" (110).

As this brief summary indicates, throughout this study Goffman highlights the system of domination, the conflict of interests between staff and inmates, and the self-serving ideology of those who rule.

THE PATIENT AS INMATE

In the second essay in *Asylums,* "The Moral Career of the Mental Patient," and in other articles as well,[4] Goffman fundamentally calls into question the prevailing policy by which behavior comes to be defined as psychotic, many aspects of the theory and practice of psychiatry, and, finally, the nature of the institutions that have purportedly been established to treat the mental patient.

How does one become a mental patient? Who decides that one is losing one's mind? It is abundantly clear that when an individual has certain experiences—imagining things, losing his orientation, hearing voices, suspecting he is being followed, and the like—he regards these as "symptoms" of illness because that is how they have been defined and stereotyped in his culture. There are a thousand reasons why an individual in our society might have such experiences and most often, even from a psychiatric standpoint, they signify nothing more than "a temporary emotional upset in a stressful situation . . . " (132).

What is important to note is that the experiences come to be defined as "symptoms" by the significant others with whom one has immediate and frequent interaction. These others begin to define forms of conduct as symptomatic of mental illness when they begin to experience that conduct as

[4] See, for example, Erving Goffman "Mental Symptoms and Public Order," in *Interaction Ritual* (Garden City, N. Y.: Doubleday Anchor Books, 1967), pp. 137–48.

troublesome or offensive. Just as we might say that common crime offends the property order, treachery the political order, incest the kinship order, homosexuality the sex-role order, and drug addiction some aspect of the moral order, so might one argue that so-called psychotic behavior offends

> what might be thought of as public order, especially one part of public order, the order governing persons by virtue of their being in one another's immediate physical presence. Much psychotic behavior is, in the first instance, a failure to abide by rules established for the conduct of face-to-face interaction—rules established that is, or at least enforced, by some evaluating, judging, or policing group. Psychotic behavior is, in many instances, what might be called a situational impropriety.[5]

In the United States, most pre-patients enter the hospital *unwillingly*: family or friends either implore or threaten them to enter "willingly," police or attendants forcefully escort them, or someone close persuades them on deceptive grounds. From the very outset, therefore, the pre-patient feels coerced, abandoned, embittered and, often, even betrayed. Wherever one might locate the psychological beginning of the pre-patients' illness, there is a definite social beginning in which some complainant takes action against the "offender."

Moreover, numerous contingencies govern the process of becoming a mental patient. Among the more obvious are socioeconomic status, conspicuousness of the "offense," proximity to a hospital, availability of treatment facilities, and the family's and community's attitude toward available treatment. Other contingencies involve what Goffman calls "atrocity tales": "A psychotic man is tolerated by his wife until she finds herself a boy friend, or by his adult children until they move from a house to an apartment; an alcoholic is sent to a mental hospital because the jail is full, and a drug addict because he declines to avail himself of psychiatric treatment on the outside; a rebellious adolescent daughter can no longer be managed at home because she now threatens to have an open affair with an unsuitable companion, and so on" (135).

But contingencies also enable individuals to avoid such a fate, just as once an individual enters a hospital contingencies determine whether and how soon he will be discharged. The official view of those in mental hospitals is that they are there because they are ill; yet insofar as those outside hospitals numerically exceed those inside, "we could say that mental patients distinctively suffer not from mental illness, but from contingencies" (135).

Almost invariably the pre-patient experiences the process of becoming a patient as a third person in an "alienative coalition." He finds that a next-of-kin or dear friend has come to some prior understanding with the professional. He is told he is being committed for his own good but he experiences this as a hostile coalition against him—which in turn leads to a fundamentally greater estrange-

[5] Goffman, "Mental Symptoms and Public Order," p. 141.

ment between himself and his next-of-relation than his initial troubles may have brought about. He feels betrayed and deserted by those who claim they love him most.

Most often, therefore, it is the very person to whom the pre-patient turns for help and protection—against forceful commitment, for example—whom the professionals also approach seeking authorization. This does not mean that when the next-of-kin appeals to the professional for help he has already planned to hospitalize the pre-patient; indeed, he may not even regard him as definitely ill. Typically it is the professional who persuades the relative that it entails no betrayal to hospitalize the pre-patient for his own health and welfare.

Once hospitalized, the "patient's" troubles really begin. Now his life begins to follow that fateful pattern common to the inmates of all total institutions—prisons, concentration camps, labor camps, and the like. Ironically, the more "medical" and therapeutic is the hospital's orientation, and the less custodial, the more the staff will strive to impose upon the inpatient a view of himself as a failure. They will press him to understand that the cause of his trouble lies within him, that his attitude toward life has been wrong, and that he must change both his way of relating to others and his conception of himself.

Goffman tells the inpatient's "sad tale" with compassion. A host of pressures converge to coerce him into taking the institution's view toward himself. Not only informally but in formal records as well, staff will describe the inpatient in terms that a "layman would consider scandalous, defamatory, and discrediting" (158). If a staff member should happen to question and doubt a patient's illness or to take seriously his complaints of abuse or malpractice, this too will avail the patient nothing. The staff meeting will soon develop a common front and a common "line," assuring the anxious staff member that the patient is really sick.

So long as an individual remains in a mental hospital he also remains deprived of the customary means of expressing the anger and alienation he now has more reason to feel than ever before. He therefore reaches out for whatever is available, including unauthorized means of obtaining his ends. Such means and practices Goffman calls "secondary adjustments." They "comprise . . . the *underlife* of the institution, being to a social establishment what an underworld is to a city" (199).

A PUBLIC INSTITUTION'S UNDERLIFE

In the mental hospital no less than in other total institutions, inmates learn to work the system. Prisons, work camps, concentration camps, and mental hospitals require some labor from the inmates. The resulting distribution of assignments creates opportunities. Whether it is the kitchen, laundry, or shoe-repair shop; or recreational facilities such as the canteen, tennis courts, or library, the worker finds ways to help himself to the "fruit of his labor." Furthermore, the work situation allows the inmate to develop a special and favored relation with his staff supervisor, which, in turn, might bring with it additional privileges.

Occasionally the work position itself provides escape from perpetual surveillance. Failing this, however, inmates seek and find places where they can hide, and with some security engage in unauthorized activities. All such places of refuge provide the inmate with a temporary sense of self-determination and relaxation. So desirable are such places that inpatients will gladly suffer severe physical discomforts if only they can be relatively free of control. Human beings always seek and frequently find "free places"—a small and temporary measure of freedom even under the most totalitarian conditions.

Some of these free places soon become the exclusive preserve of specific individuals and groups; they assert and acquire proprietary rights over these places and keep others out. Goffman cites three types of places over which patients exert unusual control: "free places" which he shares with any other patient; "group territories," which he shares with a select few; and, finally, "personal territory," which no one shares "except by [the patient's] own invitation" (243).

Seeking escape from surveillance often brings with it a severe competition for scarce places and other resources, and even the domination and exploitation of some patients by others. This was especially evident to Goffman in the "bad wards," where, he informs us, "one patient might force a mute one off a footrest, leaving the vocal patient with a chair *and* a footrest, and the mute patient with nothing at all—a difference that is not negligible considering the fact that except for breaks at mealtime some patients spend the whole of the day in these wards doing nothing but sitting or standing in one place" (246).

Indeed, naked coercion plays no small role in the relations among the patients. The weak comply with the demands of the strong simply because noncompliance would increase considerably their pain and suffering. Goffman observes that "open expropriation, blackmail, strong-arm techniques, forced sexual submission—these are the methods that can be employed without rationalization as a means of bringing the activities of another into one's own line of action" (263). Thus men continue to desire what the restrictive and repressive controls have deprived them of. To realize the objects of their desires they not only manipulate the authorities, resisting them in various ingenious ways, but also dominate and exploit their fellow patients.

The underlife of a mental hospital is a special instance of a much more general phenomenon. In every total institution—indeed, in every stratified social organization—the probability is great that one will find conduct running counter to the official view: "Where enthusiasm is expected, there will be apathy; where loyalty, there will be disaffection; where attendance, absenteeism; where robustness, some kind of illness; where deeds are to be done, varieties of inactivity" (305).

It is the particularly tragic circumstance of the mental patient that his every expression of dissatisfaction and alienation is construed by the authorities as symptomatic of the very illness

> the institution was established to deal with and as the best kind of evidence that the patient properly belongs where he now finds himself. In short, mental hospitalization out-maneuvers the patient, tending to rob him of the common expressions through which people hold off the embrace of organizations—insolence, silence, *sotto voce* remarks, unco-operativeness, malicious destruction of interior decorations, and so forth; these signs of disaffiliation are now read as signs of their maker's proper affiliation. (306)

Every alienative act thus becomes a psychotic symptom.

But resistance and opposition to authority go on. Like the inmates of other total institutions, the inpatient engages in "world building" activities that temporarily "remove" him from his oppressive conditions. At the same time he shows solidarity with his fellows when they stand against authority, occasionally even participating in elaborate plans for escape. Resistance may therefore be viewed as a way of giving his existence meaning and demonstrating to himself at least "that he has some selfhood and personal autonomy beyond the grasp of the organization" (314).

It is clear in this discussion that Goffman's purpose is not only to describe the form of domination and resistance peculiar to a specific total institution, but also to grasp the nature of the *self*. The sustained and strenuous efforts of an individual to save something of himself from the "clutch of an institution" are evident not only in closed, total institutions but in open ones as well. The efforts are "not an incidental mechanism of defense but rather an essential constituent of the self" (319). In opposition to the one-sided sociological determinism stressing as a positive fact that society shapes and forms the individual, Goffman stresses the other side of the process. In any social role, relationship, or organization, "we always find the individual employing methods to keep some distance, some elbow room, between himself and that with which others assume he should be identified" (319).

That Goffman in this context subscribes to a dialectical conception of the self becomes most evident in his suggestion that the individual ought perhaps to be defined "as a stance-taking entity, a something that takes up a position somewhere between identification with an organization and opposition to it, and is ready at the slightest pressure to regain its balance by shifting its involvement in either direction. It is thus *against something* that the self can emerge." If this is true under totalitarian conditions, "may this not be the situation . . . in free society, too?" (320).

Goffman does not explicitly employ the concept of repression or "surplus repression" (a concept I shall elaborate in Chapter 19). Nor does he explicitly employ Mead's "I," the impulsive, active, creative self. Yet these concepts are more or less implied in Goffman's view of the self as a stance-taking entity that resists and opposes domination and seeks to safeguard and widen its boundaries of freedom. As we shall see, however, he abandons these important concepts in his subsequent work.

Goffman has shown us quite effectively that the mentally ill, particularly the "functionally psychotic," may be regarded as persons who offend an area of public order—the proprieties of everyday encounters. The mentally ill are those who cause troubles for others, who soon collaborate in putting them away. The official ideology maintains that the pre-patient is hospitalized for his own good so that he may avail himself of the medical-therapeutic care he needs in order to get well. Actually, however, he is being incarcerated to keep him from constituting either a danger or a nuisance to others. The mental hospital is therefore not a service but a custodial institution, in much the same sense as the prison.

In these terms the mental hospital is only one among numerous types of custodial institutions that exist to separate "socially troublesome people" from those who find them troublesome. This is borne out not only by the prison-like structure of the mental hospital, but also by the attitude of outsiders toward the former patient once he has achieved his freedom. Having a mental-hospital record stigmatizes a man no less than having a prison record.

Goffman thus questions fundamentally the service frame of reference in terms of which mental hospitals are officially justified. It is altogether inadequate to regard the mental patient as sick, pure and simple, and to attribute to the professionals a technical competence that enables them to diagnose "pathologies" scientifically—especially when a "functional" disorder is involved. Since "pathology" is conduct that is improper, offensive, or troublesome to others, there is no purely technical means of recognizing and analyzing so-called pathologies. What constitutes a "pathology" is therefore quite problematic and may very well be a moral judgment that some, from the standpoint of their own values and interests, make of others. More, decisions regarding the so-called mentally ill tend to be of a political nature, since these decisions express "the special interests of some particular faction or person rather than interests that can be said to be above the concerns of any particular grouping, as in the case of physical pathology" (364).

Accordingly the patient views all those who collaborated in incarcerating him, particularly those who are treating him, as persons with power over him. Far from being a mere patient, he is like "a charge pleading with his master for more priviliges, a prisoner remonstrating with an unlawful jailor, or a prideful man declining to exchange communications with someone who thinks he is crazy" (367). Of course, neither the professional ideology of the psychiatrist nor the institutional ideology acknowledges any of this. Professionals and staff persist in framing their relationship with the patient in strictly technical-professional and service terms. The patient's every act is dubbed "schizophrenic," "psychopathic," etc., and even normal conduct is defined as a mere "mask or shield for the essential sickness behind it" (375).

In this way the patient is transformed into the object of a disciplinary and custodial practice that the official ideology presents as medical and therapeutic. He is crushed by a situation that provides little actual treatment and in which his improvement, if it occurs at all, does so "in spite of hospitalization, and presumably might occur more frequently in circumstances other than the deprived ones within the institution" (382).

Goffman's analysis in the essays in *Asylums* is highly illuminating because he critically questions the prevailing definition of things. By taking into account the various group interests involved in mental institutions he shows that the mental hospital is not what it is said to be. Through his analysis we come to see clearly how every stage of the patient's career is determined by his relationship with more powerful others. His career as a pre-patient begins by offending the interests and values of others; once he becomes a patient, he enters a relation of subjection to those who control the institution. Goffman thus lays bare key relationships and conflicts of interest and enables us to see behind the official ideology. By taking the standpoint of the main victims of this institutional process, he helps us to see clearly how even the victims of totalitarian rule strive for autonomy and freedom. These are the qualities that make the essays in *Asylums* so penetrating. Unfortunately, however, these same qualities are much less evident in Goffman's subsequent work.

ROLES AND FREEDOM

In the essay "Role Distance" published in 1961, Goffman addresses himself to the important question of the autonomy an individual retains within the roles he plays, exploring the limitations of the traditional role framework. He begins by distinguishing "among typical roles, the normative aspect of role, and a particular individual's actual role performance."[6] He then turns to what he calls "situated activity systems" with the aim of adapting "role concepts for use in close studies of moment-to-moment behavior." He limits himself to such behavior as it "occurs entirely within the walls of single social establishments" (95). "Situated activity system" refers to "the performance of a single joint activity, a somewhat closed, self-compensating, self-terminating circuit of interdependent actions. ... The performance of a surgical operation is an example" (96).

The point of all this, Goffman says, is to enable the student of behavior to deal more adequately with the "complexities of concrete conduct." If the

[6] Erving Goffman, "Role Distance," in *Encounters* (Indianapolis and New York: Bobbs-Merrill Co., 1961), p. 93. Page references to this essay are hereafter cited in parentheses immediately following the quoted passage.

"situation system faithfully expresses in miniature the structure of the broader social organization in which it is located," traditional role analysis is adequate. If, on the other hand, "a discrepancy is found," traditional analysis would appear to require revision.

The revision Goffman proposes revolves about the "problem of expression." Individuals police and control their expressions so that they will be consistent with the expectations and obligations of the particular role they are playing. Thus, to take the very serious role of surgeon, one can observe him both before and after he enters the operating room out of role, so to speak—that is, staring vacantly, picking his nose, or combing his hair, "all in a manner unbecoming a surgeon . . . " (101). This presents no special problems that traditional role theory cannot account for. Nor does the conduct of the three or four-year-old boy as he rides a wooden horse or a merry-go-round. In this case "doing is being," says Goffman, for the child embraces the role fully and seriously.

When the actor embraces a role as does the child, he expresses attachment to it, he demonstrates his capacities to perform it, and he shows active engagement in it. The term "embracement" refers to conduct in which all "three features are present." "To embrace a role," Goffman writes, "is to disappear completely into the virtual self available in the situation, to be fully seen in terms of the image, and to confirm expressively one's acceptance of it." (106).

In contrast, if one studies the merry-go-round behavior of a somewhat older boy, say at age five, one finds significant differences. Now the role of the wooden-horse rider is played much less seriously. He shows his complete control by clapping his hands and feet, by changing horses while in motion and without descending to the platform, by leaning "back as far as possible while looking up to the sky in a challenge to dizziness" (107). This child does not embrace his role—far from it. His every action shows irreverence for it and detachment from it. "Whatever I am," his actions are saying, "I'm not just someone who can barely stay on a wooden horse." (107). This child has detached himself, Goffman argues, from "the whole role."

This brings us closer to Goffman's main point: when a wedge is driven between an individual and his "putative role," when a definite separateness is evident and the individual shows "disaffection from or resistance against" a role, there exists "role distance" (108). There are many instances of this in the serious world of adults as well.

Goffman selects as an illustration the behavior of the chief surgeon in the operating room, on the grounds that this must surely be one of the most serious and demanding of roles. What does one find? The chief surgeon occasionally adopts a farcical, ironic tone toward the members of his team; he jokes with them; he uses humorous, nontechnical labels when requesting specific instruments, and so on. Even here, then, one finds *role* distance—which Goffman wants to explain in strictly sociological terms, that is, without abandoning "a strictly sustained role perspective" (120). The result is a functional analysis in which he seeks the "functions of role distance for surgery" (120). Paradoxically, he argues, it is precisely one's commitment to the situated activity system that prevents one from fully embracing one's role. Why? Because certain maneuvers, or system-irrelevant roles, are necessary to "integrate the system."

The situated system demands that the individual balance its "needs" against all other claims on himself, including those of his particular role. Each member of the team must be in control of himself; when such control diminishes, the chief surgeon especially must help him regain it. All team members must "keep their heads during the operation," so the chief surgeon feels he must help by subordinating what is due him by virtue of his status to the needs of the situation.

If, for example, "he exercises his situated rights openly to criticize incompetent conduct, the surgeon may only further weaken the defaulter's self-command and further endanger the particular operation" (121–22). He therefore sacrifices some dignity in order to keep the anxiety level down. By becoming a "nice guy" and demanding less deference than his official status entitles him to demand, he facilitates the smoother cooperation among team members and therefore increases the probability of the operation's success.

Goffman's argument seems to be this: the surgical operation is a highly complicated and delicate task requiring the full attention and cooperation of the team members, and hence, all are under great tension. Under these circumstances, if the surgeon were to demand from his team members the full respect his status formally enables him to demand, he would add to the already great tension, thus possibly endangering the entire operation and defeating the purpose of the situated activity.

If we generalize from Goffman's illustration, we must infer that all superordinate-subordinate relations are characterized by anxiety and tension. If the chief surgeon gave outright commands, instead of joking, he would add substantial tension to that inherent in the task itself. By refraining from adopting a fully official posture, and by exercising role distance, so-called, he contributes to the reduction of tension and anxiety to the lowest possible level under the circumstances: that inherent in the task. Moreover, only the surgeon or superordinate is in a position to maintain this level, for if a subordinate were to exercise role distance it might appear as insubordination, and hence heighten tension.

Goffman's approach does not do full justice to the problem, for he remains strictly within the confines of the sociological role perspective and never addresses himself to the ultimate sources of tension and anxiety in roles and relationships. So long as he refrains from inquiring into these sources, his solution must remain superficial. Goffman does perceive the individual as seeking a measure of freedom from his role, but he does not employ either Freud's or Mead's concepts to explain this freedom-seeking inclination. The individual, Goffman writes, "must be seen as someone who organizes his expressive situational behavior *in relation* to situated activity roles, but . . . in doing this he uses whatever means are at hand to introduce a margin of freedom and maneuverability, of pointed disidentification, between himself and the self virtually available for him in the situation" (132–33). But Goffman fails to indicate why the individual would "introduce a margin of freedom and maneuverability."

Goffman remains on the surface of an important phenomenon. Although he recognizes that there will always be "*some* discrepancy between the self emerging from a situated activity role and the self associated with the role title in the name of which the activity is carried on," he wants to account for this exclusively in terms of a closed sociological perspective. "Surgery," he writes, "requires acts unbecoming a surgeon, just as mothering requires acts that are unmaternal" (134). Thus, if the surgeon relaxes his authority, he is simply borrowing from his "nice guy" role; and if mother panics, for whatever reason—breaks out in tears and acts like a child—she is simply borrowing from the child role.

Goffman's conception of "role distance" thus resolves itself into the rather simple proposition that we tailor the roles we play to the situations we find ourselves in by borrowing materials from other roles. Roles are not monoliths. If this is all Goffman intends by his revision, however, it is hardly a revision, since it is already a part of any intelligent sociological thinking. If this is all Goffman wants to convey, he would seem to have lost the important truth he grasped implicitly in *Asylums*.

There, as we have seen, the self was a stance-taking entity that resisted domination and sought freedom. In "Role Distance," however, we read that the "various identificatory demands are not created by the individual but are drawn from what society allots him. He frees himself from one group, not to be free, but because there is another hold on him" (139). This partially valid, one-sided proposition Goffman elevates to the status of a supreme principle, thereby dissolving the self into a mere multiplicity of roles with no nonsociological residue.

The basic shortcoming here is that Goffman, like other post-Meadian symbolic interactionists, refuses to recognize the human individual as an active, creative, spontaneous being who resists roles, especially certain roles; he refuses to recognize that the detachment, distance, or freedom one seeks from social roles and other social constraints has organic roots and that the relative success or failure to achieve some measure of freedom also has organic consequences; he refuses, finally, to consider seriously the constraining and oppressive character of social roles and relationships, not only from the standpoint of certain ethical and cultural values but also from the standpoint of the expressive needs of the biologic individual we call a human being.

Goffman apparently holds to a sociologistic conception that denies that the human individual is anything more than a bundle of roles. In given situations he distances himself from some and moves closer to others and this is where "the individual's personal style is to be found" (152). Somehow Goffman overlooks that if this distancing is to be anything more than a mechanistic response to an external stimulus, anything more than a passive adapting to roles and situations, there must be an active creative side that initiates activity. This, of course, again brings us back to what is so important about Mead's conception of the self but which Goffman effectively ignores. For it is ironic that despite Goffman's concern for the freedom and autonomy of the individual, he deprives him of an autonomous self. The self we find in Goffman is all "me," never "I."

Goffman notes that under conditions of domination, subordinate individuals who cannot openly challenge those in power nevertheless show that they have not totally capitulated: "sullenness, muttering, irony, joking, and sarcasm may all allow one to show that something of oneself lies outside the constraints of the moment . . . " (114). But in his zealous devotion to strictly sociological means of understanding this important phenomenon he consistently and vehemently rejects any view according to which the individual "behaves personally and spontaneously, (phrasing the standard obligations in a way that has a special psychological fit for him)" (115). But Goffman nowhere tells us why he insists on this purely sociological approach or what one presumably gains therefrom.

PUBLIC GATHERINGS AND SITUATIONS

Returning to the question of situational proprieties and improprieties, Goffman, in *Behavior in Public Places*, centers our attention upon the implicit rules governing behavior in public and semipublic places: "The norms of face-to-face conduct in streets, parks, restaurants, theatres, shops, dance floors, meeting halls and other gathering places of any community . . . "[7] The implicit norms are "negatively eventful" in that they involve negative sanctions when we fail to act in accordance with them but otherwise remain unnoticed. Goffman frankly acknowledges that he is exploring mainly the middle-class realm of his own experience.

Since the center of his interest is behavior in the immediate physical presence of others—embodied information—he reviews the importance of physical appearance, limb discipline, apparel, and facial expressions as we move in and out of situated gatherings and participate in them. "We have party faces, funeral faces, and various kinds of institutional faces" (28), and presenting the appropriate face is something one learns only after considerable experience involving numerous rehearsals. In terms quite similar to those used in *The Presentation of Self*, Goffman explores the importance of "body idiom"—"dress, bearing, movement and position, sound level, physical gestures . . . formal

[7] Erving Goffman, *Behavior in Public Places* (New York: The Free Press, 1963), p. 4. Page references to this book are hereafter cited in parentheses immediately following the quoted passage.

decorations, and broad emotional expression"—as a form of nonverbal communication we all inevitably engage in, adapting it to the norms of propriety of our situated activities.

Among the most important of norms pertaining to face-to-face interaction are those having to do with the degree of our involvement in given situations. In face-to-face situations, we divide our attention and allocate it between "*main* and *side* involvements" (43). When we allow a major portion of our attention and interest to be absorbed, this is a main involvement; frequently, even while we are thus absorbed we engage in a minor activity, a side involvement, which does not, however, disrupt the main one. It follows that one can become overinvolved and underinvolved in situations, so that showing just the right degree of involvement is an ideal of social intercourse, a rule of propriety.

Goffman discusses various objects of involvement, including one's own body or self—what he calls auto-involvement, an extreme form of which is masturbation. There are also "creature releases" that "slip through the individual's self-control and momentarily assert his 'animal nature.' They appear to provide a brief release from the tension experienced by the individual in keeping himself steadily and entirely draped in social clothing—momentary capitulations to the itches that plague a performer who does not want to sneeze in his role" (68–69). Goffman ranges over a continuum of such creature releases. At one end are scratching, coughing, sighing, yawning and the like; at the other end "flatulence, incontinence, and the like; in the middle ranges are . . . dozing off, belching, spitting, nose-picking . . . " (69).

But there is also the phenomenon Goffman calls "away." "While outwardly participating in an activity within a social situation, an individual can allow his attention to turn from what he and everyone else considers the real or serious world and give himself up for a time to a playlike world in which he alone participates" (69). And later he writes, "individuals develop many untaxing activities as covers behind which to go into a reverie" (72).

It is clear, then, that Goffman here acknowledges a definite tension that the human individual experiences in his social roles. Accordingly, the individual seeks to reduce or to escape this tension through "creature releases," getting "away," and the like. This is therefore related to the issues raised in our earlier discussion of "role distance." For what "creature releases," "away," and "role distance" all have in common is the pronounced effort individuals make to limit embracement in a role and social situation, to loosen its grip upon them and, in a word, to achieve some measure of freedom from social constraints.

However, in this book no less than in *Encounters*, Goffman fails to recognize the human significance of what he observes. *Why* does the tension exist between the individual and his social roles? What is its significance? Goffman sidesteps these questions.

Even when Goffman tacitly acknowledges the tension between man's biological nature and the "social clothing" he steadily drapes himself in, to what does he draw our attention? To "creature releases"—sneezing, yawning scratching. In this way he brings into relief man's "animal nature" but not the organic roots of his human nature and need for freedom.

To anticipate a thesis which we shall later develop in detail, Goffman fails to grasp those aspects of the human condition to which Freud, Mead, and Marx alerted us. Freud's concept of repression states that, whatever more he may be or become, the human individual always remains a living organism from whom the socializing, or civilizing, process unavoidably exacts a heavy toll in real pain, deprivation, and suffering. Marx's concept of alienation alerts us to the fact that human suffering is immeasurably increased by the prevailing social forms of domination. What these concepts have in common and imply—indeed what Marx, Mead, and Freud insisted upon—is that the human individual is an active and insurgent being: no matter how apparently total are the forms of social control and discipline over the individual, he always retains some measure of resistance to them, some measure of freedom-seeking will. These propositions, implicit in *Asylums*, disappear from Goffman's subsequent work.

COMING FULL CIRCLE

With *Stigma* and *Strategic Interaction* Goffman returns to the problem that concerned him in the beginning: the presentation of self.

Let us first look briefly at *Stigma*. The term "stigma" refers to a sign of some discrediting attribute that an individual has. Goffman regards the process by which one becomes stigmatized as a much neglected area of study. He wants therefore to explore the process and "describe the structural preconditions of stigma . . . "[8]

Goffman sees three types of stigma: (1) physical deformities; (2) short-comings of character, especially those inferred from one's record as mental patient, prisoner, drug addict, alcoholic, homosexual, etc.; and (3) stigma associated with race, nation, and religion. Whatever the type of stigma that an individual carries, it is something he and others know about and take into account in their social interactions.

The stigmatized individual is ill at ease with so-called "normals," just as they are with him. The "normals," however, are frequently in a position to reduce the life chances of the stigmatized. Since the normals are normal against him, and since the stigmatized individual knows this very well, his main task becomes one of gaining acceptance among them. Sometimes he achieves this by removing his bodily deformity or ridding himself of his characterological defect.

[8] Erving Goffman, *Stigma* (Englewood Cliffs, N. J.: Prentice-Hall, 1963), p. 2. Page references to this work are hereafter cited in parentheses immediately following the quoted passage.

This may result, however, not in imparting to him normal status, but rather in transforming him "from someone with a particular blemish into someone with a record of having corrected a particular blemish" (9).

What interests Goffman primarily are the face-to-face encounters of normals and stigmatized, the moment when they are in the same situation and must therefore confront the stigma and take it into account. Clearly, this may require delicate, calculating impression management on both sides. The stigmatized person is anxious and self-conscious in the face of the too sympathetic or unsympathetic concern of the normal; but the latter is also anxious, regarding the stigmatized as, say, either too aggressive or too humble. The stigmatized person has the perennial problem of managing the impressions he makes as well as the inevitable tension that emerges in his encounters with normals. Frequently, moreover, his stigma is not conspicuous or apparent, so he has the additional problem of managing information—should he disclose his shortcoming or not? Often the stigmatized whose defects are not readily apparent try to "pass."

The "passer's" psychic state continues to be one of anxiety. He lives in fear of being discovered; he has found acceptance among normals who remain prejudiced against the category of persons to which, unbeknown to them, he belongs; he experiences extreme marginality. He feels himself neither fish not fowl, for he has abandoned his own "group" without gaining full and true acceptance in the other. More than the discredited person who never attempts to pass and certainly more than the normal, the "passing" but always discreditable person needs continually to employ strategies to present himself in a manner so as to minimize risk and reduce anxiety.

Now, to see the connection between Goffman's first book and his most recent, *Strategic Interaction*, and between both and *Stigma*, we must appreciate what he is arguing in the latter: we are all carriers of stigma; we are all engaged in "passing," just as we are all normal. Goffman rejects the view that would place all those "who possess a flaw that uneases almost all their social situations" into one pile (the "stigmatized") presumably distinct from the other (the "normals"). There is only one pile, not two.

> The most fortunate of normals is likely to have his half-hidden failing, and for every little failing there is a social occasion when it will loom large, creating a shameful gap between virtual and actual social identity. Therefore, the occasionally precarious and the constantly precarious form a single continuum, their situation in life analyzable by the same framework. (127)

We are all therefore engaged in passing and covering, for these are "a special application of the arts of impression management, the arts, basic in social life, through which the individual exerts strategic control over the image of himself and his products that others gain from him" (131). If impression management entails the strategic control of one's image, it is an "information contest," a game, a form of strategic interaction.

In *Strategic Interaction* Goffman comes full circle. As in *The Presentation of Self*, he again explores "exuded expressions" and "expressed information" but presumably with more explicit attention to "the individual's capacity to acquire, reveal, and conceal information."[9] The communality of theme between the two books is quite evident. In *Strategic Interaction* the focus of interest is still upon face-to-face communication that derives particularly "from paralinguistic cues such as intonation, facial gestures, and the like—cues that have an expressive, not semantic, character" (9). People "inhibit and fabricate" their expressions; they are therefore engaged in "expression games."

So Goffman adds to the vocabulary of expression a vocabulary of games. There is the "unwitting move," an act unoriented to an observer's assessment; a "naive move," a subject's act that an observer takes as it appears; a "control or covering move," a subject's deliberate act designed "to produce expressions that he thinks will improve the situation if they are gleaned by the observer" (12). This is a form of impression management because the "subject . . . tends to make use of the observer's use of his behavior before the observer has a chance to do so" (13).

Observer and subject attempt in this way to gain information from the expressive behavior of the other. Each participates in a "contest of assessment," controlling his own expressions while assessing the other's. The contest involves moves, covering moves, uncovering moves, and "counter-uncovering moves" (19).

Much of what Goffman has to say here is a translation of Mead's conception of role taking into the language of games (47). To appreciate what Goffman's translation implies it is necessary to recall the context and purpose of Mead's theory. For Mead, the complex process of taking the attitude of the other, including the emergence of the reflexive self and mind, facilitates man's rational quest for freedom. The reflective process illuminates men's ways as they strive to solve their most pressing practical problems and to remove the obstacles obstructing their way to higher forms of cooperation.

This Goffman transforms into an expression contest, a Hobbesian "war of each against all." By some sleight of hand, he soon abandons the realm of face-to-face interaction in everyday life and draws his illustrations almost exclusively from the world of espionage, spy games, and cops and robbers. Indeed, the impression is unavoidable that the condition he calls "degeneration of expression"—taking nothing at face value, constantly suspecting other's motives, seeing traps everywhere—is typical, not exceptional.

The inevitable effect of Goffman's game metaphors and the illustrations drawn from double agentry is to portray the world of everyday life as if it were a

---

[9] Erving Goffman, *Strategic Interaction* (Philadelphia: University of Pennsylvania Press, 1969), p. 4. Page references to this work are hereafter cited in parentheses immediately following the quoted passage.

world of gamesmen, a world in which there is no obviously innocent expression—that is, after all, precisely the impression that "a guilty expert gamesman would give" (69).

Goffman himself reveals some ambivalence toward his metaphors but resolves it rather easily. It is true, he says, that in a number of important respects "agents are unlike ordinary mortals." But the analogy is nonetheless warranted because "Getting oneself through an international incident involves contingencies and capacities that have a bearing on the games that go on in local neighborhoods" (79).

Goffman wants thus to transform all of us into agents who expose and discredit others, fearing all the while that we ourselves shall soon be discovered and exposed. In this way Goffman attributes to the whole of everyday social intercourse a fundamental cynicism. It may be true, as Goffman observes, that "every adult who has had a friend or spouse has had occasion to doubt expression of relationship and then to doubt the doubt even while giving the other reasons to suspect that something is being doubted" (81). But it is an unwarranted interpretation that Goffman makes of this—an interpretation couched in vulgar exchange-theory terms—when he adds, "In every social situation we can find a sense in which one participant will be an observer with something to gain from assessing expressions, and another will be a subject with something to gain from manipulating this process. . . . [This] renders agents a little like us all and all of us a little like agents" (81).

The modifier "little" does not minimize by much the power of the agent metaphor. Goffman, whose speciality is the able use of metaphor, himself appreciates how game metaphors and attitudes may fatefully determine the human condition. He observes that many regarded President Kennedy's handling of the Cuban missile crisis—"however successful in terms of the game—[as] a bad omen of the penetration of game attitudes into wrong places" (67). The same might be said of Goffman's application of double-agentry terms to everyday life.

16

Herbert Blumer's
Symbolic Interaction

It was Herbert Blumer who, in 1937, in an article entitled "Social Psychology," coined the term "symbolic interaction" to denote the approach represented by such thinkers as Charles H. Cooley, W. I. Thomas, Robert E. Park, E. W. Burgess, Florian Znaniecki, William James, John Dewey, and George Herbert Mead.[1] In a later essay, "Society and Symbolic Interaction," Blumer argues that Mead, more than any of the others, laid out the main premises of this approach, though he did not "develop its methodological implications for sociological study."[2] I take this essay to be Blumer's statement of the main principles laid out by Mead and a programmatic effort at sketching out the method that follows from those principles. Let us examine it in detail.

Symbolic interaction, writes Blumer, "refers ... to the peculiar and distinctive character of interaction as it takes place between human beings." Actors do not simply react to each other but interpret and define each other's actions. An actor's response is not immediate and direct but rather based on an assessment of the meaning of the act. Human interaction is therefore mediated by the use of symbols, "by interpretation or by ascertaining the meaning of another's actions" (180).

Blumer then goes on to other premises, which may be summarized as follows: The human being has a "self," that is, he can make himself the object of his own actions, or act toward himself as he might act toward others. This enables the individual to make indications to himself, and these self-indications are what we call consciousness. Anything the individual is conscious of, ranging

[1] Herbert Blumer, "Social Psychology," in *Man and Society*, ed. E. Schmidt (New York: Prentice-Hall, 1937), p. 153.

[2] Herbert Blumer, "Society and Symbolic Interaction," in *Human Behavior and Social Process*, ed. Arnold M. Rose (Boston: Houghton Mifflin, 1962), p. 180. Page references to this work are hereafter cited in parentheses immediately following the quoted passage.

from the ticking of a clock to an abstruse meaning is a self-indication, and the conscious life of the human being is a steady flow of such self-indications. Further, the self and its constitution mediated by language enables the human being to abstract something from his surroundings, and to give it meaning—to "make it into an object" (182). The object is no mere stimulus but is constituted by the individual's disposition to act. In these terms, humans tend to construct and reconstruct their actions and hence their world.

The main premises of the symbolic interactionist approach are, therefore,

> that human society is made up of individuals who have selves (that is, make indications to themselves); that individual action is a construction and not a release, being built up by the individual through noting and interpreting features of the situations in which he acts; that group or collective action consists of the aligning of individual actions, brought about by the individual's interpreting or taking into account each other's actions. (184)

Symbolic interaction, it is important to note, is opposed to positing "factors" or "forces" and explaining human conduct in those terms. Even when such forces are lodged in the "social system," "social structure," etc., this procedure is opposed by symbolic interactionists because it treats individuals as "media through which such factors operate" and denies or ignores that it is individuals who act "by making indications to themselves" (185).

Similarly, symbolic interaction opposes psychological factors and forces: "the "self" is not brought into the picture by introducing such items as organic drives, motives, attitudes, feelings, internalized social factors, or psychological components. Such psychological factors have the same status as the social factors mentioned: they are regarded as factors which play on the individual to produce his action. They do not constitute the process of self-indication" (185).

This brief summary should be sufficient to show how Blumer, in his effort to avoid the reification of dimensions of human interaction, presents us with a philosophical conception that flattens out both "society" and the "individual." On the one hand he insists on a society without structure: human society refers to the "empirically observable activity" of acting units, whether individuals or groups, and therefore one cannot speak of "units that do not act—for example, social classes in modern society" (187). On the other hand, he insists on individuals without organic drives.

This is a conception of reality that carries with it an ironic epistemological twist. For if we take this argument literally in its refusal to speak about "units that do not act," it becomes a crude positivism or empiricism for which the only reality is the immediately observable. If one accepts this view, one has no right to employ concepts that have no direct empirical referent. How can one speak of "social classes" if one cannot observe them acting? At the same time Blumer's fear of reification leads him to deny drives, motives, attitudes, and feelings—to deny everything but the "self" indicating itself, whether alone or in alignment with other such self- or other-indicating selves. "Society" is thus nothing more than a plurality of disembodied selves interacting in structureless situations.

Methodologically this means that what is most important is to "catch" the interpretive process of interaction "as it occurs in the experience of the acting unit which uses it" (188), and above all to avoid viewing "human society in terms of structure or organization" and treating "social action as an expression of such structure or organization" (189).

The desire to avoid the reification of concepts is noteworthy. Nonetheless, the *use* of concepts should not be confused with their reification. What epistemological principle gives one the right, let us ask, to employ the concept of "self" and to deny to others the use of the concept "social class," "impulse," etc.? Is the concept "self" more empirically verifiable than the concept "social class"?

It is one thing to say that "organizations and changes in it [sic] are the product of the activity of acting units and not of 'forces' which leave such acting units out of account" (189). The first part of the proposition, through the word "forces," is a fruitful reminder that only individuals act, not organizations or "forces"; however, the remainder of the sentence simply calls attention to a mystical reification of "forces" in an organizational context or to bad sociology, or to both. Only those sociologists who do in fact posit "forces" in society independent of acting individuals have need for Blumer's methodological injunction.

But Blumer appears to want to rule out the possibility of speaking of social organization and "forces" even when one does in fact take account of the acting individuals. What else can it mean to say that "the organization of a human society is the framework inside of which social action takes place and is not the determinant of that action" (189). If we take this at face value it is either meaningless or false. Are the relationships, formal or informal, in terms of which men interact, merely impotent frameworks? If some men control property and other resources while other men do not, and the latter are able to earn their livelihood only by working for the former, would Blumer deny that this relationship is a determinant of action? If those who are high in a bureaucratic hierarchy command while those who are low obey, is that organization a "mere" framework, or a determinant of action? Is prison a mere framework? school? family?

If Blumer meant to indicate by this infelicitous formulation that individuals are not totally or passively shaped by their participation in organizations or position in formal relationships, then he would be pointing to an important truth. It is apparent, however, that Blumer intends more than this, for he has a definite theory about society: "In the case of human societies, particularly modern societies, in which streams of new situations arise and old situations become unstable, the influence of organization decreases" (190). Modern society is an increasingly classless, structureless, "criss-crossing of lines of action . . . in which the actions of participants are not previously regularized and standardized" (190).

Here Blumer has abandoned Mead's dialectical philosophy and has presented in its place a one-sided interpretation that denies altogether social relationships, social structure, and social organization. Society, from this standpoint, becomes a plurality of disembodied, unconstrained selves floating about in amorphous situations. Little wonder that this perspective has been dubbed "symbolic interaction."

By and large Blumer's conception, not Mead's, has prevailed and dominates symbolic-interactionist thinking and research today. We cannot begin to review the work of the numerous adherents of his "school" here. There are now available, in any case, several collections of representative writings. A quick glance at any one of the most recent of these collections will reveal the way in which contemporary adherents have centered on one dimension of Mead's conception to the virtual exclusion of all others, treating social interaction and socialization as if these processes were nothing more than symbolic communication.[3] Society is dissolved into discourse. The fact that language is essential to man apparently is taken to mean that human interaction and socialization can be understood as if they were symbolic processes and nothing more. There is a great gulf between present-day symbolic interactionist theory and the dialectical theory of the founder.

[3] See, for example, Jerome G. Manis and Bernard N. Meltzer, eds., *Symbolic Interaction: A Reader in Social Psychology*, (Boston: Allyn and Bacon, 1967).

17

The Dialectical Philosophy of George Herbert Mead

If one had to sum up the philosophical efforts of George Herbert Mead in a few words, one might say that he sought to overcome the bifurcation of nature. Here is the object of experience, and there the experiencing subject, and never the twain shall meet. Matter effectively occupies a place in space; it resists the tendency of other matter to occupy the same place; it has mass, and also mobility, when it overcomes inertia. This conception implies that all of natural reality can be reduced to terms of extended matter in motion. On the other hand, anything which cannot so be reduced, such as color, sound, subjectively experienced temperature, taste, and odor, reside not in nature, but in "mind." The organism mediating between "nature" and "mind" must itself be understood as a natural object, or matter in motion. Under the impact of this physical science legacy that could be traced to Galileo, a physiological, mechanistic psychology emerged that attempted to comprehend human actions and conduct as mere behavior—i.e., matter in motion. In this psychology there was no place for "consciousness" or "mind" except as states accompanying the material conditions of the physio-nervous system conceived as a mechanical whole. Thus the original bifurcation led to the doctrine of parallelism: mind and consciousness were simply the epiphenomena of physical particles in motion, and the "connection between the experiencing individual and the things experienced— conceived in their physical reality—were reduced to a passive conditioning of states of consciousness by a mechanical nature."[1]

For Mead, the traditional bifurcation of nature into "mind" on the one hand and physical nature on the other was unsatisfactory. The philosophical result was that either nature was divested of all independence and devoured by

[1] George Herbert Mead, *The Philosophy of the Act* (Chicago and London: The University of Chicago Press, 1938), p. 359.

mind, as among the various idealists, or mind was effectively extinguished by reducing it to material particles, as among the materialists.

Mead saw clearly that these extreme and defective views could not be applied fruitfully to the study of human action or conduct. Beginning in *Mind, Self, and Society*, and continuing throughout his works, Mead undertook a single task: to overcome the traditional dualism by means of a dialectical conception of the relation of man to man and of man to nature. In Mead's view, the individual as a sensitive, active, social being contributes to the constitution of his effective environment as truly as the environment (natural and social) conditions his sensitivity and action; and Mead emphasizes that "the individual is no thrall of society. He constitutes society as genuinely as society constitutes the individual."[2]

In these terms, Mead's philosophical critique of the traditional dualism and his repudiation of both idealism and mechanistic materialism are reminiscent of Marx's efforts in this regard. This suggests that selected aspects of Mead's approach may be compatible with Marx's, and that a fusion of Meadian and Marxian elements might yield a more fruitful social psychology than is presently available. Before we can explore this possibility, however, we need to review Mead's thought with particular attention to its much neglected dialectical character.

MIND, SELF, AND SOCIETY

There are aspects of human behavior and interactions that are immediate, that is, mediated by little or no thought, and which therefore bear a marked resemblance to the interaction of animals. In Mead's famous illustration of the dog fight each dog's gesture is a stimulus for the other's response, which in turn becomes a new stimulus. They are engaged in a *conversation of gestures*, though these gestures are not significant ones, for they carry no meaning. The dogs interact with each other, each anticipating the position of the other reflexively, as it were.

Similarly, two boxers or fencers, Mead argues, respond to each other's gestures reflexively, without consideration or deliberation. On the basis of our present knowledge we presume that all animals remain at this level of interaction: conversation of nonsignificant or meaningless gestures. In the case of man, in contrast, this constitutes a relatively small proportion of his total interactions. A man can strike another without intending to do so or recoil from something before he knows why. But he can also shake his fist in anger, displaying a deliberately hostile attitude. There is an *idea* behind his gesture.

[2] George Herbert Mead, *Mind, Self, and Society*, (Chicago and London: The University of Chicago Press, 1934), p. xxv. Page references to this work are hereafter cited in parentheses immediately following the quoted passage.

Indeed, when a gesture carrying with it a specific meaning arouses in the other individual the same idea it arouses in the first, Mead says, "we have a significant symbol" (45). This is what we commonly mean by "language," or communication by means of symbols; among men's meaningful gestures the vocal ones are the most important.

Gestures and significant gestures are therefore phases and aspects of acts that facilitate cooperation or the carrying out of tasks. However, a significant gesture offers a much greater facility for cooperation because it evokes the same attitude in the other actors or participants as it does in the individual making it. The gesture as a significant symbol arouses in the individual making it the same response (meaning) he intends to arouse in the other. A conversation of significant gestures thus requires that one take "the attitude of the other toward his own gestures" (47). Gestures come in this fashion to call forth commonly understood acts and responses in given groups, communities, and societies.

It is precisely by means of these significant gestures and symbols that *thinking* takes place; this is what one means by "mind." The essence of thinking, Mead insists, is the experientially internalized conversation of meaningful gestures that we also carry on externally, that is, with others.

For Mead, then, mind presupposes a social process. Mead tacitly subscribes to Marx's dictum that social being determines social consciousness. In opposition to Wundt and others, who posited selves as antecedent to the social process, Mead argues that "selves must be accounted for in terms of the social process, and in terms of communication . . . " (49). It is only within that process that minds and selves can emerge. If one begins with mind and derives social process from it "then the origin of minds and the interaction among minds become mysteries" (50). If in contrast one assumes the priority of the social process and communication—priority in the sense that they are antecedent to any given individual mind or self and in the further sense that neither mind nor self can emerge as phenomena except in relation to the social process—then the mystery ceases. For Mead there can be no equivocation here: "Mind arises through communication by a conversation of gestures in a social process or context of experience—not communication through mind" (50).

The origin of peculiarly human communication, language, cannot be derived from imitation. Mead's discussion in this regard sheds further light on the fundamental difference between gestures pure and simple and significant gestures. In man and other higher animals imitation in the sense used by Gabriel Tarde plays a very minimal role. Monkeys, dogs, and foxes, for instance, do not purely imitate; they learn and even learn very quickly. The young fox runs away from man not merely because this is what the older fox does; he rather comes to link the response of flight to the stimulus of man's scent. This is learning, not imitation.

Animals do learn. Their behavior is not strictly instinctive or imitative. They acquire patterns that facilitate their adaptation to a given environment by responding adequately to specific stimuli. Among such stimuli is the gesture. In the conversation of gestures common to both animals and men, the stimulus and response differ: one animal's threat leads to another's flight; the baby's cry leads to the mother's care; a boxer's jab leads to the other's block. In all these cases the response is different from the stimulus. In the conversation of significant gestures, in contrast, stimulus and response are identical for all participants.

Mead perhaps handicaps himself here by attempting to explain this fundamental difference in the vocabulary of behaviorism. He makes the point clearer when he uses the concepts idea, symbol, content, and language. "What language seems to carry" he writes, "is a set of symbols answering to certain content which is measurably identical in the experience of the different individuals. If there is to be communication as such the symbol has to mean the same thing to all individuals involved" (54).

Although the most intelligent animals learn to behave appropriately and even to cooperate, the stimulus-gesture of one can never evoke the identical response-gesture in another. So long as this is true, they do not have significant symbols or language. There is no way of getting from the animal condition, in which stimulus and response differ, to the human condition, in which stimulus and response can be identical. The latter requires the mediation of that exclusively human capacity for creating and transmitting symbols, meanings, ideas, and content.

The vocal gesture, and man's physiological ability to form a great variety of complex sounds, may involve a small element of imitation: we imitate when we learn to pronounce certain words. But by no means can vocal symbolic communication be accounted for by a theory of imitation. No amount of vocal imitation will ever produce meaning—it never has among canaries.

This qualitative difference between humans and animals probably requires little elaboration. It is a uniquely human capacity to symbolize and to interact with others and oneself by means of abstractions, generic concepts and universals. This has been understood for a very long time. Yet the Darwinian theory of evolution, together with the various currents of mechanistic behaviorism, fostered a conception of man according to which he differed hardly at all from other animals. Darwin, for instance, posited a merely quantitative difference between man and his closest zoological relatives. Psychologists like Watson denied mind and consciousness altogether; while others like Wundt simply posited mind. Mead's essays must be viewed in this context, as polemically directed against these positions. Mead insists upon the validity of the concepts "mind," "consciousness," and "meaning," but rejects a metaphysical interpretation of them.

Meaning is generated in the social process, and remains intimately associated with that process. Meaning can be objectively present, Mead argues, even in the absence of awareness or consciousness. "Meaning," he says, "is . . . a development of something objectively there as a relation between certain phases of the social act; it is not a physical addition to that act and it is not an 'idea' as traditionally conceived" (76). The adjustive response of one organism to another is its meaning: "in fencing the parry is an interpretation of the thrust . . . " (78).

When one becomes conscious of one's own and the other's gestures and responses, and their context, gestures become significant symbols. But this does not mean that the interpretation is exclusively in the mind; interpretation is also an external process in an "actual field of social experience." Mead continues: "Meaning can be described, accounted for, or stated in terms of symbols or language at its highest and most complex stage of development (the stage it reaches in human experience), but language simply lifts out of the social process a situation which is logically or implicitly there already" (79). Today most symbolic interactionists would reserve the terms "meaning" and "interpretation" for the complex human stage involving symbols and consciousness, and avoid these terms at the nonsymbolic levels. But Mead wishes to suggest that meaning resides in the total social process and not in mind as a separate province.

It is within the social process of interaction that men communicate and constitute their thought objects. In a formulation not unlike the one we have already encountered in Schütz, Mead says that the social communicative process is in a sense responsible for the existence of objects, "indeed for the existence of the whole world of common-sense objects" in "the sense in which it determines, conditions, and makes possible their abstraction from the total structure of events, as identities which are relevant for everyday social behavior; and in that sense, or as having that meaning, they are existent only relative to that behavior" (80).

The constitution of objects requires abstract concepts and universals. Animals can only relate to specific others, objects, and gestures; men can relate to abstract objects, to concepts and categories of things and organisms. "Dog" as a universal simply has no meaning or existence for dogs; but dog and man in general are the very kind of universals that men communicate with and about. This ability in man enables him to break out of narrowly and inevitably specific responses.

Now, if when we say "dog," "tree," or "hammer," we think not of a particular dog, tree, or hammer, but of a universal, this means that we are thinking about something "not given in the particular occurrence which is the occasion of the thought. The thought transcends all occurrences. Must we assume a realm of such entities, essences or subsistents to account for our thinking?" (88). Such a realm is of course assumed by all realists, i.e., philosophical idealists since Plato. Mead, however, rejects this assumption.

If one individual indicates to himself the same thing he indicates to others, they share a meaning. One individual indicates to the other from his own perspective and to himself from the other's perspective. And since that which is indicated is identical to all observers or participants, regardless of their different perspectives, it must be a universal. Indeed, the tendency to generalize or universalize is developed in the process of socialization, whereby any given individual goes beyond all particular attitudes toward himself and soon crystallizes "all these particular attitudes into a single attitude or standpoint which may be called that of the generalized other" (90).

This ability and tendency to generalize, to hold on to the general or universal and to communicate it, gives men their unique ability to think and reflect. Reflection takes place when one has stopped acting, if only for a moment. By means of thinking and reflecting men can explore alternative courses of future action without taking actual steps in any of the apparently available directions. Men can assess the consequences of their acts before actually engaging in them. And they can also convey the character of that future state to their fellow men without the latter engaging in actual acts. A dog can pick out a specific odor but he cannot indicate that odor to another dog. A man can indicate how to bring about a future state: he can identify another man to a detective; a dog can only follow a scent himself. This absolutely distinguishes man from beast or, as Mead says, the detective from the bloodhound.

Man can draw attention, his own and others, to specific aspects of the situation or field and thus control and guide his action. An animal has no such capacity to focus on an analyzed element; it can only make its "combinations" in actual trial and error and by interacting with the specific and concrete on the knife-edge here and now. Men can make their combinations symbolically; they construct and deconstruct by means of creative imagination.

It is this complex capacity to explore "alternative possibilities of future response" which contrasts fundamentally with behavior that is either reflexive, habitual, or instinctive. There are therefore significant degrees of freedom in human conduct not found in animal behavior. Substantial elements of creativity, selectivity, spontaneity, and contingency are unique to the human condition.

In these terms—and Mead emphasizes this throughout—man's actions are never strictly determined by the past events and therefore cannot be precisely predicted in advance. Because of the elements of creativity and spontaneity, and because man's ideas of the future and its alternatives enter his present conduct as determinants, man's conduct is inherently unpredictable. For man the future is an active determinant of his action, though he never knows *precisely* the nature of that future. If other animals exist on a knife-edge present, man exists in a temporal realm which includes past, present, and future.

Men thus have a unique capacity for intelligent action: the ability to solve present problems or cope with present adversity on the basis of past experience and in terms of possibly future consequences. As Mead says, they are able to act "in the light of or by reference to, both the past and the future . . . both memory and foresight" (100). All this is made possible by the fact that man can become an object to himself by taking the role of another toward himself; in this way his "self" emerges and hence his ability to project the self into reflective situations in which he is now subject, now object. Self, like mind, emerges and develops as an aspect of the social process of interaction.

THE SELF

The self, for Mead, is a social entity distinct from the physical organism, although, of course, it could not emerge except on the basis of that organism. The self appears in a specific context of social experience and interaction, and continues to develop in relation to the social process and the individuals within it. Eventually the self becomes an object to itself and hence the center about which all bodily experiences are organized. I experience this hand, this foot, this back as mine, because I am aware of my self and all that "belongs" to it. The hand, foot, and back belong to the self in a way that the dog never can experience the tail as his own.

The self is both subject and object; it is an object to itself. This is what fundamentally differentiates man from other animals; for the ability to become an object to oneself means that one can achieve *self*-consciousness, not just consciousness. And self-consciousness means that one can adopt an objective and impersonal attitude toward oneself and the situation in which one acts. Man's capacity for intelligent and rational action rests squarely on this uniquely human ability to look upon oneself *objectively*.

Indeed, in the development of the self it is the objective side that appears first. The self is an object before it is a subject, because one's first experiences of oneself are indirect, i.e., from the standpoint of others. If we borrow Harry Stack Sullivan's concept of "significant other," a term Mead did not use but is certainly implied in his theory, we can say that an individual's first experience and awareness of self are indirect, impersonal, and objective because he first becomes an object to himself by taking toward himself the attitudes of the significant others about him. Clearly it is symbolic communication that makes this phenomenon possible. The individual, the very young child, begins to relate to himself as others do by means of these symbols: he addresses himself, responds to himself, talks and replies to himself, so that soon a subjective side emerges and he becomes both subject and object.

The self, then, is a "social structure" (Mead's term) and once formed achieves a certain autonomy—that is, it "provides for itself its social experiences . . . " (140). We can therefore conceive of an adult hermit who has only himself as human companion and talks to himself as he would with others; but what is absolutely inconceivable is a "self arising outside of social experience" (140).

Conversation with oneself is an essential aspect of communication with others. When one speaks to another one speaks to oneself; one affects oneself while one affects the other so that in the very process of speaking one checks, controls, and guides one's speech by assessing its effect on others according to its effects on oneself. One also takes account of the specific other to whom one is relating, and speaks and acts accordingly. In this way one becomes many selves, exhibiting one self here and another there. The self is therefore no static structure; it is a dynamic aspect of the interaction process.

Each of us, then, has multiple and different selves, depending on our relationships and associations. "A multiple personality is in a certain sense normal" (142), Mead notes. It is equally true, however, that each of us is a unified self, exhibiting some degree of consistency in our personality characteristics, a relatively stable configuration. The character of this unified self and the degree of its stability or changeability Mead sees as a function of one's most significant social relationships.

It is not the conversation of gestures but the conversation of significant gestures that makes the emergence and development of self possible. In the absence of language or communication by symbols, or universals, neither self nor mind is conceivable. All symbols are universal, Mead reminds us: "You cannot say anything that is absolutely particular; anything you say that has any meaning at all is universal" (146). The term "universal" conveys the fact that thinking and talking involve symbols that, in a given group, community, or society, evoke in others the same response they evoke in oneself. Symbols enable one to say to oneself what one says to others. "Such a symbol is a universal of discourse . . . " (147). Only after Helen Keller was symbolically communicated with and then herself got into communication with others could she arouse in others the response she aroused in herself. In the absence of this process she never would have developed either a mind or a self—she would have remained "subhuman."

THE "I" AND THE "ME"

We now arrive at a very complex part of Mead's theory, a part that must be carefully examined and adequately grasped. Perhaps the best way to begin is to say that the "I" is a processual dimension of the self that one can never capture except after the fact. The "I" is the actual process of thinking and acting; the "me" is the reflective process. By taking the attitudes of others, one introduces the "me" to which one reacts as an "I." One can never catch oneself as "I"; for one cannot literally observe oneself or be aware of oneself at the same time as one thinks, speaks or acts. "The 'I' therefore appears only in memory and by that time it has become a 'me.' The 'I' of this moment is present in the 'me' of the next moment. The " 'I' in memory is there as the spokesman of the self of the second, or minute, or day ago. As given, it is a 'me,' but it is a 'me' which was the 'I' at the earlier time. If you ask, then, where directly in your own experience the 'I' comes in, the answer is that it comes in as a historical figure" (174).

If the "me" is the organized attitudes of others that one assumes toward oneself, the "I" responds to the "me" and the "me" reflects the "I" in an ongoing dialectical process. The "I," moreover, is rooted in the organism (a point we shall soon elaborate to show that Mead does in fact take into account the biologic individual).

Still another characteristic of the "I" is its relative uncertainty or unpredictability. What one does as "I" one does not precisely know in advance. The "I" responds (exists) in the specious, knife-edge present, as it were, which means one can become aware of the "I" only as a memory image (176), as a part of a "me." The "I" is action whose results one cannot know in advance; it is the actual steps one takes into the future with the uncertainty that this necessarily entails; the "I," then, is never entirely calculable and is associated with spontaneity, novelty, freedom, and initiative.

For Mead, the most important implication of the "I" is that men can never be wholly passive or totally socialized; they are never mere reflections. The "I" changes the world, however infinitesimally. It is the response to the organized attitude that in turn changes that attitude. Men reconstruct the world in this limited sense even as they act in and upon it; for in every act there is an element of originality, of reconstruction, however humble or small.

MEAD'S BIOLOGIC "I"

Mead's "I" involves a paradox: on the one hand it represents freedom, spontaneity, novelty, initiative; on the other hand, however, because the "I" is essentially biologic and impulsive, it is blind and unconscious, a process we become aware of only when it is a fait accompli. It is the biologic "I"'that is involved in our enjoyment and excitement in the present. "It is the realization in some sense of this self that we are continually seeking" (204). But it is also this self that laughs when an individual falls. If he breaks "a leg we can sympathize with him, but it was funny, after all, to see him sprawling out." Laughter is a release from the strenuous effort involved in our identification with the individual, empathetically falling with him and then rising up. But laughter also involves a "sense of the superiority of the person standing toward the person on the sidewalk" (206). In a formulation not too remote from Freud's, Mead goes on to say that the sophisticated "me" soon gains control of the naive "I": "One behaves perfectly proper, suppresses his laughter, is very prompt to get the fallen person on his feet again. There is the social attitude of the "me" over against the "I" that does enjoy the situation . . . " (207). Similarly, Mead argues that in the artist's attitude the "me," the "conventional form is reduced to a minimum," while the "I," "the element of novelty is carried to the limit" (209). Employing Freud's concepts Mead elucidates the relation between the "I" and "me": "Impulsive conduct is uncontrolled conduct. The structure of the 'me' does not there determine the expression of the 'I.' If we use a Freudian expression, the 'me' is in a certain sense a censor" (210).

The "me" sets the limits within which the "I" must appropriately act. "But," Mead continues, "let the stress become too great, these limits are not observed, and an individual asserts himself in perhaps a violent fashion. Then the 'I' is the dominant element over against the 'me' " (210). So Mead, like Freud, posits a definite tension between the "me" and the "I." But the "me" also "enables the 'I,' so to speak, to use the 'me' as the means of carrying out what is the undertaking that all are interested in" (210).

Let us explore further the nature of Mead's impulsive "I" and its relation to the "me." Men have a definitive need to express themselves, to loosen and widen social restraints so that they may express their "I." "Those social situations in which the structure of the 'me' for the time being is one in which the individual gets an opportunity for that sort of expression of the self bring some of the most exciting and gratifying experiences" (213).

What is important to note here is a point that has been severely neglected in interpretations of Mead's theory. The "I" is a manifestation of human natural needs; it, or the energy behind it, is "deeply imbedded" in man's biological nature. That is why Mead calls it the "biologic I." Furthermore, the biologic "I" is definitely in a state of tension with the social "me." In this respect Mead's conception is not as remote from Freud's as has often been assumed. A major function of the "me" is that of Freud's censor: "The situation in which one can let himself go, in which the very structure of the "me" opens the door for the "I," is favorable to self-expression. [When the "me"] opens the door to impulsive expression one gets a peculiar satisfaction . . . the source of which is the value that attaches to the expression of the "I" in the social process" (213).

Mead is very explicit, then, in emphasizing "that which is involved in the 'I' as over against that involved in the 'me.' " The "me" represents the values of the group, which under "extreme moral and religious conditions call out the sacrifice of the self for the whole." On the other hand is the "I" resisting the "me" and its underlying social relationships. The dialectical relation of these dimensions of self Mead underscores throughout. "The response of the 'I' involves adaptation, but an adaptation which affects not only the self but also the social environment which helps to constitute the self; that is, it implies a view of evolution in which the individual affects its own environment as well as being affected by it" (214). This is the position Mead explicitly holds, rejecting the view that "the individual is really passive as over against the influences which are affecting it all the time" (214). And in the same vein: it is with "the 'I', over against the situation in which the 'I' finds itself, that important social changes take place" (217).

Mead thus gives a very prominent place to the biologic individual (an emphasis increasingly ignored by subsequent symbolic interactionists). The "I" is a biologic entity—it is the impulsive tendency to act or react to a certain stimulus "under certain organic conditions. Hunger and anger are illustrations of such impulses" (337). The term "impulse" enables Mead to avoid two extremes: totally purging human beings of a biological nature or endowing them with "instincts." Because this has been so neglected a part of Mead's conception of man, it is desirable to quote at length his rough catalogue of impulses making up the biologic individual:

> There are, first of all, the adjustments by which the individual maintains his position and balance in motion or at rest; (2) the organization of responses toward distant objects, leading to movement toward or from them; (3) the adjustment of surfaces of the body to contacts with objects which we have reached by movement and especially the manipulation of these objects by the hand; (4) attack on and defense from hostile forms of prey, involving specialized organization of the general impulses just noted; (5) flight and escape from dangerous objects; (6) movements toward, or away from, individuals of the opposite sex and the sexual process; (7) securing and ingesting food; (8) nourishment and care of child forms, and suckling and adjustment of the body of the child to parental care; (9) withdrawals from heat, cold, and danger, and the relaxations of rest and sleep; and (10) the formation of various sorts of habitats . . . (348–49).

The biologic component of the self is active, impulsive, and blind—and if this were the only component of self man would be indistinguishable from animals. But, of course, there is another component of the self, a component whose origins and development Mead brilliantly traces. In so doing he resolves a potential contradiction: If man's biological, active, impulsive side is blind and unconscious, how can it be the source of freedom? What good is spontaneity and initiative if one does not know what one is doing, and becomes aware of one's acts only after they are accomplished facts?

Mead's resolution rests on the nature of the self as a dialectical, processual unity, enabling man to act and *reflect* on his acts, modifying them accordingly. In Mead's homely example, it is strictly impulsive simply to tug harder and harder at a drawer that refuses to open. The process of reflection enters when we think intelligently and analytically about the drawer: it is a wooden thing; it may be swollen here and there; it has contents that may account for the drawer's resistance; and so forth.

When we act under impulse the drawer is strictly something to be tugged at, and once the knobs come off, all we can say is "What have I done?" With reflection, in contrast, the "drawer has ceased for the time being to be a mere something to be pulled" (356). Reflection and analysis accompany and guide action, so we can say, "What am I doing?" or "What is to be done?" Here action and theory are more nearly a unity.

But reflection never takes us totally out of the field of impulses, for we continue to use our hands, feeling for resistance and trying to overcome it. Reflection is the unique human capacity according to which we analyze and recombine our impulses "in the presence of obstacles and inhibitions" (362).

Mead assigns central importance in this process to the hands, which mediate human interactions with objects and provide a "contact that is vastly richer in content than that of the jaws or the animal's paws" (363). Reflection is the process in which man's acts are no longer direct, unconscious reactions to stimuli but rather reactions to his object-self. The guidance that the impulsive "I" receives from the reflective self gives the otherwise blind "I" the possibility of conscious and intelligent action.

SOCIETY

We have already seen that Mead refuses to derive human society from preexisting minds and selves. Quite to the contrary, he insists on the temporal and ontological priority of social experience and behavior. The social process of interaction among human beings or, more correctly, quasi-human beings "must have been there in advance of the existence of minds and selves in human beings, in order to make possible the development, by human beings, of minds and selves within or in terms of that process" (227). Here it is important not to confuse the capacity for mind, intelligence, and self-consciousness with their actual development. The potential capacity was the product of biological evolution; its actualization was a product of social development. One process preceded and made the other possible, but once minds and selves emerged, the two processes became interdependent.

For Mead, there is a social aspect to the behavior of all higher organisms: the fundamental biological impulses such as hunger and sex "involve or require social situations and relations for their satisfaction by any given individual organism . . . " (228). These fundamental impulses also play an essential role among human beings. If the reader needs still further evidence of the importance of biologic man in Mead's theory he will find it in Mead's discussion of "society." Among the fundamental impulses, Mead says, "the one which is most important in the case of human social behavior, and which most decisively or determinately expresses itself in the whole general form of human social organization (both primitive and civilized) *is the sex or reproductive impulse* . . . " (228, italics added).

Mead does not go on, as did Freud, to analyze the main dyadic relations within the family, developing on that basis the Oedipal and other theories with which we are familiar. Nor does he systematically and explicitly develop the concepts of the "unconscious" or "repression" as does Freud. Nevertheless, Mead perceives a definite tension between individual, biological man and civilization.

The relation between the rational or primarily social side of the self and its impulsive or emotional or primarily anti-social and individual side is such that the latter is, for the most part, controlled with respect to its behavioristic expressions by the former; and that the conflicts which occur from time to time among its different impulses—or among the various components of its impulsive side—are settled and reconciled by its rational side. (230n)

Of course, this is not precisely Freud's view; Mead does not explore directly the process of "repression," i.e., the price the human being pays for subordinating the impulsive to the social side. Nevertheless, repression is implicit in Mead's conception throughout.

Mead's conception of human "society" also stresses the peculiarly human mode of *praxis*, in which the *hand* mediates man's interaction with nature and with other men. He underscores the interdependence of practical experience, mediated by the hand, and the emergence and development of speech, consciousness, and self-consciousness: "Speech and the hand go along together in the development of the social human being" (237). Similarly, in a famous essay entitled "The Part Played by Labor in the Transition from Ape to Man," Frederick Engels argued that man's various faculties "developed only side by side with the development of the human hand itself through the medium of labor."[3] The concept of labor here refers to the practical activities of men in the process of interacting with nature and of cooperating with one another, and is basically what Mead means by practical experience. Mead, Engels, and Marx are also in basic agreement that the practical cooperative experiences of the protohominids antedate speech, consciousness, and self-consciousness. Engels writes: "First labor, after it and then with it speech—these were the two most essential stimuli under the influence of which the brain of the ape gradually changed into that of man . . . " And Mead:

> It is true that some sort of co-operative activity antedates the self. There must be some loose organization in which the different organisms work together, and the sort of co-operation in which the gesture of the individual may become a stimulus to himself of the same type as the stimulus to the other form, so that the conversation of gestures can pass over into the conduct of the individual. Such conditions are presupposed in the development of the self (240).

Earlier we saw how Mead consistently places the accent on the dialectical character of man's interaction with his environment: man actively determines his environment even while it determines him. This mutual determination is also true of animals: "the individual organism determines in some sense its own environment by its sensitivity. The only environment to which the organism can react is one that its sensitivity reveals. The sort of environment that can exist for

---

[3] Karl Marx and Frederick Engels, *Selected Works* (Moscow: Foreign Languages Publishing House, 1951), 2:74–85.

the organism, then, is one that the organism in some sense determines" (245). This is all the more true of man because of the qualitatively greater control man has achieved over his material surroundings by virtue of the practical actions his *hand* makes possible.

The animal acts directly and immediately upon the environment; there is no real separation of the beginning of the act from its consummation. The dog can "utilize his jaws for carrying, but that is the only extension possible beyond their actual utilization for the process of devouring" (248). The human, in contrast, can separate the beginning of an act from its consummation. He can *manipulate!* So much of man's environment is the product of his own hands that one can properly say that man makes his world and hence himself. By separating the beginning of an act from its consummation, through the hands and their implements, men can relate means to ends. Analytical consciousness thus has its counterpart in man's practical ability to form objects, using them as implements to make still other objects, and to put them together and take them apart. In this way, premeditated, planned action directed toward definite ends distinguishes man fundamentally from even his most intelligent zoological relatives.

The complex nervous system, the hand and its implements, language, and self-consciousness all contribute to man's unique ability to separate the early phases of an act from its later ones and also to delay his response—to cease acting while he thinks or reflects. His actions thus typically involve his reflection on the reciprocal relations of his self to others, and to other objects—giving rise in turn to self-consciousness and self-criticism, again distinctively human processes.

THE PHILOSOPHY OF THE PRESENT

In the essays collected under the title *The Philosophy of the Present*, Mead's dialectical conception of reality is seen even more clearly. This conception involves two others, "emergence" and "relativity." One source of the doctrine of emergence was German classical philosophy, particularly Hegel, a tradition Mead knew rather well. This doctrine, Mead believed, held the key to a naturalistic conception of "life" and "consciousness" with which one could avoid the alternative extremes of mechanistic materialism and philosophical idealism.

The methodological approach that Mead fashioned primarily for application to the social world appeared to be further validated by developments in contemporary physics, notably Einstein's theory of relativity. We may best grasp the dialectical character of Mead's philosophy by reviewing his approach to the present.

The locus of reality is the present. But that "which marks a present is its becoming and its disappearing. . . . Existence involves non-existence."[4] Permanence involves change. The past is in a sense irrevocable, yet the past, as experienced, changes for each subsequent generation. Insofar as we are involved in them, pasts are "both irrevocable and revocable." In this sense there is no "real" or static past that one may discover more and more accuratley. The past is always relative to a present emergent event; when looked at from the "standpoint of the emergent, [it] becomes a different past." Once an emergent appears it "is always found to follow from the past, but before it appears it does not, by definition, follow from the past" (2). We never capture the past as it actually was but rather construct and reconstruct it. This is as characteristic of the historian's work as of the conduct of the intelligent being generally.

Some historians act as if there is a past that can be grasped objectively, as it actually was; for them past events have an "absolute correctness" and each subsequent historical treatment comes closer to this absolute. But the "correct" past of one generation is quite different from that of a later one and, indeed, one past changes from year to year and even more frequently. "The picture which this offers is that of presents sliding into each other, each with a past which is referable to itself, each past taking up into itself those back of it, in some degree reconstructing them from its own standpoint." New pasts emerge relative to the standpoint of the experiencing subject.

There is then a dialectical relation between the individual and his world resulting in the reconstitution of both. There is no necessity rigidly determining the present "out of a past which is independent of that or any present" (10). Rather "the present in which the emergent appears accepts that which is novel as an essential part of the universe, and from that standpoint rewrites its past" (11). "The long and short of it," says Mead, "is that the past (or the meaningful structure of the past) is as hypothetical as the future." And this clearly implies that the past is involved in the present and has consequences for the future. The past "determines" man's action but only insofar as he actively selects from it and rewrites it in preparation for the future. He participates in his becoming as both author and actor. Man's being is a process of becoming in which, potentially at least, he consciously and actively realizes himself.

We hypothetically reconstruct the past that is involved in what is going on, and on this basis construct the future already arising. The chief reference of a present, then, is the emergent event, which can never be accounted for strictly in terms of antecedent processes, which is therefore more than the processes that led up to it, and which finally, by its change, persistence, or disappearance imparts to later passages of time a character "they would not otherwise have possessed" (23).

With every emergent, nature assumes a new character and hence changes

---

[4] George Herbert Mead, *The Philosophy of the Present* (La Salle, Ill.: The Open Court Publishing Company, 1932), p. 1. Page references to this volume are hereafter cited in parentheses immediately following the quoted passage.

somewhat. The new calls forth a responsive adjustment, and the old enters into a relation with the newly arisen. For Mead, the concept of "social" illuminates this process in the natural as well as the social world. If a new biological form is to survive it must receive an adequate response from its environment; and indeed its sensitivity, selectivity, and activity do call forth such a response, so that one may say that the animal determines his environment and is not merely determined by it. The processual stage between the old system (the ordered universe prior to the advent of the emergent) and the new (the changed universe after it has adjusted to the newcomer) is firmly a feature of reality.

Mead thus speaks of the "social character of the universe," by which he refers to the process of the emergents partaking of both the old order and the new: "sociality is the capacity of being several things at once" (49). Emergence never takes us completely out of old systems to place us exclusively in the new: an element belonging to one system, whose nature is determined by its relations to other members of that system, "will carry over into its process of readjustment in the new system something of the nature of all members of the old" (52).

The emergence of consciousness does not mean that one's biophysical and biochemical systems become irrelevant. In Mead's words:

> The conduct of the conscious organism is determined both by a physiological system from behind and also by a consciousness which reaches into the future. This can of course take place only in a present in which both the conditioning past and the emergent future are to be found; but as these problems indicate, what is further called for is the recognition that in the present the location of the object in one system places it in the others as well. It is this which I have called the sociality of the present (63).

All this has further implications for the development of consciousness and of the self.

For Mead, animals also are involved in a teleological process; unlike plants, animals react "purposively," as wholes, to conditions of their own organisms. Animals thus manifest feeling, or the "lowest form of consciousness" (69). What distinguishes an unconscious form from a conscious one is that the latter is capable of making "phases of its own life-process parts of its environment" (70). The plant's rootlets take water because it needs water; the animal, however, *feels* his need for water (though he does not *know* he is thirsty, as man calls his own state of needing water). The animal "not only ingests food, he also tastes it. . . . [It] not only selects objects, but senses them as well" (70). Its responses to its own feelings constitute a part of its objective environment. This gives the sensing, feeling animal a new type of control over its organism: it invests, in a nonsymbolic sense, the objects of its environment with "values" and "meaning:" this is food, that poison; this creature is a friend, that is an enemy; this is pleasurable, that painful.

If the animal lives in more than one system thus effectively enhancing the control of its life process, man has the unique ability to pass symbolically from one system to another and therefore even to occupy mutually exclusive worlds. In a system in motion he can take the standpoint of a system at rest and vice versa. His train, though moving, seems to be at rest relative to another; or conversely, his train though at rest seems to be moving relative to another. Mind and self-consciousness enable him to be a *relativist*, i.e., "to hold on to two or more mutually exclusive systems within which the same object appears, by passing from one to the other" (81).

For Mead these systems are real without requiring a Minkowski world in which space and time transcend our frames of reference and become not the dimensions of events but subsistent entities; they are real for Mead because in mind one can occupy in passage both systems. This is what we encounter in Einstein's theory: two individuals connected with each other by light signals occupy a common world because each places himself in the other's system as well as his own. What makes this possible is the reflexive self, which can pass from one self to another and occupy both. Not simultaneously, of course, because "the temporal dimension of sociality is essential to its existence. One cannot be in Chicago and Berkeley at the same instant even in thought . . . " (82).

Thus man's ability to communicate symbolically, to arouse the same meaning in himself that he arouses in another, to take the role of others towards himself, enables man to do what the other animals cannot do—become an object to himself as a whole. By means of symbolic communication he can move from one system to another, from one attitude to another and consequently occupy both.

Sociality in its highest human form is the principle that gives rise to consciousness. Only the human being can pass through numerous situations in which, say, the dog, frog, lion, and elephant appear, and yet occupy all these attitudes "in so far as they all include the common attitude toward 'an animal' " (86).

Thus man thinks with and acts in terms of universals, symbols and ideas. Consciousness of self and others takes place in the functional present, which, in turn, is delimited by the social act in which one is engaged. The functional present is wider than the specious, knife-edge present and always carries with it the pasts and futures that belong to it. "They arise out of it and are criticized and tested by it" (88). This conception, Mead says, "frees us from bondage either to past or future. We are neither creatures of the necessity of an inexorable past nor of any vision given in the Mount" (90).

THE PHILOSOPHY OF THE ACT

In the brilliant essays of *The Philosophy of the Act* we find a further enrichment of Mead's theory of sociality. According to Mead, sociality characterizes in varying degrees the relationship of all organisms to their environments. Building on William James's "insurgent character" of the organism and on John Dewey's essay "Reflex Arc Concept in Psychology," Mead goes on to accentuate the active side of all organisms and the reciprocal determination of organism and environment.

The main trend in biological science and correlatively in philosophy had been to portray the organism as passively adapting to an environment that actively determined and controlled it. This view is thoroughly defective, Mead insists, and must be replaced by another: an organism actively seeks to express its impulses, and it is only in terms of these impulses that it attends to, or has "interest" in a given stimulus. The stimulus becomes such only insofar as it corresponds to the organism's sensitivity and impulsive needs. The organism thus actively constitutes the objects of its environment. And of course, what is true of the "lower" organisms is true a fortiori of man.

Animals in general, and not man exclusively, engage in social acts. The general stages of the social act Mead calls: impulse, perception, manipulation, and consummation. An animal that man describes as hungry has an impulse to eat; this impulse impels it to act—to seek food. This determines what will stand out in the environment as a stimulus to guide the developing action; the animal approaches the stimulus object, clawing, biting and downing it; finally it eats, consummating the act with the satisfaction of the original impulse. In man the social act involves reflection, and assumes a new quality: impulse is illuminated by reason, and action takes place in a world of meaning.

THE PROCESS OF REFLECTION

Thinking and reflection, for Mead, are instrumental problem-solving activities the main function of which is to facilitate and guide action. Thought and action are moments in a dialectical processual unity. It is precisely when action is checked that reflective thinking arises to test the hypothetical alternative ways of resuming the action. The exploration of alternatives that animals can engage in only directly by trial and error, men can engage in reflectively. Thinking is part of the process by which men solve the problems and overcome the obstacles inhibiting their practical activities. Science is a more formally organized form of reflection.

Mead draws no sharp line between the thinking of the scientist and that of Everyman in everyday life. Mead's conception of science is not that of the positivists for whom facts are unproblematic; for whom "what is observed is, as a fact of experience, there in a sense in which it never can be false."[5] Mead criticizes the positivists for whom there is cause here and effect there, but no process. But he criticizes equally the kind of thinking that never goes outside of itself and remains "shut up inside of the syllogism" (85). Whether it is the scientist's reasoning or Everyman's, the point is "to get back to some process taking place" (87). And a real process cannot be grasped with either the mechanistic thinking of the positivists or the metaphysical categories of the idealists.

Even when science has "all the facts," so to speak, there are qualities of process that remain unpredictable. Knowing all we do about the separate elements H_2O, Mead asks, "would that state to us in advance the character of water, as water? We would be able to determine the positions of the atoms, but water is something more than H_2O. We obtain certain wholes as a result of various compositions which have character not given in the parts themselves" (87–88). One cannot predict in advance, from an examination of the separate elements, what qualities will emerge in the processual order of the universe. There is a creative dimension in both natural and social processes.

Man can treat physical objects as if they were independent of his physiological organism. This ability rests on the social nature of the self, through which he can address and observe himself by taking the role of the other. The active self speaks to the self that is the result of past action. It is the past or former self that states and reorders the world as past and present so as to guide and orient the action at hand. In this way the interaction of selves illuminates the individual's conduct somewhat, but his conduct nevertheless results in a changed situation. The individual is creative and the social world "would not be what it is without his conduct. The change may be slight, but it is unquestioned. The same is true insofar as his conduct is that of invention and discovery" (89). In both science and everyday knowing, then, the individual tests his theories of the world (necessarily a world that is passing) by means of his present action or practical experience. To know the world we must act upon it; and that very action changes the world, however little. Our theories of this changing world are true insofar as they enable us to act intelligently and rationally—that is, anticipate as fully as possible the consequences of our acts.

Knowledge from Mead's pragmatic standpoint is therefore the process of active discovery that enables us to solve the problems and overcome the obstacles that have thwarted our action. If we are able to resume acting, more or less realizing our purposes, our knowledge has proved itself adequate and practicable. This kind of knowledge, Mead maintains, is the only kind that justifies our confidence in it.

The past is shaped by the functional present. We select from memory and history as our interests seem to require it. "One past displaces and abrogates

---

[5] Mead, *The Philosophy of the Act,* p. 47. Page references to this volume are hereafter cited in parentheses immediately following the quoted passage.

another as inexorably as the rising generation buries the old" (95). The reality we find in the past (whether memory or history) is that which we hypothesize has relevance for the present. We search in the past in order better to understand the present problematic world. And the only test we have of whether we understand it or not is our ability to change the condition that has stymied us. The goal of reflective thinking, whether in everyday life, science, or historiography, is therefore practical!

Mead recognized very well that this pragmatic point of view many found offensive. He writes,

> Pragmatism is regarded as a pseudo-philosophic formulation of that most obnoxious American trait, the worship of success; as the endowment of the four-flusher with a faked philosophic passport; the contemptuous swagger of a glib and restless upstart in the company of the mighty but reverent spirits worshipping at the shrine of subsistent entities and timeless truth; a blackleg pacemaker introduced into the leisurely workshop of the spirit to speed up the processes of thinking *sub-specie aeternitatis*; a Ford efficiency engineer bent on the mass production of philosophical tin lizzies. (97)

To these allegations Mead responds quite effectively. It is simply not true that the pragmatic view is opposed to "leisured contemplation and enjoyment of the past." The aesthetic experience is an activity "like all other human activities, and like these it faces its own problems, those of appreciation, and solves them by reflection" (98). Mead does not deny the value of aesthetic activity and its works be they literary, artistic, dramatic, architectural, or whatever.

The process by which the character of objects enters into the experience of the self is an eminently *cooperative* one, Mead insists. "The physical object must literally do as much as we do if we do anything." For this physical "other" to enter an individual's experience, he must "in a premonitory fashion . . . take the attitude of acting as the physical thing will act, in getting the proper adjustment for his own ultimate response" (109). Cooperation or a "conversation of attitudes," in this sense, is therefore essential for man's knowledge of his objects and himself. The world can never be comprehended or known apart from these complex interactive relationships of man to man and man to object in which man becomes both subject and object.

ONTOLOGICAL AND EPISTEMOLOGICAL ASSUMPTIONS

The relation of the individual to his world is an active process. It is only within this processual relation that things become what they are. In man this dialectical relation gives rise to *reflection*, which is also a form of action in which the individual converses with others and himself and therefore evokes in himself the same response (meaning) he does in others. The process of cooperating with others or other objects man carries over into himself. This process enables the individual to isolate stages of the act, those that lie in him from those that lie in its completion. It is within this process that spatial and temporal dimensions emerge: the individual distinguishes distance from contact experiences, and seeks their identity in action, at the same time distinguishing the specious, knife-edge present from the future and the past.

It is the inhibited or interrupted social act that gives rise to reflective thinking, a process in which the individual represents his relational experiences in the world to himself through images and symbols. The interruption of the act and the resulting reflection make abstraction possible. Man can analytically separate his objects from himself, one sensory experience from another, contact experience from distance experience, the experiences of the specious present from those of the past and the future, the spatial from the temporal, and so on. He can grasp aspects of process and represent them to himself symbolically. Only man becomes "metaphysical" in this sense when his action is thwarted.

The foundation of Mead's epistemology is therefore the active relation of man to man, and of man to his natural-social objects. The universe existed long before men ever appeared on earth and will continue to exist long after they have disappeared. In this sense the world exists independently of man. But that world can never be known; for the world man does know is the world he acts in. His observations and actions result in the reconstruction of the world, which is therefore never a world reality independent of his relation to it. When man engages in an experiment, whether as scientist or as Everyman, he does so with respect to the specifically and immediately problematic aspects of his experience in the world. In doing so he assumes an ultimate universe independent of himself. This ultimate universe is an expression of his assured reference to a world of experience that he is not immediately questioning. We test a "hypothesis not by a world of ultimate reality but by a world within which we are living and acting successfully except at the point which has become problematic" (280). In science as in everyday life, man treats his knowledge of reality as the rational ability to anticipate the results of his conduct.

The fact that man's knowledge is relational or perspectival does not mean that it is subjective. Quite to the contrary, while it is true that a particular perspective emerges out of the relation of the observer to the observed, the perspective "is as objectively there as anything can be" (281). Our distance experience of a coin is that it is oval. We are not sure whether it is oval or round. Nonetheless,

> the ultimate experience of contact is not subject to the divergences of distance experience. It is that into which every perspective can be

translated. The round solid coin in the hand is the ultimate fact of every oval of vision. It is a translation when a problem arises respecting the coin. Barring such a problem, it is the identical coin as we walk about it, and it opens from a straight line through all the ellipses into the circle of frontal vision. Evidently perspectives are there and are determined by the relation of the perceiver to the perceived. It is a falsification not only of immediate experience but also of optics to regard them as subjective. (281)

Similarly the traditional philosophical dichotomy between "secondary qualities," i.e., color, sound, taste, odor, etc., as "subjective," and "primary qualities," i.e., extension, occupation of space, motion, etc., as "objective," is a false one. What the philosophers have called "secondary qualities" are simply the character objects have in distance experience while the "primary qualities" are the character they have in contact experience. Both depend on the relation of the individual to his environment.

Mead regards as uncritical the discrimination between the so-called primary and secondary qualities and rightly insists that neither is more objective than the other since neither is independent of the active, sentient, observing, knowing individual. It is nevertheless understandable why the distinction has been made: the association of subjectivity with distance experience and objectivity with contact experience is "natural" because we test "the reality of what affects us from a distance . . . by coming into contact with it" (285).

As we touch and feel the object, it retains its color, sound, odor, etc. With further handling it "crumbles," analytically speaking, until we reach its ultimate elements, particles of energy, "so minute that they could not subtend a light vibration" (286). In this way science creates the hypothetically ultimate elements of material reality, and translates into abstract mathematical models an assumed contact experience in which distance experience disappears or becomes impossible. This theory of nature and of material reality has its experiential basis in everyday life—"in the fact that the hand naturally breaks things up into parts which can be rolled between the thumb and the finger" (296). But while the crumbled object in the hand retains *both* its distance and contact values, the scientifically analyzed object substitutes contact value for distance value—but a contact value of an assumed or hypothetical character.

In these terms, the emergence of the "physical thing," and its accompanying concept, must be seen in the context of the social act—or more precisely in relation to its interruption at the manipulatory stage by the human hand. It is in the context of this stage that "matter" appears, and "which under the crumbling analysis of the hand suggests the hypothetical atom" (326).

For Mead, the relation of the individual to the world is therefore not a simple cognitive one. The individual does not merely reflect or represent the environment; he does not merely acquire a consciousness of what is objectively there. Throughout Mead underscores that the individual's relation to the world is selective, constitutive, and determinative. Even with respect to organisms other than man, Mead consistently repudiates the mechanistic theories according to which living things passively adapt to antecedent changes in external nature: the plant twists toward the light and has an active, striving side.

Every organism, not only reflective man, "stratifies" its environment and selects its objects, thereby determining the contents of objects: what constitutes food, who is an enemy, what is an obstacle, and so forth. These contents the organism determines in the course of carrying out its life processes. All life process involves a future and hence uncertainty.

> That which will happen is always different in some respect from what has happened, and this different quality is something that cannot be predicted. In a sense we can predict the future, but what we can predict is always something less than that which happens. Theoretically we can predict to the extent that we can make our statement in mechanical terms, and this implies, as we have seen, that we have abstracted from the determining relation of the organism upon the environment. (413)

There are problems that can perhaps be stated more or less adequately in mechanical terms; but the adequacy of these terms is confined to processes that interest us for their cyclical recurrent character, e.g., eclipses. In such cases we are not actually predicting the future but stating the past. Prediction, so-called, is actually retrodiction.

When, however, we are dealing with the *action* of organisms, it is not true that if we had enough information about their past and present we could predict their future. The living being's action is a creative process in which he selects, determines, and reconstructs the world. He thus lives partly in the future. Even if we included the physical organism, its elements, and their motions in the problem, we would still not know the future goal of the act,

> for the physical organism so stated is a part of the abstraction. It also contains necessary conditions, but not the novel objects that may appear. The novel element may be very slight, especially in comparison with the given world within which it appears, but in the experience of the individual it was not involved as a necessity of its past. The statement of the abstract motions could not have included the necessity of the particular act.
>
> This amounts to the affirmation that all the novelties of living experience are as novelties essential parts in the universe; the fact that when they arose they were unpredictable means that in the universe as then existing they were not determinable nor in the universe as then existing did there exist the conditions that were the sufficient reasons for their appearing. (419–20)

Action always has a creative and novel and hence unpredictable aspect. Thus

Mead generalizes Henri Bergson's conception of creative evolution to include social development as well as biological evolution.

Hegel's philosophy, it is clear, contributed immensely to the formation of Mead's dialectical conception of being and consciousness. This philosophy, Mead notes, marks "the first time that the self had been definitely given a function in the experience of reaching the truth" (634).

Moreover, Mead's attempts to transcend Hegel's standpoint are reminiscent of Marx's efforts:

> If we take the starting point of the appearance of the reflective attitude in society, we can locate an Hegelian moment in the social development; the self realizing itself over against the individuals of the community so that it finds itself in opposition to the other as essentially a social being. That is, when a man finds himself in opposition to some social order, as in labor conflicts, then the attitude between labor and employer is one of hostility, which we call class war. It appears, of course, in the conflict with the employer over such control as is expressed in wages and labor conditions, but the laborer as such under those conditions has to realize himself in relation to the employer. This characteristic, as we know, appears in class war. Individuals do realize themselves definitely in their oppositions to one another. Those oppositions are the starting point for the development of the new social order. This is characteristic of social development as such, not simply of such modern problems as labor troubles . . . (655)

Epistemologically, Mead's principles may be regarded as largely compatible with Marx's. They become even more so if we apply a particular critique to Mead's conception. Let us therefore first explore this compatibility and then indicate the kind of criticism that must be made of Mead in order to integrate his view with Marx's.

18

The Rudiments of Marx's Epistemology and Social Psychology

Let us begin with the most evident point: like Mead but long before him Marx developed his own dialectical approach by repudiating and transcending both idealism and mechanistic materialism. It is well known that Marx early dissociated himself from the metaphysical premises of Hegel's philosophy, in which thinking was separated from the life process and transformed into "the idea," "into an independent subject [as] the demiurgos of the real world . . . "[1] Marx rejected Hegel's metaphysics as well as philosophical idealism in general.

Yet Hegel did bring out the *active* side of man, for he gave the self a creative and determining role in his philosophy—though it was only in a form abstracted from real human history and social activity. There was thus an important "rational kernel" in Hegel's mystical shell; and it is this kernel, the rational form of Hegel's dialectic, that Marx wished to salvage and apply in his own social theory. In Marx's words:

> In its rational form [the dialectic] is a scandal and abomination to bourgeoisdom and its doctrinaire professors, because it includes in its comprehension an affirmative recognition of the existing state of things, at the same time also, the recognition of the negation of that state, of its inevitable breaking up; because it regards every historically developed social form as in fluid movement, and therefore takes into account its transient nature not less than its momentary existence; because it lets nothing impose upon it, and is in its essence critical and revolutionary.[2]

At the same time Marx found the prevailing form of materialism equally

---

[1] Karl Marx, *Capital* (Moscow: Foreign Language Publishing House, 1954). 1:19.
[2] Ibid., 1:20.

unacceptable. He firmly opposed the mechanistic and reductionist standpoint according to which man's mental activity was nothing more than matter in motion. Chemical bodily processes, according to this doctrine, were sufficient to explain men's ideas and emotions. Materialists of this kind contended that "Ideas stand in the same relation to the brain as bile does to the liver or urine to the kidneys."[3]

The *locus classicus* of Marx's critique of mechanical materialism is his famous "theses on Feuerbach." There Marx clearly rejects any doctrine that ignores the active, creative and determining side of man, that ignores the dialectical relation of man to his conditions. In his first thesis on Feuerbach, Marx writes:

> The chief defect of all hitherto existing materialism—that of Feuerbach included—is that the thing [*Gegenstand*] reality, sensuousness, is conceived only in the form of the *object* [*Object*] or of contemplation [*Anschauung*], but not as *human sensuous activity, practice*, not subjectively. Hence it happened that the *active* side, in contradistinction to materialism, was developed by idealism—but only abstractly, since, of course, idealism does not know real, sensuous activity as such. Feuerbach wants sensuous objects, really differentiated from the thought objects, but he does not conceive *human activity* itself as objective [*gegenstandliche*] activity.[4]

Feuerbach missed the active side of human activity, which meant that he missed its objectively practical and revolutionary significance.

The dialectical and pragmatic character of Marx's theory (and therefore its anticipation of Mead's) is further evident in Marx's remaining theses on Feuerbach. Marx writes:

> The question whether objective [*gegenstandliche*] truth can be attributed to human thinking is not a question of theory but is a *practical* question. In practice man must prove the truth, that is, the reality and power, the this-sidedness [*Diesseitigkeit*] of his thinking. The dispute over the reality or non-reality of thinking which is isolated from practice is a purely *scholastic* question.
>
>   .   .   .   .
>
> The materialist doctrine that men are products of circumstances and upbringing, and that therefore, changed men are products of other circumstances and changed upbringing, forgets that it is men that change

[3] Franz Mehring, *Karl Marx* (Ann Arbor: Ann Arbor Paperbacks, University of Michigan Press, 1962), p. 280.

[4] Karl Marx and Frederick Engels, *Selected Works* (Moscow: Foreign Languages Publishing House, 1951), 2:365.

circumstances and that the educator himself needs educating. . . . The coincidence of the changing of circumstances and of human activity can be conceived and rationally understood only as *revolutionizing practice.*

.   .   .   .

Feuerbach resolves the religious essence into the *human* essence. But the human essence is no abstraction inherent in each single individual. In its reality it is the ensemble of the social relations.

.   .   .   .

Social life is essentially *practical.* All mysteries which mislead theory to mysticism find their rational solution in human practice and in the comprehension of this practice.

And, finally, the famous eleventh thesis:

The philosophers have only interpreted the world, in various ways; the point, however, is to change it.[5]

It is clear then, that for Marx as for Mead man actively constitutes himself. The external world is a man-shaped world that men mold and change by means of their theoretical-practical activity. Man's practical activity "creates" the world in the sense that he produces his tools and external objects with the materials of nature, thus modifying nature, his means of acting upon it, and his relations with his fellow men. It is only as he changes the world that he may adequately interpret or know it. In these terms the eleventh thesis on Feuerbach is an epistemological principle and not just an expression of Marx's moral commitment.

For Marx as for Mead, nature is not objective in the sense that it is independent of men's will, or that it would be the same nature in the absence of men. The "world" or "nature" is always the man-made world and the man-shaped nature. Man is no tabula rasa passively receiving impressions from the outside world and responding to external stimuli. Quite to the contrary, man is an active cognizing subject who comes to know reality as he acts upon it. To account for experience adequately, therefore, requires that we recognize the contributing activities of the knower-actor to the object and consider the specific social-historical context of knower and object.

Like Mead (and Dewey, to whom we shall return in a moment) Marx thus disposes of the traditional epistemological problem concerning the existence of the world. Marx has no need either to prove or disprove the existence of the world. Such problems result from false premises regarding the relation of man to nature—premises according to which man is a detached contemplative observer. For Marx, man is an integral part of nature; therefore to question the external

[5] Ibid., pp. 365–67.

world or to regard it as in need of proof is to question his own existence—an extreme to which even Descartes and Berkeley refused to go.

It is evident from this that Marx's conception of man and nature substantially anticipates Dewey's instrumentalism[6] and Mead's philosophy of the act. Dissociating himself from both idealism and materialism, Marx describes his standpoint as "naturalism or humanism [that] is distinguished from both idealism and materialism and at the same time constitutes their unifying truth."[7]

Further evidence of Marx's naturalism and its affinity with Mead's may be found in Marx's *Economic and Philosophic Manuscripts of 1844*[8] and in his *German Ideology*. In the manuscripts in particular Marx affirms that man is a natural being but at the same different from animals. Marx's dialectical-naturalistic approach to man anticipates the substance of Mead's social psychology. "Man *lives* on nature—means that nature is his body, with which he must remain in continuous intercourse if he is not to die. That man's physical and spiritual life is linked to nature means simply that nature is linked to itself, for man is a part of nature" (74).

The animal, however, "is immediately identical with its life activity. It does not distinguish itself from it. It is its life-activity. Man makes his life-activity itself the object of his will and of his consciousness. He has conscious life-activity. . . . Conscious life-activity directly distinguishes man from animal life-activity" (75). This is Marx's way of saying that man has what Mead calls "mind" and "self." For man is conscious of his "species-being" and as such "his own life is an object for him" (75).

How does man prove himself to be a "conscious species-being?" By "creating an *objective world*," Marx replies,

> by his practical activity, in *working-up* inorganic nature. . . . Admittedly animals also produce. They build themselves nests, dwellings, like the bees, beavers, ants, etc. But an animal only produces what it immediately needs for itself or its young. . . . It produces only under the dominion of immediate physical need, whilst man produces even when he is free from physical need and only truly produces in freedom therefrom. . . .
> It is just in the working-up of the objective world, therefore, that

[6] Bertrand Russell called attention to this anticipation; see his *Freedom and Organization* (London: George Allen Unwin, 1934), p. 192. Dewey, however, denied any affinity between Marx's view and his own, and even accused Marx of the one-factor fallacy and the elevation of environment over man. See his *Freedom and Culture* (New York: G. P. Putnam's Sons, 1939), pp. 75–76, where he betrays his fundamental misunderstanding of Marx.

[7] Karl Marx, *Economic and Philosophic Manuscripts of 1844*, (Moscow: Foreign Languages Publishing House, 1961), p. 181. Page references to this work are hereafter cited in parentheses immediately following the quoted passage.

[8] It is in these manuscripts that we find Marx's most explicit discussion of *alienation*—a process which is severely neglected by Mead, and which we shall consider later in our critical observations.

man first really proves himself to be a *species being*. This production is his active species life. Through and because of this production, nature appears as *his* work, and his reality. (75–76)

What is distinctively human production, then, is creative and free activity, as in the case of the artist whose work is not dictated by immediate physical need. Indeed, when man's activity is degraded to a means to his physical existence, his activity becomes coerced and alienated labor or, in a word, dehumanizing activity.

Although Marx's main purpose in this context is to specify the sources of alienation, he nevertheless puts forward a central proposition that anticipates Mead almost verbatim:

"We must bear in mind," writes Marx, " . . . that man's relation to himself only becomes *objective* and *real* for him through his relation to the other man" (79). And Marx continues, "If [man's] own activity is to him an unfree activity, then he is treating it as activity performed in the service, under the dominion, the coercion and the yoke of another man" (79). To be sure, Marx's application of the proposition is not only scientific but critical, in that he wants to lay bare the root cause of dehumanization in the relations of man to man—that is, in a specific historical form of domination. In these terms there is a world of difference between his application and Mead's—a point to which we shall soon return. But Marx does recognize and employ the principle of the self-other dialectic that Mead does, namely, that man becomes an object to himself only in the process of taking the roles and attitude of others toward himself. Man's "own sensuousness first exists as human sensuousness for himself through the *other* man" (111).

In common with Mead, Marx rejects any reification of society. "What is to be avoided above all," Marx insists, "is the re-establishing of 'society' as an abstraction vis-á-vis the individual. The individual is *the social being*. His life, even if it may not appear in the direct form of a *communal* life carried out together with others—is therefore an expression and confirmation of *social life*" (105).

Marx like Mead and indeed like Freud, also refuses to ignore the fact that man as a part of nature has a biologic-organic nature with all the needs that this implies—although, of course, there are important differences in this respect among the three thinkers. Under capitalism Marx saw that man was not only dehumanized, but that he was becoming less than human without even fulfilling his animal needs.

Even the need for fresh air ceases for the worker. Man returns to living in a cave, which is now, however, contaminated with the mephitic breath of plague given off by civilization, and which he continues to occupy only *precariously*, it being for him an alien habitation which can be withdrawn from him any day—a place from which if he does not pay, he can be thrown out any day. For this mortuary he has to pay. A dwelling in the *light* which Prometheus in Aeschylus designated as one of the greatest boons, by means of which he made the savage into a human being ceases to exist for the worker. Light, air, etc.—the simplest *animal* cleanliness—ceases to be a need for man. *Dirt*—this stagnation and putrefaction of man—the *sewage* of civilization (speaking quite literally)—comes to be the *element of life* for him. Utter, unnatural neglect, putrefied nature, comes to be his *life-element*. None of his senses exist any longer, and not only in his human fashion, but in an *inhuman* fashion, and therefore not even in an animal fashion. . . . It is not only that man has no human needs—even his *animal* needs are ceasing to exist. (117)

The convergence of Marx in this regard with Mead and Freud becomes even clearer when Marx writes:

Man is directly a *natural* being. As a natural being and as a living natural being he is on the one hand furnished with *natural powers of life*—he is an *active* natural being. These forces exist in him as tendencies and abilities—as *impulses*. [Note here that Marx uses precisely the same term as Mead.] On the other hand, as a natural, corporeal, sensuous, objective being he is a *suffering* conditioned and limited creature like animals and plants. That is to say, the objects of his impulses exist outside him, as *objects* independent of him; yet these objects are *objects* of his *need*—essential *objects*, indispensable, to the manifestation and confirmation of his essential power. . . . Hunger is a natural need; it therefore needs a *nature* outside itself, an *object* outside itself in order to satisfy itself, to be stilled . . . (156–57)

"But man," Marx continues, "is not merely a natural being: he is a *human* natural being. That is to say, he is a being for himself. Therefore he is a *species being*, and has to confirm and manifest himself as such both in his being and in his knowing" (158). As a human-natural being man not only retains his natural needs (hunger and sex) but acquires new ones as well—love, to single out the most important: "If you love without evoking love in return—that is if your loving as loving does not produce reciprocal love; if through a living expression of yourself as a loving person you do not make yourself a loved person then your love is impotent—a misfortune" (141).

Even Mead's theory of language is anticipated by Marx in his *German Ideology*:

Language is as old as consciousness, language is practical consciousness, as it exists for other men, and for that reason is really beginning to exist for me personally as well; for language like consciousness only arises from the need, the necessity, of intercourse with other men. . . . Consciousness is therefore from the very beginning a social product, and remains so as long as men exist at all.[9]

[9] Karl Marx, *German Ideology*, (New York: International Publishers, 1947), p. 19.

19

Toward a Synthesis of Marx, Mead, and Freud

As we have seen, George Herbert Mead's dialectical naturalism brings out with considerable clarity the relation of man to man and of man to nature. Because his philosophy of human action is at once dialectical and naturalistic, and because it emphasizes the active and creative side of man, it parallels Marx's conception in several important respects and provides *some* of the important elements of a social psychology that adequately comprehends the human condition.

Nevertheless, important elements are also absent. If we take a critical look at Mead we begin to see what is either missing or blurred in his work.

First, although for Mead socialization is not uniformly good, he gives no sustained attention to domination and coercion—that is, to the internally and externally imposed constraints on the individual that socialization necessarily entails. Mead's "biologic I" and its relation of tension with the "me" is central to his philosophy, yet Mead himself fails to elaborate the important implications of this tension. "Repression," for example, is certainly implicit in the relation of the "I" and "me." But Mead provides no extended analysis of the "price" the individual pays in the course of institutionalization and internalization.

Second, because Mead was not primarily concerned with social structure, particularly property and power relations, his conception of society appears to carry with it a certain political naiveté and technocratic bias. Often one gets the impression that to solve its problems all society needs is intelligent social engineering and better communication.

These criticisms revolve about two concepts: domination and repression. Both concepts have the highest importance for an understanding of man and his world, and neither occupies a central place in Mead's framework. If it is from Marx that we learn much about historically specific forms of domination, it is from Freud that we learn about repression. It should therefore be highly illuminating to explore Herbert Marcuse's critical reinterpretation of Freud in the light of Marx's theory. In reviewing particular aspects of Marcuse's work I hope to specify the elements that must be built into Mead's conception and accentuated if a truly adequate social psychology is to emerge.

MARCUSE'S REINTERPRETATION OF FREUD

At the very center of Freud's theory is what he regarded as an irremediable antagonism between the human individual and civilization.[1]

An unavoidable antagonism prevails between the instinctual needs of the human organism and the requirements of the civilizing process. The development of the ego and superego necessarily involves a subordination of the individual's organic needs (the pleasure principle) to the demands of the socializing agencies (the reality principle). The result is the repressive transformation of the instincts with all that this implies—deep unhappiness, mental disorder, and a powerful tension generally between the individual and society. A tragic and permanent contradiction prevails in which men paid and will continue to pay an enormous price for the advance of civilization. This is the pessimistic view one finds in Freud's late writings, notably *Civilization and Its Discontents.*

A powerful reaction to Freud's pessimism soon emerged from the "left," leading eventually to the fundamental revisions of Freud's theory associated with such neo-Freudians as Erich Fromm, Karen Horney, and Harry Stack Sullivan. Essentially, their critique may be summed up as follow: the ego faces not some abstract, unchanging civilization but a historically changing social world. By obscuring this fact Freud's reality principle becomes conservative and justificatory, for it transforms contingency into necessity, generalizing to all social reality what is only characteristic of specific sociohistorical forms.

Clearly, this criticism has validity. But "its validity," argues Marcuse, "does not vitiate the truth in Freud's generalization, namely, that a repressive organization of the instincts underlies *all* historical forms of the reality principle in civilization" (31). It is here that the neo-Freudian revisionists of the left have made their fundamental error: they have *flattened out* man's instinctual needs. "In minimizing the extent and depth of the conflict [between the human organism and any society], the revisionists proclaim a false but easy solution" (229).

If this critique, as leveled against the neo-Freudians, is significant, it is even more significant when directed toward the social psychologies examined in this book. For, if the neo-Freudians have flattened out man's organism and its needs,

[1]The present discussion is based on Herbert Marcuse, *Eros and Civilization: A Philosophical Inquiry into Freud* (New York: Vintage Books, 1962). Page references to this work will be cited in parentheses immediately following the quoted passage.

the sociological psychologies have effectively ignored them. This is conspicuously true of the symbolic interactionists who followed Mead—though not of Mead himself. To be sure, Mead did not draw from the tension between his "biologic I" and "society" all the conclusions Freud drew from his pleasure principle—reality principle dichotomy. Nevertheless, the organism's vital need to express and satisfy its impulsive needs and society's thwarting of them is an integral part of Mead's social psychology.

What is the importance of the general proposition that man is an active biologic individual and that his needs (whether we call them "instinctual" with Freud or "impulsive" with Mead) can never be wholly reconciled with society? Why is it important to recognize the tension inevitably generated by the repressive transformation of man's biologic needs in the process of socialization? This proposition has the greatest importance because it affirms that the individual is never totally socialized into his society, and that even under what is apparently the most complete socialization, there remains a residue of resistance to the prevailing roles, relationships, and institutions imposed upon him.

This proposition brings into relief what has been either grossly neglected or ignored in sociological theories—namely, that while man's roles and relationships constrain, shape, and determine him, he also determines them. More, he resists those relationships, hence changing and reconstituting them. This is the dialectical conception we find so well formulated in Marx and Mead. Both thinkers stressed the active and even insurgent character of the human organism and its deep-seated need for freedom.

But Freud's theory of the conflict between the individual and society also points directly to this truth—though his critics have underscored its conservative implications. Freud's theory, they have argued, implies that social change is pointless since repression and therefore discontent will remain under *any* form of civilization. Indeed, man has certain attributes that not only account for the destructive, antihuman character of hitherto existing society, but that also severely limit the scope and depth of social change. This conservative interpretation of Freud is unwarranted, Marcuse argues. If we analyze his reality principle into components that are implicit but that he himself never developed, the traditional interpretation is reversed. We then not only succeed in fashioning a theory that is scientifically more accurate, we also bring out the critical implications of Freud's view.

SURPLUS-REPRESSION

For Freud society is necessarily a repressive organization of the instincts. His theory of the irreconcilability of the pleasure and reality principles, Marcuse contends, "expresses the historical fact that civilization has progressed as organized *domination*" (32). Freud's awareness of the historically changing forms of *domination* and their repressive role is manifest in *Moses and Monotheism, Totem and Taboo* and other works where he imaginatively reconstructs what he regards as the transition from the patriarchal despotism of the primeval horde to the "internalized despotism of the brother clan."

Freud's purpose in these works was not to write scientific history or anthropology. His purpose was rather heuristic: to show that all civilizations have been forms of organized domination. In their original form, then, Freud's concepts are reified and ahistorical. They do have an implied historical character, however, which might be clarified, Marcuse suggests, by modifying Freud's basic terminology.

Marcuse here introduces two terms that one can justifiably extrapolate from Freud's:

1. *Surplus-repression.* This refers to the "restrictions necessitated by social domination. This is distinguished from (basic) *repression*: the 'modification' of the instincts necessary for the perpetuation of the human race in civilization."

2. *Performance principle.* This is "the prevailing historical form of the *reality* principle" (32).

Marcuse's point here is that it is quite true that man's historical struggle with scarcity (*Lebensnot*) has forced upon him "constraint, renunciation, delay." To satisfy his needs he has had to engage in labor and painful arrangements and tasks. And, Marcuse continues: "For the duration of work, which occupies practically the entire existence of the mature individual, pleasure is 'suspended' and pain prevails. And since the basic instincts strive for the prevalence of pleasure and for the absence of pain, the pleasure principle is incompatible with reality, and the instincts have to undergo a repressive regimentation" (33).

This necessary process, however, should not be confused with the deprivation, pain, and suffering that the historically specific organizations of scarcity have imposed on man. These have never distributed scarce resources in accordance with individual needs. On the contrary, by means of violence and the rational use of power this scarcity has always been controlled by the powerful and distributed in accordance with their interests. Therefore, Marcuse continues,

> no matter how useful this rationality was for the progress of the whole, it remained the rationality of *domination,* and the gradual conquest of scarcity was inextricably bound up with and shaped by the interest of domination. Domination differs from rational exercise of authority. The latter, which is inherent in any societal division of labor, is derived from knowledge and confined to the administration of functions and arrangements necessary for the advancement of the whole. In contrast, domination is exercised by a particular group or individual in order to sustain and enhance itself in a privileged position. Such domination does not exclude technical material and intellectual progress, but only as an unavoidable by-product . . . (33–34)

It has therefore not been the reality principle pure and simple but the performance principle that has subjected man to such great suffering. Added to the repressive control required by any form of human association, man has endured the controls accompanying "specific institutions of domination"—in a word, surplus-repression.

Historically the reality and performance principles and their respective forms of necessary and surplus repression have been inseparable. However, Freud himself appears to have acknowledged that when a section of the populace gains the upper hand and exploits the rest for its own advantage, "Fear of a revolt among the oppressed then becomes a motive for even stricter regulations."[2] The pleasure principle has been hedged in and suppressed not simply because men's struggle and control of nature required it, but also and perhaps mainly because the privileged interests of those who dominated demanded it.

Is it possible to pull together the points in Marcuse's extrapolation of Freud's concepts and relate them to both Mead's and Marx's work? I think it is. As applied to Mead, one might make the point this way: Mead's "me" and "generalized other," and their impact upon the "biologic I," do not sufficiently recognize the element of domination in the process of taking the role of the other and in internalization. To use Freud's terms as modified by Marcuse, Mead recognizes repression (although not as explicitly as Freud and without the focus on sexuality) but not surplus-repression. In other words, he fails to take systematic account of the very condition that Marx placed at the center of his investigation. Just as we are able to extrapolate from Freud's concepts, so are we able to extrapolate from Mead's. Everything in Mead's work suggests that surplus-repression is wholly compatible with his theory. Indeed, by building this concept into his framework, we enhance greatly the compatibility of his dialectical conception with Marx's.

For it is clear that what Marcuse calls surplus-repression is an important dimension of what Marx called alienation. In a passage reminiscent of Marx's *Economic and Philosophic Manuscripts*, and probably inspired by them, Marcuse writes:

> For the vast majority of the population, the scope and mode of satisfaction are determined by their own labor; but their labor is work for an apparatus which they do not control, which operates as an independent power to which individuals must submit if they want to live. And it becomes the more alien the more specialized the division of labor becomes. Men do not live their own lives but perform pre-established functions. While they work, they do not fulfill their own needs and faculties but work in *alienation*. Work has now become general, and so have the restrictions placed upon the libido: labor time, which is the

[2] Sigmund Freud, *Civilization and Its Discontents* (London: Hogarth Press, 1949), p. 74; cited in Marcuse, *Eros and Civilization*, p. 37.

largest part of the individual's life time, is painful time, for alienated labor is absence of gratification, negation of the pleasure principle (41).

Hence there is a definite compatibility between Marx and a reinterpreted Freud. And a similar harmony may be justifiably attributed to Marx and Mead. This, I hope, has become evident from the general presentation of Mead's thought. It becomes even more evident in Mead's conception of freedom and its opposite—though he did not use the word "alienation" to denote that condition. In the last of his "Miscellaneous Fragments," entitled "Freedom," Mead writes:

1. The organism enters entirely into the act as a whole, and this is freedom. The action is the action of the organism and not of the separate parts. We cannot gather ourselves together when we do not feel free, and this happens frequently. But in freedom the personality as a whole passes into the act. Compulsion disintegrates the individual into his different elements, hence there are degrees of freedom in proportion to the extent to which the individual becomes organized as a whole. It is not often that the whole of us goes into any act so that we face the situation as an entire personality. Moreover, this does not necessarily spell creation, spontaneity; it spells the identification of the individual with the act. Freedom, then, is the expression of the whole self which has become entire through the reconstruction which has taken place.

2. If one is reconstructing one's situation, one's action may be called rebellion. This is the attitude of the reactionary, who believes that reformers are bolsheviks. But freedom lies definitely in a reconstruction which is not in the nature of a [mere] rebellion but in the nature of presenting an order which is more adequate than the order which has been there.[3]

With the foregoing critical modifications, the Freudian and Meadian frameworks acquire a definite congruence with Marx's—and this despite the different purposes, contexts, and values of Marx, Freud, and Mead. Mead's dialectical conception lends itself to this reinterpretation and the value of his social psychology, great in any case, is thereby substantially enhanced.

[3] George Herbert Mead, *The Philosophy of the Act* (Chicago and London: The University of Chicago Press, 1938), p. 663.

Epilogue

Our exploration of the main currents in contemporary sociological theory has come to an end. The explicitly "constructive" part of the study is, first, the programmatic essay outlining the intellectual advantages of a Marx-Weber model and, second, the consideration of Mead, Marx, and Freud and the feasibility of a synthesis. But the "negative," critical task was also essential to indicate some of the shortcomings of the theories examined in this book. Perhaps we will better see the validity of the critique and the virtues of the orientation advocated if I make a final methodological comment.

An adequate comprehension of the human condition entails a twofold task. We must give attention to the processes tending to constrain and determine men's actions; but we must also illuminate the active and creative efforts men make to diminish and remove constraints by changing institutions and practices that are unnecessarily repressive. Men are active, creative beings who make their history, though not "just as they please."

There are two types of errors that often result from a misunderstanding of this conception of man, society, and history. The first is to minimize or ignore altogether the constraining influences of social relationships and institutions. This error results in regarding men as supermen who are able, presumably, to transform their existential conditions at will. The opposite error is to exaggerate the staying power of institutions, to objectify them, thereby unjustifiably underestimating the ability of men to modify their circumstances. This error leads to a pronounced diminution of human stature and potential. By avoiding these errors, we may be genuinely able to learn of real human possibilities.

By the phrase "real human possibilities" I do not refer to what might be possible in some distant future, but to the possibilities for change and development that promise all of us greater freedom and self-realization. To uncover these possibilities, we must not study man or his conditions in the abstract, as is so frequently done. This can only lead us to allegations about "man's eternal nature" and his "necessary institutions." Instead we must grasp the extent to which men's conduct and institutions are rooted in historically specific and transitory social conditions. Any sociology failing to recognize the historical character of society and its forms is bound to conceal from our view what is most essential. We must not deal with one frozen moment of a process but with the process itself.

Index

Aberle, D. F., 4, 6, 23, 24
Action systems, 22
Action theory, 17, 18, 22, 23
"Adaptation," 9, 10, 11, 42
"Adaptive advantage," 56
"Adaptive capacity," 52, 53
Adjustment. *See* Adaptation
Affectual action, 169
Alienated labor, 247, 256
Alienation, 164, 211, 247, 255, 256
"Alter." *See* Ego and Alter
Animal life-activity, 246
"Anomic," 19
Anomie, 38
Appresentation, 172
Aron, Raymond, 119
Ascription-Achievement dichtomy, 25
Authoritarian Regime, 24
Authoritariniasm, 39
Authoritarian-submissive (complex), 39
Authority, concept of, 88, 89, 92, 93

"Back region," 194
Ball, John, 99
Beauvoir, Simone de, 194
"Because motives," 177, 178
Behaviorism, 17, 20, 141, 167
Bendix, Reinhard, 136
Bergson, Henri, 174, 242
Berkeley, George, 246
Biemel, Walter, 145
Biologic I, 228, 251, 253, 255
Biologic man, 230
Blau, Peter, 66, 80–98
Blumer, Herbert, 215–218
Bodin, Jean, 103
Bottomore, Thomas B., 19, 42, 49, 120
Bourgeois ideology, 160
Bourgeoisie, 41
Bourgeois revolution, 41
Brentano, Franz, 140, 145
Broom, Leonard, 31
Burgess, E. W., 215
Burke, Kenneth, 192
Burnham, James, 112

Cancian, Francesca M., 7, 8, 10, 11
Capital accumulation, 127
Capital concentration, 130, 131
Capitalism, 38, 111, 112, 113, 127, 128, 155, 157, 247
Capitalist class, 113, 126
Capitalist development, 157
Capitalistic principles, 122
Capitalist-industrial society, 112
Capitalist interests, 134, 135
Capitalist mode of production, 110, 111, 126, 157
Capitalist society, 115, 120, 124
Capitalist system, 109, 159
Capital ownership, 111
Capitals, conflict among, 127
"Caste," 12
Cathectic, 22
"Civil death," 198
Class conflict, 104, 112, 114, 115, 116, 117, 128, 160
Class consciousness, 128, 129
Classes, 35, 37, 40, 109, 112, 126
Classical political economy, 159
Classical tradition of sociological thinking, 10, 123, 125
Class interests, 35, 128
Class structure, 36, 39, 126
"Class situation," 129, 130
Class struggle, 159, 160, 242
"Cognitive dissonance," 90, 91
Cohen, A. K., 4
Collins, Paul W., 13, 14
Collins, Randall, 136
"Common value system," 18, 30, 42, 44, 45, 97, 98
Communism, 30, 33
Competitive capitalism, 126, 127
"Complementarity of expectation," 21, 98
Comte, August, 154, 155, 156
Comtean dogma, 55
Conflict model, 35, 104
Conflict-coercion theory, 115, 116, 139
Conflict of interests, 33, 106, 107, 113, 159, 199, 205

Conflict theorists, 38, 116
Conflict theory, 103, 104, 109, 117
Conscious life-activity, 246
Conversation of gestures and significant gestures, 220, 221, 222, 226, 231, 238
Cooley, Charles H., 215
Coser, Lewis, 103–107
Cottrell, Leonard S., Jr., 31
Creature releases, 210, 211
Culture, 17, 21, 22, 24
Cybernetic model, 11, 13, 14

Dahrendorf, Ralf, 103, 109–121, 126, 133
Daimyo, 40, 41, 42
Darwin, Charles, 222
Darwinism, 52, 163, 222
Davis, A. K., 4
Davis, Kingsley, 10
Descartes, René, 145, 246
Dewey, John, 215, 236, 245, 246
Dialectical process, 118, 203, 226, 232, 243, 251, 254–256
Differentiation, 28
Dilthey, Wilhelm, 143, 153, 167
Division of labor, 28, 254, 255
Doctrine of emergence, 82
Domination, 33, 251, 253, 254
Durkheim, Emile, 10, 14, 18, 19, 52, 64, 95, 96, 154, 156, 193
"Dysfunction," 6, 7, 9, 10

"Economic determinism," 124
Edie, James M., 149
Egalitarian Societies, 29
Ego and Alter, 20, 21, 31, 173, 252
Einstein, Albert, 232
Emerson, Richard M., 86
Engels, Frederick, 157, 231, 244
English political economy, 159
Environmentalism, 141
Epicurus, 165
"*Epoché*," 174, 182
Equilibrating systems, 11
Equilibrium, 18, 24, 31, 32, 41, 44, 192
Equivalents, structural and functional, 8
"Ethical neutrality," 159
Ethnomethodology, 183–188
"Eufunction," 6, 7
"Eustructure," 6
Evolutionary theory, 51, 53, 54
Evolutionary universals, 52, 53, 54, 56
Exchange relations, 69, 70, 71, 77, 78, 80, 86, 94, 95, 96, 98
Exchange theory, 63–99, 139, 214
Existentialists, 19
Exploitation, concepts of, 92, 93, 94, 95, 98, 115, 116, 119
"External horizon," 148

"Face-to-face" interaction, 172, 209, 210, 212, 213
"Fallacy of misplaced concreteness," 175
"False consciousness," 116
Family, 26, 27, 105, 230
Fascism and Fascist movements, 24, 38, 42
Ferguson, Adam, 103
Feudalization of the bourgeoisie, 36, 41
Feuerbach, Ludwig, 124, 244
Festinger, Leon, 90
"Finite provinces of meaning," 174
Force, 25, 30, 46
Formal functional analysis, 11, 13, 14
Free labor, 128
Free love, 26
"Free places," 202
Freud, Sigmund, 165, 207, 211, 227, 228, 230, 247, 248, 252–257
Fringes, 150
Fromm, Erich, 252
"Front region," 194
"Functional equivalents," 8
"Functional imperatives," 41
Functionalism, 10, 13, 14, 23, 24, 27, 33, 35, 53, 54, 57, 63, 103, 104, 117, 136, 139
Functionalist–evolutionary perspective, 56
Functionalists, 5, 20, 23
Functional requisites and prerequisites, 4–6, 23, 24

Galileo, 219
Garfinkel, Harold, 183–188
Geiger, Theodore, 113
Geisteswissenschaften, 17, 19
Gellner, Ernest A., 8
Gemeinschaft, 24
"Generalized other," 255
German classical philosophy, 232
German ideology, 40
Gerth, H. H., 30, 131
Gesellschaft, 24
Giddens, Anthony, 50
"Goal attainment," 42
Goffman, Erving, 191–214
Gouldner, Alvin, 31, 35, 85, 93, 95
Gumplowicz, L., 103
Gurvitch, George, 33

Harris, Marvin, 11, 12, 13
Hegel, Georg W. F., 42, 242, 243
Henderson, L. J., 63
Hindu taboo, 12
"Historical inevitability," 157
Hobbes, Thomas, 5, 17, 43, 103, 165
Hobson, J. A., 134
Homans, George C., 63–87
Horney, Karen, 252

Hume, David, 103, 140, 142
Husserl, Edmund, 139–150, 152, 158, 159, 171, 172, 174, 178, 179, 182

"I," concept of, 164, 226, 227, 228
Imperatively coordinated associations, 133
Imperialism, 134, 135
Impression management, 192, 194, 196, 212, 213
Industrial conflicts, 115, 120, 121
Industrial societies, 114, 115, 122, 125
"Inner durée," 174
"In-order-to" motives, 177, 178
Instinctual behavior, 161, 162
Instrumentalism, 246
"Insurgent organism," 236
"Integration theory," 103, 115–117
Intentionality of consciousness, 145–148, 150
"Interchangeability of standpoints," 173
"Internal horizon," 148
"Intersubjectivity," 148, 149, 150, 170, 171

James, William, 150, 164, 172–174, 215, 236
Japanese social structure, 40–42
Junker class, 36, 37, 39, 42
Justice, concept of 68, 70–76

Kant, Immanuel, 142, 144, 165
Kantian view, 144
Keller, Helen, 226
Kelley, H. M., 77
Khaldun, Ibn, 103
Kibbutz, 29
Kinship, 26, 29
Knight, Frank H., 128
Koch, Sigmund, 141
Kockelmans, Joseph J., 140, 144, 146

Lauer, Quentin, 142
La Mettrie, Julien O. de, 165
Lebensphilosophie, 152
Lebenswelt, 145, 148, 149, 150, 171, 172, 181
Leeds, Anthony, 12, 13
Lenin, V. I., 134
Levy, Marion J., Jr., 4, 6
Linton, Ralph, 25
Lipps, Theodor, 140
Locke, John, 17, 140, 144

Machiavelli, Niccolo, 103, 165
Malinowski, Bronislaw, 63, 64
Malthus, Thomas, 103
"Managerial revolution," 113
Mandel, Earnest, 131

Manis, Jerome G., 215
Mannheim, Karl, 59, 152, 158, 159, 179, 183
Marcuse, Herbert, 252, 253, 254, 255
Market economy, 36
Martindale, Don, 103
Marxism, 26, 46, 51, 55, 118, 123, 126
Marxists, 26, 38, 131
Marx, Karl, 7, 10, 14, 46, 55, 99, 109–116, 120, 123–132, 136, 154–160, 165, 211, 220, 231, 242–257
Marx's concept of "separation," 131, 132
Marx's paradigm, 125
Marx–Weber model, 125, 136, 139, 257
Material incentives, 28
"Materialist conception of history," 156
Mauss, Marcel, 84
Mayo, Elton, 73
McCarthyism, 20, 42, 49
Mead, George Herbert, 150, 164, 165, 172, 193, 207, 209, 211, 213, 215, 218–257
Means of production, 78, 110–112, 116, 126–128, 132, 133, 136
Means of scientific research, 132
Mechanistic materialism, 232
"Me," concept of, 150, 164, 226–228, 251, 255
Mehring, Franz, 244
Meiji reforms, 40, 41
Meltzer, Bernard N., 218
Merleau-Ponty, Maurice, 139, 140
Merton, Robert K., 3, 7, 8, 9, 10, 31
Meyerhoff, Hans, 161
Mikhailovsky, Nikolai, 157
Mills, C. Wright, 30, 33, 45, 46, 103, 113, 121, 123–125, 131
"Mind," concept of, 246
Minkowski, H., 235
Mode of distribution, 129, 130
Mode of productions, 125, 126, 155
Modern capitalism, 128
Modern imperialism, 134
"Modernization," 24, 56
Monopoly control, 131
Moore, Barrington, Jr., 24, 27, 32, 94
"Morgenthau plan," 39
Mosca, Gaetano, 119, 120, 134
Morgan, Lewis Henry, 51
Motivational orientation, 22
"Myth of the Sacred Cow," 11

Nation-State, 4
"Natural attitude," 147, 173, 174
"Naturalism," 141, 143
"Natural selection," 53
"Naturwissenschaften," 17, 19
Nazism, 20, 35, 37, 39, 42
"Negative theory," 165

Neo-Freudians, 252
"Neutral attitude," 147
"New middle class," 113, 114
Noetic analysis, 147, 148

"Objectification," 163, 164
"Objectivism," 141, 143
"Objectivity," 159
Oedipal theory, 230
"Organic composition of capital," 127
"Organic solidarity," 19

Pareto, Vilfredo, 10, 18, 63, 119, 120, 134
Park, Robert E., 215
Parsons, Talcott, 3–59, 96–98, 183, 186
Pattern variables, 24
Pearce, Brian, 131
"Performance principle," 254
"Performance team," 193, 194, 195
Peripheralism, 141
"Person," 172
Personality, 21, 24
"Personal territories," 202
Phenomenological psychology, 141
Phenomenological reduction, 145, 146, 147, 150, 159
Phenomenologists, 19
Phenomenology, 139, 140, 144, 149, 151, 175, 183
Philosophical anthropology, 161
Philosophical idealism, 232
Philosophy of the Act, 236, 246
Philosophy of the Present, 232
"Plain Marxists," 123, 124
Plato, 223
Pleasure principle, 252, 253, 254, 255, 256
Positivism, 154, 167
Positivists, 17, 18, 19, 156, 236, 237
Postcapitalist society, 110, 111, 114, 115, 118, 119, 120–122, 133
"Postulate of adequacy," 181
"Postulate of logical consistency," 180
"Postulate of subjective interpretation," 180
Power, 25, 26, 30, 33, 40, 43, 46, 47, 49, 50, 54, 77–99, 115, 133
Power elite, 45, 46, 121
"Practical equilibrium," 70
Pragmatism, 238
"Principle of least interest," 77, 84
Private property, 110, 111
Process of reflection, 229
Productive forces, 125, 126, 157
"Profit motive," 29
Property relations, 30, 110, 125, 126, 129, 130
"Psychologism," 140, 141, 143, 167

Quasi-Marxian approach, 38, 40–42

Rational action, Weber's concept of, 168
"Realfaktoren," 155
Reality principle, 252, 253
Reflective self, 235
Reflective attitude, 242
Reflective thinking, 236, 238, 239
Relations of production, 110, 111, 125, 126, 157
"Relativity," 232
Repression, 165, 211, 230, 231, 251, 252
Rickert, Heinrich, 167
"Role distance," 205, 206, 207, 208, 210
Rose, Arnold M., 215
Roth, Guenther, 128, 168
Ruling class, 36, 53, 116, 120, 157, 158
Russell, Bertrand, 246

Samurai, 40, 41, 42
Sartre, Jean-Paul, 19, 193
Scheler, Max, 150–169, 178
Schmitt, Richard, 145, 146
Schütz, Alfred, 149, 169, 171–184, 186, 187, 223
"Second industrial revolution," 130
Self, 203, 215–217, 224–226, 229, 234, 246
"Self-consciousness," 163, 164
Self-other dialectic, 247
Self-regulating systems, 11, 13
"Sentiment," Pareto's concept of, 18
"Significant other," 225
Simmel, Georg, 18, 104, 105
Small, Albion, 103
Smelser, Neil J., 50, 77
Smith, Adam, 103
Social change, 14, 32, 38, 54, 55
Social classes, 26, 32, 38, 109, 121, 127–129, 216, 217
Social conflict, 26, 38, 97, 104, 106, 107
Social Darwinism, 65
Social equilibrium, 31
Social evolution, 51, 52
"Social self," 150, 164
Social structure, 36, 39, 106, 107, 115, 116, 216, 225
"Social system," 4, 7, 14, 15, 17, 19–29, 32, 37, 44, 54, 105–107, 114, 216
"Society," concept of, 4, 7, 17, 21, 23, 24, 45, 53, 133, 156, 216, 217, 230, 253
Sociology of knowledge, 152, 156, 158
Socrates, 7
Sombart, Werner, 151
Sorel, George, 134
Sorokin, Pitrim, 6, 7, 9, 10
Soviet Union, 26, 27, 29, 30

Spencer, Herbert, 57
Spiegelberg, Herbert, 139, 144, 147, 150
S-R Orientation, 141
State, 17, 32, 36, 120, 121, 133
"Status congruence," 76
Staude, John R., 152, 155, 157, 158
Stratification, 25, 28, 29, 113
"Stream of thought," 150
Structural functionalism, 3n
Stumpf, Carl, 140
"Subjective," concept of, 168
Subjectivism, 143
Subuniverse, 150, 173, 174
Sullivan, Harry Stack, 225, 252
Sumner, William Graham, 103
Superego, 252
Surplus-repression, 253, 254, 255
Sutton, F. X., 4
Symbolic interaction, 170, 191, 215, 218, 235
System equilibrium, 24
"System integration," 42
"System needs," 3, 4, 6, 9, 11, 24, 41, 52

Tarde, Gabriel, 221
Theory of action, 19, 20
Theory of relativity, 232
Thibaut, J. W., 77
Third World countries, 125
Thomas, W. I., 215
Toennies, Ferdinand, 18, 24
Tokugawa, Japan, 40–41
"Total institutions," 197, 198, 201, 202, 203
Traditional action, 169
Traditional functionalism, 7–11, 14, 15, 107
Transcendental ego, 145

Trotsky, Leon, 133
Tyler, Edward Burnett, 51

"Unconscious," 230
"Underdeveloped" societies, 11, 56
Universal imperatives, 29
Utilitarians, 17

"Value consensus," 116
Vayda, Andrew P., 12, 13
Verstehende Soziologie, 171, 175
"Vested interests," 32, 33, 38, 39, 97
"Voluntarism," 19–20
Von Wiese, Leopold, 33

Wann, T. W., 141
"War of all against all," 4, 17, 44, 213
Watson, J., 222
Weber, Max, 10, 14, 18, 19, 29–31, 38, 49, 57, 58, 85, 88, 118, 121, 125, 127, 128, 131–134, 136, 143, 147, 151, 153, 158, 159, 167–171, 176, 178–183
Weimar Republic, 36
Weltanschauung philosophy, 143, 152, 153, 154, 167
Wertbeziehung, 58, 59, 147, 159
Wertfreiheit, 58, 59, 147, 159
Wertrationales Handeln, 169
Whitehead, Alfred North, 175
Whyte, William F., 71
Windelband, Wilhelm, 167
Wissenschaft als Beruf, 58, 144
Wissensoziologie, 152, 154, 165
Wittich, Claus, 128, 168
Wundt, Wilhelm, 140, 221, 222

'Zero sum' concept, 45, 48
Znaniecki, Florian, 215
Zweckrationales Handeln, 168